Administration, Personnel, Buildings and Equipment

HANDBOOKS FOR LIBRARY MANAGEMENT

Administration, Personnel, Buildings and Equipment
Acquisitions, Collection Development, and Collection Use
Reference Services and Library Instruction
Cataloging and Catalogs
Circulation, Interlibrary Loan, Patron Use, and Collection Maintenance
Library Education and Professional Issues

Administration, Personnel, Buildings and Equipment
A Handbook for Library Management

David F. Kohl

Foreword by Bernard Kreissman

ABC-Clio Information Services
Santa Barbara, California
Denver, Colorado
Oxford, England

This book is Smyth sewn and printed on acid-free paper to meet library standards.

Library of Congress Cataloging in Publication Data

Kohl, David F., 1942–
    Administration, personnel, buildings and equipment.

    1. Library administration—Handbooks, manuals, etc.
2. Library personnel management—Handbooks, manuals, etc.
3. Library buildings—Handbooks, manuals, etc.
I. Title.
Z678.K63   1985   025.1   84-24267

ISBN 0-87436-431-0 (v. 1)
ISBN 0-87436-399-3 (set)

10 9 8 7 6 5 4 3 2 1

ABC-Clio Information Services
2040 Alameda Padre Serra, Box 4397
Santa Barbara, California 93103

Clio Press Ltd.
55 St. Thomas Street
Oxford OX1 1JG, England

Manufactured in the United States of America

CONTENTS

1.

Administration

Contents

2.

Personnel

3.

Buildings and Equipment

FOREWORD

For decades, library professionals have cited some of their major reference tools by abbreviated titles (for example, "Roget's," "Bartlett's," "Granger's," or "Webster's Second"), and the universal recognition of those abbreviations stands as a signal of the status of those seminal volumes. In the last two to three decades, a number of library publications—by virtue of their strong influence or broad use—have won similar recognition and are referred to as "Sheehy" (though I still cite it as "Winchell"), or "Metcalf," or "Magill." To that list of distinguished volumes, librarians of the next decade will now have to add "Kohl," for David Kohl has produced a work of library research information that may legitimately take its place among those major productions. His publication, *Administration, Personnel, Buildings and Equipment: A Handbook for Library Management,* is both a distinguished work of quantitative research and a mine of information for any library administrator or decision-making group.

His concept is a model of simplicity. From thirty-four core library journals, he has isolated the central findings of each of the research articles published since 1960 (research interpreted here to include surveys and similar information-gathering techniques). He has grouped the isolated selections into well-chosen topical categories and then arranged the findings by type of library (public, academic, school, special) and date. He provides a succinct summary of each and every research finding. He completes the work with an array of indexes: an index from each summary to the full citation, resulting in an extensive subject bibliography of more than 800 articles, a reference from the full citation back to the summary, an author index to the Bibliography of Articles, and a bibliographic listing of the journals surveyed.

Any librarian who has struggled through an intensive, time-consuming, and often unproductive literature search in the course of decision making will almost immediately recognize the extraordinary value of David Kohl's *Handbook.* In the future, I expect that librarians facing a decision requiring a literature search—whatever their type of library or position in the library—will turn first to "Kohl" and, in all likelihood, find the desired information quickly and efficiently.

I am among those library administrators who have long wished for such a management tool and, indeed, the idea must have occurred to other disappointed searchers. However, the sheer volume of effort involved would have daunted any but the most dedicated bibliographic polygraph. This first volume on "Administration, Personnel, Buildings and Equipment" indexes and summarizes more than 800 research articles and will be succeeded by five complementary volumes covering "Acquisitions, Collection Development and Collection Use," "Reference Services and Library Instruction," "Cataloging and Catalogs," "Circulation, Interlibrary Loan, Patron Use, and Collection Maintenance," and "Library Education and Professional Issues," for an additional 4,000 to 4,500 entries. A staggering achievement.

While the sheer volume of the work in the *Handbook* is impressive, it must take second place to the degree of discrimination used in organizing the information. The "Administration" section, for instance, which includes such topics as "Affirmative Action," "Institutional Comparisons and Rankings," "Chain of Command," and "Unions—Professional," is broken down into 164 categories! As a result, Kohl has provided subject indexing in a depth beyond that which one normally finds in analagous print or online compilations. The *Handbook* allows each of us to become instantly knowledgable about all of the fields indexed.

Some months back, I had an occasion to run an extensive computer literature search on the subject of organizational patterns within libraries. Unfortunately, as often happens in literature searches, the results were barely useful for the purposes I had in mind, and I was forced to supplement the online process with manual searches in a variety of other sources. Had "Kohl" been available at the time, his subject headings: "Organization," "Organization—Chain of Command," "Staffing Levels," and "Staffing Standards" in the section on Administration would have led me immediately to the relevant summarized information.

Equally important, given the comprehensiveness of the *Handbook,* if the results of a search in "Kohl" were found to be few in number, this would provide quick verification of the probable paucity of quantitative literature on the subject. Since one of the most difficult points of a search is the confirmation of little or no literature on a subject, Kohl's inclusive compilation allows us to make a speedy and strong probable decision in that regard. In simple terms, if it's recently conducted research and it's not in the *Handbook,* it probably hasn't been reported in the journal literature.

The library profession is currently skeptical of the continuing role of voluminous printed sources of information in this period of computer-driven information sources, and in the main I am on the side of the skeptics. It is, therefore, enlightening for me to realize that for a work like Kohl's *Handbook,* the computer will act only as an auxiliary supplement to the printed page. With the publication of the six *Handbooks for Library Management,* I foresee that most literature searches for the period 1960 to 1983 will begin and end with "Kohl." Mr. Kohl has produced an outstanding work of reference. The library profession is in his debt.

—Bernard Kreissman
University of California–Davis

INTRODUCTION

The *Library Administrator's Handbook* series has been designed for library managers and decision makers who regularly need information, but who are chronically too short of time to do involved and time-consuming literature searches each time specific, quantitative information is desired. This unusual tool, rather than abstracting complete studies or providing only citations to research, instead presents summaries of individual research findings, grouped by subject. By looking under the appropriate subject heading in the *Handbook,* librarians can find summaries detailing the research findings on that topic. For example, what percentage of reference questions are answered correctly, and does it make a difference whether professional or nonprofessional staff are doing the answering? As a result, helpful information can be found in minutes and without an extensive literature review. Furthermore, if a more complete look at the study is desired, the user is referred to the bibliographic citation number so that the full study can be consulted.

Arrangement

The series consists of six volumes, with each volume covering two or more of the sixteen basic subject areas that divide the volumes into parts. While most of these basic subject divisions reflect such traditional administrative divisions of library work as administration, circulation, and reference, at least two subject areas go somewhat further. "Library Education" may be of interest, not just to library school administrators, but to faculty and students as well, and "Professional Issues" should be of interest to all career-oriented library professionals. Each basic subject division is further divided by specific subject headings, which are further subdivided by type of library: General (more than one library type), Academic, Public, School, and Special. For example, readers seeking information on book loss rates in academic libraries would consult the basic subject division "Collection Maintenance" and look under the specific subject heading "Loss Rates (Books)," in the "Academic" libraries subdivision. There they would find the summarized results of studies on book loss rates in academic libraries followed by the number referring to the full citation in the Bibliography of Articles.

Each volume in the series follows the same basic pattern: The introduction; a list of the journals surveyed; a detailed table of contents listing all subject headings used in that volume; the research findings arranged by subject; the complete bibliography of articles surveyed for the series with page numbers indicating locations of corresponding research summaries in the text; and an alphabetically arranged author index to the Bibliography of Articles.

The summaries of the research findings also tend to follow a standard format. First the study is briefly described by giving location, date, and, when appropriate, population or survey size and response rate. This information is provided to help users determine the nature, scope, and relevance of the study to their needs. The actual findings, signaled by an italicized *"showed that,"* follow and include, when appropriate, such supporting data as significance level and confidence interval. Information in brackets represents editorial comment, for example "[significance level not given]" or "[remaining cases not accounted for]," while information in parentheses merely represents additional data taken from the article.

The Sample Entries on page xxi identify the elements and illustrate the interrelationships between the subject organization of the volume, research summaries of the text, corresponding article citations in the bibliography, and the author index entries.

Scope

In order to keep the *Handbook* series manageable, a number of scope limitations were necessary. The time period, 1960 through 1983, was selected since it covers the time when quantitative research began to come of age in library research. Only journal literature has been surveyed, because the bulk of quantitative library research is reported in that medium, and because the editorial and refereeing process required by most journals helps ensure the quality of the research reported. This limitation does ignore a number of important studies reported in monographic form, however, and we hope to cover this area at a later date. Further, only North American journals and research were reviewed since they constitute the main body of quantitative library research reported. Again, this ignores several journals reporting significant library research, particularly journals from Great Britain. We plan to expand our focus and include these in later editions or updates of the *Handbook* series.

Although we generally followed the principle that research good enough to publish was research worth including in the *Handbook* series, several caveats must be stated. First, no research findings with statistical significance exceeding .05 were reported. This follows general Social Science practice and, in recent years, almost universal library research practice. Second, occasional findings, and sometimes whole studies, were not reported in the *Handbook* series when there were serious problems with internal consistency and/or ambiguous and confusing text. At issue here is not the occasional typographical error or arithmetical miscalculation, but those situations where charts and text purportedly presenting the same information differed in substantial and unaccountable ways. Fortunately, such problems were not excessive. And third, as a general rule, only original and supported findings were used in the *Handbook* series. Findings that were reported second-hand, or where the study documentation was reported elsewhere (often the case with doctoral research), were generally not used in the series. Only in those instances when the second-hand data were used to show a pattern or otherwise resulted in new data by their juxtaposition, were such findings reported.

Finally, under the category of unsought limitations, we, like many library users, were not always able to find all the journal articles we needed in the time available to us. However, the excellent holdings and services of the University of Illinois Library Science Library provided us with access to almost all of the journal issues actually published and received by March 1984—a fact that should probably be listed as a record rather than as a limitation.

Acknowledgements

As might be expected, a project of this size required assistance from many quarters. Both the University of Illinois Library Research and Publication Committee and the University of Illinois Research Board provided invaluable assistance in the form of financial support for graduate assistants. The assistants themselves, Becky Rutter, Nicki Varyu, and Bruce Olsen, constituted a dedicated, bright and hardworking team. The Undergraduate Library staff deserve special thanks for their support and cooperation, as do the Library Science Library staff, who were unfailingly courteous and helpful in making their truly outstanding collection available. The staff at ABC-Clio, particularly Gail Schlachter and Barbara Pope, provided much needed encouragement and good advice, even in the face of several delays and at least one nasty shock. And last, but by no means least, I would like to acknowledge the patience and support of my wife, Marilyn, and my son, Nathaniel, who have given up much in the way of a husband and father so that this *Handbook* series could be completed on schedule.

—David F. Kohl
Urbana, Illinois

SAMPLE ENTRIES

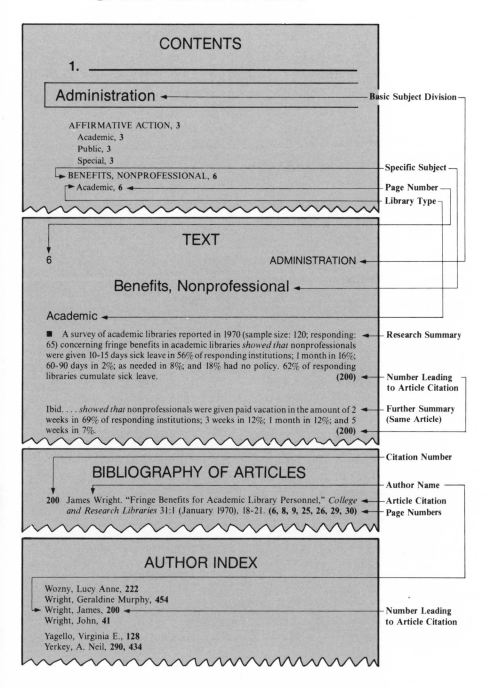

CONTENTS

1. _____

Administration ◄——————————————————————— Basic Subject Division ┐

AFFIRMATIVE ACTION, 3
  Academic, 3
  Public, 3
  Special, 3 ——————————————————————— Specific Subject ┐
└► BENEFITS, NONPROFESSIONAL, 6
  ┌►Academic, 6 ◄——————————————————————— Page Number ┐
    Library Type ┐

TEXT

6   ADMINISTRATION ◄

Benefits, Nonprofessional ◄———————————————

Academic ◄—————————————————————

■ A survey of academic libraries reported in 1970 (sample size: 120; responding: ◄—— Research Summary
65) concerning fringe benefits in academic libraries *showed that* nonprofessionals
were given 10-15 days sick leave in 56% of responding institutions; 1 month in 16%;
60-90 days in 2%; as needed in 8%; and 18% had no policy. 62% of responding
libraries cumulate sick leave.   **(200)** ◄—— Number Leading
                                   to Article Citation

Ibid. . . . *showed that* nonprofessionals were given paid vacation in the amount of 2 ◄—— Further Summary
weeks in 69% of responding institutions; 3 weeks in 12%; 1 month in 12%; and 5   (Same Article)
weeks in 7%.   **(200)** ◄

                            Citation Number

BIBLIOGRAPHY OF ARTICLES

                              Author Name ┐

200 James Wright. "Fringe Benefits for Academic Library Personnel," *College* ◄—— Article Citation
  and Research Libraries 31:1 (January 1970), 18-21. **(6, 8, 9, 25, 26, 29, 30)** ◄—— Page Numbers

AUTHOR INDEX

Wozny, Lucy Anne, **222**
Wright, Geraldine Murphy, **454**
►Wright, James, **200** ◄——————————————————— Number Leading
Wright, John, **41**   to Article Citation

Yagello, Virginia E., **128**
Yerkey, A. Neil, **290, 434**

LIST OF JOURNALS SURVEYED

American Libraries. Chicago: American Library Association, 1970–. Monthly. LC 70-21767. ISSN 0002-9769. (Formerly *ALA Bulletin,* 1907–1969.)

American Society for Information Science. Journal. (JASIS) New York: John Wiley & Sons, 1970–. Bimonthly. LC 75-640174. ISSN 0002-8231. (Formerly *American Documentation,* 1950–1969.)

Canadian Library Journal. Ottawa: Canadian Library Association, 1969–. Bimonthly. LC 77-309891. ISSN 0008-4352. (Formerly *Bulletin,* 1944– March 1960; *Canadian Library,* 1960–1968.)

Catholic Library World. Haverford, PA: Catholic Library Association, 1929–. Monthly. LC 39-41. ISSN 0008-820X.

Collection Building. New York: Schuman, 1978–. Quarterly. LC 78-645190. ISSN 0160-4953.

Collection Management. New York: Haworth Press, 1975–. Quarterly. LC 78-640677. ISSN 0146-2679.

College and Research Libraries. Chicago: American Library Association, 1939–. Bimonthly. LC 42-16492. ISSN 0010-0870.

Drexel Library Quarterly. Philadelphia: Centrum Philadelphia, 1965–. Quarterly. LC 65-9911. ISSN 0012-6160.

Harvard Library Bulletin. Cambridge: Harvard University Library, 1947–. Quarterly. LC 49-1965//R802. ISSN 0017-8136.

International Journal of Legal Information. Camden, NJ: International Association of Law Libraries, 1982–. 6/yr. LC 82-643460. ISSN 0731-1265. (Formerly *Bulletin. International Association of Law Libraries,* 1960–1972; *International Journal of Law Libraries,* 1973–1979.)

International Library Review. London: Academic Press, 1969–. Quarterly. LC 76-10110. ISSN 0020-7837.

Journal of Academic Librarianship. Ann Arbor, MI: Mountainside Publishing, 1975–. Bimonthly. LC 75-647252. ISSN 0099-1333.

Journal of Education for Librarianship. State College, PA: Association of American Library Schools, 1960–. 5/yr. LC 63-24347. ISSN 0022-0604.

Journal of Library Administration. New York: Haworth Press, 1980–. Monthly. LC 80-644826. ISSN 0193-0826.

Journal of Library Automation. Chicago: American Library Association, 1968–. Quarterly. LC 68-6437//R82. ISSN 0022-2240.

Journal of Library History, Philosophy and Comparative Librarianship. Austin, TX: 1966–. Quarterly. LC 65-9989. ISSN 0275-3650. (Formerly *Journal of Library History,* 1966–1975.)

Law Library Journal. Chicago: American Association of Law Libraries, 1908–. Quarterly. LC 41-21688//R6. ISSN 0023-9283.

Library Acquisitions: Practice and Theory. Elmsford, NY: Pergamon Press, 1977–. Quarterly. LC 77-647728. ISSN 0364-6408.

Library Journal. New York: R.R. Bowker, 1876–. Semimonthly, except July–August. LC 76-645271. ISSN 0363-0277.

Library Quarterly. Chicago: University of Chicago, 1931–. Quarterly. LC 32-12448. ISSN 0024-2519.

Library Research. Norwood, NJ: Ablex Publishing, 1979–. Quarterly. LC 79-643718. ISSN 0164-0763.

Library Resources and Technical Services. Chicago: American Library Association, 1957–. Quarterly. LC 59-3198. ISSN 0024-2527. (Formed by the merger of *Serial Slants* and *Journal of Cataloging and Classification.*)

Library Trends. Champaign: University of Illinois at Urbana-Champaign, 1952–. Quarterly. LC 54-62638. ISSN 0024-2594.

Medical Library Association. Bulletin. Chicago: Medical Library Association, 1911–. Quarterly. LC 16-76616. ISSN 0025-7338.

Microform Review. Westport, CT: Meckler Publishing, 1972–. Quarterly. LC 72-620299. ISSN 0002-6530.

Notes. Philadelphia: Music Library Association, 1942–. Quarterly. LC 43-45299//R542. ISSN 0027-4380.

Online. Weston, CT: Online, 1977–. Quarterly. LC 78-640551. ISSN 0416-5422.

Public Libraries. Chicago: American Library Association, 1978–. 4/yr. ISSN 0163-5506. (Formerly *Just Between Ourselves,* 1962–1969; *PLA Newsletter,* 1962–1977.)

RQ. Chicago: American Library Association, 1960–. Quarterly. LC 77-23834. ISSN 0033-7072.

RSR Reference Services Review. Ann Arbor, MI: Perian Press, 1972–. LC 73-642283//R74. ISSN 0090-7324.

School Library Journal. New York: R.R. Bowker, 1954–. Monthly except June and July. LC 77-646483. ISSN 0362-8930.

School Library Media Quarterly. Chicago: American Library Association, 1981–. 4/yr. LC 82-640987. ISSN 0278-4823. (Formerly *School Libraries,* 1951–1972; *School Media Quarterly,* 1972–1980.)

Special Libraries. New York: Special Libraries Association, 1910– . 4/yr. LC 11-25280rev2*. ISSN 0038-6723.

Wilson Library Bulletin. Bronx, NY: H.W. Wilson, 1914– . Monthly except July and August. LC 80-9008(rev.42). ISSN 0043-5651.

1.

Administration

Affirmative Action

Academic

■ A survey reported in 1978 of 407 academic and public libraries who had filled professional positions (61% [no number given] responding with 233 or 57% usable responses) *showed that* 71% of the academic libraries reported affirmative action of "somewhat" or "considerable" importance in the hiring process compared to 41% of the public libraries so reporting. In both groups 5% of the positions were filled with ethnic minorities, and both groups estimated that about 5% of the applicant pool consisted of ethnic minorities. **(227)**

Ibid. . . . *showed that* in academic libraries females were hired in 47% of the cases with the pool estimated at 48%, while in public libraries 37% of positions were filled by females out of an estimated pool of 30%. **(227)**

Public

■ A survey reported in 1978 of 407 academic and public libraries who had filled professional positions (61% [no number given] responding with 233 or 57% usable responses) *showed that* 71% of the academic libraries reported affirmative action of "somewhat" or "considerable" importance in the hiring process compared to 41% of the public libraries so reporting. In both groups 5% of the positions were filled with ethnic minorities, and both groups estimated that about 5% of the applicant pool consisted of ethnic minorities. **(227)**

Ibid. . . . *showed that* in academic libraries females were hired in 47% of the cases with the pool estimated at 48%, while in public libraries 37% of positions were filled by females out of an estimated pool of 30%. **(227)**

Special

■ A survey reported in 1980 of 23 special librarians who became officers in their organizations *showed that*, of external factors (those over which the respondent had little control) influencing the appointment to officer rank, the one "most frequently mentioned" was a supportive management. The "next most frequently cited external factor" was the women's movement and affirmative action. **(431)**

Automation—General Issues

General

■ A 1976 survey of RASD members (population: 4,062; sample size: 738; usable responses: 542 or 73.4%) concerning their attitudes toward automated information retrieval services *showed that* the 3 greatest barriers to developing automated information retrieval sources in libraries reported by respondents were costs (88.2%), lack of trained library personnel (51.1%), and overworked staff (49.6%).   **(148)**

■ A study reported in 1979 comparing staff productivity in a program office of the National Science Foundation (4 program officers and a secretary) over a 21-month period both before and after computer augmentation (automated work stations for each individual at work and portable terminals for each program officer to take home; a system allowing for online word processing, interoffice communication, and filing) *showed that* automation increased productivity 22% for program officers and 33% for the secretary.   **(618)**

Academic

■ A 1979 survey of library automation in post-secondary educational institutions in Canada (survey size: 423 libraries; responding: 283 or 67%) *showed that*, of an average of 256 respondents for each of the following items, the distribution of automated activities was as follows (multiple responses allowed):

cataloging	47.2%	respondents	
online bibliographic searching	34.2%	respondents	
COM catalog	24.2%	respondents	
circulation	19.8%	respondents	
ordering	16.5%	respondents	
photo-sense ID	7.7%	respondents	
online catalog	3.2%	respondents	**(556)**

Ibid. . . . *showed that* the larger the library (in terms of number of books) the more it was likely to be automated. The composite average for 7 categories of automation (based on the number of libraries automated in each category) distributed by size of library was as follows:

1,000-20,000 volumes	12.5%	composite average
21,000-50,000 volumes	15.9%	composite average
51,000-100,000 volumes	22.7%	composite average

continued

> 101,000-250,000 volumes   22.2% composite average
> 251,000-3,500,000 volumes   53.2% composite average   **(556)**

Ibid. . . . *showed that* of those libraries that had not automated [no number given] the 3 most frequent reasons for not automating were small size (33%), lack of funds (27%), and lack of trained personnel (8%).
(556)

■ A 1980 survey of Catholic colleges with collections containing less than 300,000 bibliographic items (survey size: 105 libraries; responding: 62; usable: 60 or 57.1%) *showed that* automation had not been implemented in any library function in 24 (40%) libraries, while 36 (60%) libraries had some form of library automation. Of these 36 libraries, 13 (21.7% of the total) libraries had automated more than 1 library function.   **(754)**

Ibid. . . . *showed that* grant funding played an important role in providing automation in these libraries. Of the 36 libraries with automation, 20 (56%) reported the receipt of grant funding for the purposes of automating. 17 (47% of the 36 libraries) reported receiving Kellogg Foundation grants, while only 3 (8% of the 36 libraries) received automation grants from other sources.   **(754)**

■ A 1981 survey of faculty, students, staff, and community users of the University of Cincinnati Libraries (sample size: 4,074; responding: 912 or 22.4%, including 436 or 39% faculty response and 218 or 11% student response) *showed that*, although the University of Cincinnati Libraries operated on manual systems, "approximately 25%" of the students, community users, and university administrators reported experience with computerized library systems, while 33% of the faculty and 37% of the library staff reported experience with automated library systems.   **(522)**

Special

■ A study reported in 1979 comparing staff productivity in a program office of the National Science Foundation (4 program officers and a secretary) over a 21-month period both before and after computer augmentation (automated work stations for each individual at work and portable terminals for each program officer to take home; a system allowing for online word processing, interoffice communication, and filing) *showed that* automation increased productivity 22% for program officers and 33% for the secretary.   **(618)**

Benefits, Nonprofessional

Academic

■ A survey of academic libraries reported in 1970 (sample size: 120; responding: 65) concerning fringe benefits in academic libraries *showed that* nonprofessionals were given 10-15 days sick leave in 56% of responding institutions; 1 month in 16%; 60-90 days in 2%; as needed in 8%; and 18% had no policy. 62% of responding libraries cumulate sick leave.

(200)

Ibid. . . . *showed that* nonprofessionals were given paid vacation in the amount of 2 weeks in 69% of responding institutions; 3 weeks in 12%; 1 month in 12%; and 5 weeks in 7%.   **(200)**

Ibid. . . . *showed that* nonprofessionals were granted time off for funerals for relatives in the following amounts: 1-4 days in 37% of responding institutions; week plus in 3%; as needed in 8%; and no policy in 45%. Time off for friends' funerals was 1 hour to 1/2 day in 12% of cases; 1-4 days in 8% of cases; as needed in 5% of cases; and no policy in 74% of cases.   **(200)**

Ibid. . . . *showed that* time allotted for jury duty and voting was the same for both professional and nonprofessional staff in responding libraries with "as needed" or "no policy" reported by 95% and 90% of responding institutions, respectively.   **(200)**

Benefits, Professional—General

Academic

■ A 1964 survey of 60 private liberal arts colleges (49 responding) *showed that* 13 institutions gave sabbatical leave to all librarians; 8 gave it to the head librarian only; 2 gave it to the head librarian, assistant librarian, and department head; and 26 had no definite policy or did not answer the question. Where sabbaticals are granted, the most usual pattern is full pay for 1 semester or half pay for 2 semesters.   **(170)**

■ A 1967 survey of 4-year state colleges and universities (sample size: 321; responding: 200 or 62.3%; usable: 183 or 57%) *showed that* faculty and librarians were most likely to be treated alike with regard to fringe benefits (89.6% institutions), tenure criteria (77.6% institutions), sabbatical leave (74.3% institutions), participation in faculty government (71.0% institutions), and use of academic titles (65.0% institutions). They were least likely to be treated alike in rate of pay (29.0% institutions), academic vacations (33.9% institutions), and promotion policies (49.7% institutions). **(186)**

■ A survey reported in 1968 of all ARL directors plus all other state university library directors concerning the degree to which librarians participate in traditional faculty activities (72 responding) *showed that* 2/3 of respondents reported that librarians are given time from their schedules to teach, and 89% of respondents reported that librarians teach courses in their institutions. Further, librarians were reported as teaching library science and bibliography only slightly more than subjects outside of the library field. **(182)**

Ibid. . . . *showed that* 76% of respondents reported allowing time for research, and 83% provided some sort of financial assistance. About 60% reported that the research need not be related to library operations or problems. **(182)**

Ibid. . . . *showed that* 86% of respondents reported giving time off for free consulting, while 74% would give the time when the consultant was paid. For surveys, 83% of respondents reported giving time off for free surveys, while 72% would give the time when the surveyor was paid. **(182)**

Ibid. . . . *showed that* all respondents reported giving time for professional activities, and 99% said they pay [some] expenses. 78% of respondents said they paid some expenses to national meetings for staff not on programs or committees. **(182)**

Ibid. . . . *showed that* respondents from 43% of the institutions reported that librarians have been given leave for study or foreign assignments within the last 3 years. **(182)**

Ibid. . . . *showed that*, for participation in nonlibrary professional work, time off is given by 85% of the institutions, but expenses are paid "probably to a very limited extent" by only 47%. **(182)**

Ibid. . . . *showed that*, for participation in nonprofessional local activities, 39% of respondents reported that they neither gave time nor any expenses. In terms of time alone, 59% of respondents give it, while 39% do not.

(182)

■ A survey reported in 1976 of the libraries in the largest private and largest public college/university in each state of the continental U.S. (sample size: 100 [sic]; responding: 79 or 79%), *showed that* 82% of the responding libraries have established procedures for [requesting permission to] attend professional meetings. "Over 90%" of the respondents make both time and money available for such attendance, although 79% of respondents require that the meetings be work-related.   **(413)**

Ibid. . . . *showed that* 59% of the respondents had formal procedures for [requesting attendance] at professional workshops, although 80% provide time and money. 84% of the respondents indicated that these workshops must be work-related.   **(413)**

Ibid. . . . *showed that* less than 50% of the respondents reported providing time and funding for independent research on the part of [professional] library staff.   **(413)**

Ibid. . . . *showed that* 75% of the respondents reported money was available for [professional] library staff to take formal classes (the number of classes that may be taken is limited), but only 50% allow release time for this activity (and the classes must be work-related), and only 16% "encourage" attendance at institutions other than their own.   **(413)**

Ibid. . . . *showed that* 39% of the respondents report availability of in-service training, while only 27 respondents (36%) provide supervisory training for [professional] staff members.   **(413)**

■ A survey of academic libraries reported in 1970 (sample size: 120; responding: 65) concerning fringe benefits in academic libraries *showed that* professionals were given 10-15 days sick leave in 38% of responding libraries; 1 month in 19%; 60-90 days in 2%; as needed in 23%; and there was no policy in 17%. 62% of responding libraries cumulate sick leave.

(200)

Ibid. . . . *showed that* professionals were given paid vacation in the amount of 2 weeks in 10% of responding institutions; 3 weeks in 6%; 1 month in 65%; and 5 weeks in 19%. **(200)**

Ibid. . . . *showed that* professionals were granted time off for funerals for relatives in the following amounts: 1-4 days in 34% of responding institutions; week plus in 4%; as needed in 10%; and no policy in 51%. Time off for friends' funerals was 1 hour to 1/2 day in 12% of responding institutions; 1-4 days in 8% of cases; as needed in 6% of cases; and no policy in 73% of cases. **(200)**

Ibid. . . . *showed that* time allotted for jury duty and voting was the same for both professional and nonprofessional staff in responding libraries with "as needed" or "no policy" reported by 95% and 90% of responding institutions, respectively. **(200)**

■ The annual survey of law school libraries and librarians conducted in 1980 by the American Bar Association, American Association of Law Libraries, and Association of American Law Schools (population not given; response: 168 libraries) *showed that* the median dollar amount of fringe benefits received by U.S. head law school librarians was overall $6,160, while by size of library it was as follows:

small (under 70,000 vols.)	$7,789
medium (70,000-99,999 vols.)	$5,054
medium-large (100,000-199,999 vols.)	$6,030
large (200,000+ vols.)	$7,623 **(382)**

Ibid. . . . *showed that* the median dollar amount of fringe benefits received by full-time professional law school librarians in the U.S. (excluding head law school librarians) was overall $2,850, while by size of library it was as follows:

small (under 70,000 vols.)	$1,880
medium (70,000-99,999 vols.)	$2,447
medium-large (100,000-199,999 vols.)	$2,805
large (200,000+ vols.)	$3,263 **(382)**

■ A survey reported in 1980 of Association of Research Libraries directors in academic libraries (population: 94; responding: 68 or 72%) concerning publication requirements for professional library staff *showed that* 7 (10%) institutions allowed specific release time for working on publications; 28 (41%) allow librarians to apply for release time for publication; and 33 (49%) do not allow release time for work on publications.   **(480)**

Ibid. . . . *showed that* (multiple responses allowed) 18 (23%) institutions provide funding for research within the library; 40 (51%) reported research funding is available from the university; and 20 (26%) reported that research funding is not available.   **(480)**

■ A 1980 survey of academic librarians in Alabama, Georgia, and Mississippi concerning faculty status (sample size: 416; responding: 271; usable: 267 or 64.2%) *showed that* 12.0% of the respondents received release time for proposal development, while 14.2% received release time for research and publication.   **(502)**

■ A survey reported in 1981 of library directors in 4-year colleges and universities in 7 Rocky Mountain states (survey size: 76; responding: 64 or 84%) concerning faculty status of librarians *showed that*, although sabbatical leaves were reported possible for librarians in 33 (83%) institutions, research leaves were only available in 32 (80%) institutions, and research funds were only available in 28 (70%) institutions.   **(492)**

■ A survey reported in 1983 of the U.S. academic members of the Association of Research Libraries concerning faculty status for professionals (population: 89 libraries; responding: 89 or 100%, including 57 state and 32 private institutions) *showed that* the benefits and privileges given librarians in state institutions versus private institutions were as follows:

faculty rank	20 (35.1%) state;	1 (3.1%) private
indefinite tenure	34 (59.6%) state;	4 (12.5%) private
research funds	51 (89.5%) state;	13 (40.6%) private
travel funds	all libraries	
research leave	47 (82.5%) state;	25 (78.1%) private
sabbatical leave	35 (61.4%) state;	10 (31.3%) private
tuition break	41 (71.9%) state;	28 (87.5%) private
option of 9-month appointment	15 (26.3%) state;	7 (21.9%) private

                                                                                                                (788)

Special

■ A 1973 survey of all county law libraries listed in the 1972 American Association of Law Libraries *Directory of Law Libraries* (population:

260; responding: 86 or 33.1%) *showed that,* of 64 librarian respondents, 58 (91%) reported that time off was given for professional activities. **(392)**

■ A 1980 survey of the private law library and corporate law library membership of the American Association of Law Libraries, excluding part-time librarians (population: 585; responding: 382; usable: 360 or 61%), *showed that* librarians received the following benefits:

95% of the private/governmental respondents and 92% of the corporate respondents reported that 100% of AALL dues were paid by employer;

89% of the private/governmental respondents and 95% of the corporate respondents reported receiving health insurance for self, while 52% of the private/governmental respondents and 75% of the corporate respondents reported receiving health insurance for the family;

67% of the private/governmental respondents and 92% of the corporate respondents reported employer-supported pension plan, while 78% of the private/governmental and 100% of the corporate respondents reported employer-supported life insurance plans;

46% of the private/governmental respondents and 45% of the corporate respondents reported employer-supported business cards. **(377)**

■ The annual survey of law school libraries and librarians conducted in 1980 by the American Bar Association, American Association of Law Libraries, and Association of American Law Schools (population not given; response: 168 libraries) *showed that* the median dollar amount of fringe benefits received by U.S. head law school librarians was overall $6,160, while by size of library it was as follows:

small (under 70,000 vols.)	$7,789
medium (70,000-99,999 vols.)	$5,054
medium-large (100,000-199,999 vols.)	$6,030
large (200,000+ vols.)	$7,623 **(382)**

Ibid. . . . *showed that* the median dollar amount of fringe benefits received by full-time professional law school librarians in the U.S. (excluding head law school librarians) was overall $2,850, while by size of library it was as follows:

small (under 70,000 vols.)	$1,880
medium (70,000-99,999 vols.)	$2,447

continued

medium-large (100,000-199,999 vols.) $2,805
large (200,000+ vols.) $3,263   **(382)**

Branches

Academic

■ A study reported in 1982 at the University of California, Berkeley, concerning the added costs of operating a branch library (library science library) over the costs of providing those services through a centralized system, *showed that* the labor costs appeared to be 42.5% greater and materials costs (due to duplication) 7% greater.   **(577)**

Public

■ A survey of libraries in cities whose populations range from 20,000 to 2,000,000+ (sample size: 126; responding: 93) involving establishment of branch libraries in shopping centers *showed that* 40 of the responding libraries reported receiving gift branches for a total of 141 gifts/branches. The gifts were received from the Andrew Carnegie Foundation (81), families (20), individuals (14), industrial corporations (6), mercantile corporations (3), and other sources (17). 21 of the 40 libraries receiving gifts have or will name libraries after donors.   **(070)**

Ibid. . . . *showed that* free store space was donated by promoters for branches in 5 cases; special space separate from store groupings was donated by promoters in 4 additional cases; the merchants of the shopping area had donated space in 3 other cases; and in 4 cases promoters had donated free store space for at least a year to be followed by minimum rent after the initial free period.   **(070)**

Budget—General

Academic

■ A 1965 survey of U.S. university-connected medical school libraries to determine the degree they operate within the context of the medical school administration (decentralized) versus that of the university library (centralized) (survey size: 70 libraries; responding: 68 or 97.1%) *showed that* the predominant pattern for medical school libraries was decentralized, both in terms of budgets (48 or 71% libraries received their budgets from the medical school) and in terms of operations, e.g., acquisitions, cataloging, processing (54 or 79% libraries operated independently of the university library).   **(673)**

Ibid. . . . *showed that* there was a greater tendency for medical school libraries in publicly supported institutions to have a centralized budget than for medical school libraries in privately supported institutions to have a centralized budget. Specifically, 42% of the medical libraries in publicly supported institutions had centralized budgets, while 83% of the medical libraries in privately supported institutions had centralized budgets.

(673)

■ A study reported in 1977 at the Purdue University Libraries and Audio-Visual Center to determine and allocate library and audiovisual costs to teaching departments and user groups *showed that*, based upon library use as determined by circulation of materials, costs would be allocated as follows:

undergraduates	43.9% of the costs
graduate students	36.7% of the costs
faculty	9.5% of the costs
other (includes staff)	9.9% of the costs **(459)**

Ibid. . . . *showed that* of the various ways of allocating costs, the differences between allocating costs on the basis of intended use (i.e., on the basis of the specific group expected to use the materials) rather than on the basis of actual use (i.e., on the basis of how much actual use is made by specific groups) were "generally smaller" than the differences between allocating costs on the basis of faculty salaries and allocating them on the basis of intended use. **(459)**

Ibid. . . . *showed that* the distribution of library and audiovisual costs by school based on actual use were as follows:

humanities, social sciences and education	38.7% of total costs
science	16.3% of total costs
engineering	14.1% of total costs
agriculture	9.8% of total costs
home economics	8.9% of total costs
management	6.2% of total costs
technology	3.0% of total costs
pharmacy	1.9% of total costs
veterinary medicine	1.1% of total costs **(459)**

■ A study of 1977 survey information gathered by the National Center for Educational Statistics (U.S. Office of Education) concerning the degree to which 1,146 college and university libraries (Liberal Arts Colleges I and II; Comprehensive Universities and Colleges I and II) met the 1975

Standards for College Libraries (ACRL) *showed that* 84% of the libraries were underfunded in terms of the standard. Standards specify that at least 6% of the institution's budget (excluding capital and physical maintenance expenditures) should be allocated to the library. 84% were allocated less than 6%, while 38% were allocated less than 4% of the institutional budget.   **(486)**

Ibid. . . . *showed that* the annual (1977) average operating budget for reporting libraries was $364,000 with a median of $200,000; that the average salaries and wage budget was $188,000 with a median of $103,000; and that the materials budget averaged $124,000 with a median of $64,000.
                                                                      (486)

■ A study reported in 1981 of data on 1,146 2-year colleges as reported in the 1977 Higher Education General Information Surveys and compared to the 1979 Association of College and Research Libraries standards *showed that*, overall, 89% of the respondents including 87% of the privately supported and 91% of the publicly supported schools reported that library expenditures were less than 7% of general and educational institutional expenditures. Standards recommend that library expenditures be 7-12% of total general and educational institutional expenditures.   **(500)**

Ibid. . . . *showed that* overall the average library operating expenditures totaled $166,000 with median expenditures totaling $102,000, including average expenditures for privately supported schools (235 reporting) of $42,000 and average expenditures for publicly supported schools (911 reporting) of $198,000; that overall the average library materials budget was $39,000 with a median of $27,000, including average expenditures for privately supported schools (235 reporting) of $11,000 and average expenditures for publicly supported schools (911 reporting) of $46,000; that overall the average library salaries and wages budget was $99,000 with a median of $55,000, including average salaries and wages budgets in privately supported schools (235 reporting) of $23,000 and average salaries and wages budgets in publicly supported schools (911 reporting) of $118,000.   **(500)**

■ A study reported in 1983 of 3 surveys made by the American Medical Association's Division of Library and Archival Services in 1969, 1973, and 1979 concerning the status of health sciences libraries in the U.S.(survey size for each survey ran between 12,000-14,000 health-related organizations with a response rate for each survey around 95%) *showed that* in 1979 the average operating expenditures of hospital health sciences libraries by size of hospital was as follows:

99 beds or smaller	$10,181 per library	
100-199 beds	$15,546 per library	
200-299	$23,818 per library	
300-399	$31,939 per library	
400-499	$47,108 per library	
500 beds or larger	$71,127 per library	**(747)**

Public

■ An analysis of data on municipal expenditures reported annually in the *City Government Finances in 19—*[sic] (U.S. Bureau of Census) for the period 1950 through 1968-69 *showed that* during this period municipal expenditures on libraries remained relatively constant, with total city expenditures for all cities going from 1.0% of city expenditures in 1950 to 1.2% of total city expenditures in 1968-69 compared to police (7.9% to 8.6%) and public welfare (6.8% to 7.0%) for the same period. This reflected an increase in absolute expenditures for libraries of 496.8% compared to police (464.9%) or public welfare (403.5%) during the same period. **(088)**

Ibid. . . . *showed that* during this period municipal expenditures on libraries in cities with over 1 million population decreased slightly going from 1.4% of total city expenditures in 1950 to 1.1% in 1968-69. This reflected an increase in absolute expenditures for libraries of 405.9% compared to police (357.4%) or public welfare (240 million to 1,457 million) during the same period. **(088)**

■ A study reported in 1977 of 32 county libraries in Florida that related 4 variables (level of education in county, potential users, per capita operating cost, and per capita library collection) *showed that* allocating library budgets on the basis of circulation was likely to favor communities with higher levels of education and strong collections since both level of education and per capita collection were highly correlated with per capita circulation. Specifically, while the 4 variables taken together accounted for "about 74%" of the variance in per capita library circulation, the 2 most important variables were "level of education" (beta weight = .60) and "per capita library collection" (beta weight = .44). The regression coefficients of both of these variables were reported as statistically significant, although no significance level was reported. **(617)**

■ A review reported in 1982 of data on local public library financial support primarily taken from U.S. Department of Commerce, *Government Finance* during the period FY 1965-66 through FY 1979-80 *showed that* such support increased from $449 million in FY 1965-66 to $1,566 million in FY 1979-80. In relation to the total direct general expenditures allocated to all government functions, however, this represents a decrease from .836% of all local government spending to .700% of such spending. While library expenditures had increased by 249%, all local government expenditures had increased by 317%.   **(363)**

Ibid. . . . *showed that*, while local government appropriations to libraries had increased by 249% over this period, local government appropriations to health and hospitals increased 461%, sewerage and sanitation appropriations increased 401%, police/fire protection appropriations increased 355%, parks and recreation appropriations increased 342%, and education appropriations increased 270%.   **(363)**

Ibid. . . . *showed that* the largest relative declines occurred in FY 1965-66 through FY 1971-72.   **(363)**

Ibid. . . . *showed that* from FY 1966-67 through FY 1979-80 local library expenditures rose from $486 million to $1,566 million for an increase of 222%, while for the same period GNP rose 230% and the Municipal Cost Index rose 172%.   **(363)**

■ A survey of 53 U.S. public libraries (all responding) reported in 1983 concerning circulation and expenditures *showed that*, using 1980 as a base year (index value = 100), expenditures rose 10% by 1981 (index value 110), while expenditures had risen a further 11% by 1982 (index value 121). However, when expenditures were adjusted for inflation using the Consumer Price Index, there was no increase in real expenditures in 1981 (index value = 100), although there was a 4% real increase in expenditures the following year, in 1982 (index value = 104). Further, between 1980-82 the amount of expenditures spent on salaries rose from 63% to 64%, while the amount of expenditures spent on materials dropped from 16% to 15%. The amount spent on "other" remained constant at 21%.   **(791)**

School

■ A 1983 survey of a systematic sample of school library media centers concerning data for fiscal year 1982-83 (survey size: 2,000 centers; responding: 1,297; usable: 1,251 or 62%) *showed that* the budget was prepared (or received) as follows:

received stated amount from
  administrators (no budget input)   685 (55.47%) respondents

continued

budget prepared on basis of
    perceived needs and/or objectives   292 (23.64%) respondents
budget based on per pupil
    allocation and stated objectives   206 (16.68%) respondents
reported spending until told
    to stop (no budget)   23 (1.86%) respondents
reported that no funds were
    allocated to the media center   9 (0.73%) respondents
other   20 (1.62%) respondents **(56)**

Special

■ A 1965 survey of U.S. university-connected medical school libraries to determine the degree they operated within the context of the medical school administration (decentralized) versus that of the university library (centralized) (survey size: 70 libraries; responding: 68 or 97.1%) *showed that* the predominant pattern for medical school libraries was decentralized, both in terms of budgets (48 or 71% libraries received their budgets from the medical school) and in terms of operations, e.g., acquisitions, cataloging, processing (54 or 79% libraries operated independently of the university library). **(673)**

Ibid. . . . *showed that* there was a greater tendency for medical school libraries in publicly supported institutions to have a centralized budget than for medical school libraries in privately supported institutions to have a centralized budget. Specifically, 42% of the medical libraries in publicly supported institutions had centralized budgets, while 83% of the medical libraries in privately supported institutions had centralized budgets. **(673)**

■ A 1973 survey of all county law libraries listed in the 1972 American Association of Law Libraries' *Directory of Law Libraries* (population: 260; responding: 86 or 33.1%) *showed that* 51 (59.3%) respondents received their financial support from fees of one kind or another; 39 (45.3%) received their financial support from the general fund; 8 (9.3%) received their financial support from membership fees; and 13 (15.1%) received their financial support from other miscellaneous sources. **(392)**

Ibid. . . . *showed that* 15 (18%) respondents reported that their funding was inadequate for the present, while 35 (49%) reported that their funding was inadequate for the future. An earlier survey in 1953 *showed that* 14% reported their funding inadequate for the present, while 28% reported their funding inadequate for the future.   **(392)**

Ibid. . . . *showed that* 46 (53.5%) respondents reported being audited annually, 12 (14.0%) reported audits every 2 to 3 years, 5 (5.8%) reported audits infrequently, and 1 (1.2%) reported never being audited (no data given for the remaining respondents).   **(392)**

■ A 1974 survey of a random sample of U.S. museum libraries (including history, art, and science museums) listed in the 1973 *Official Museum Directory* (population: 2,556; sample size: 856; responding: 374 or 43.7%) *showed that*, of 159 responses including budgetary information, the most frequently reported budget was zero, the average was $6,130, and the median was $1,001.   **(412)**

Ibid. . . . *showed that* 60.4% of the respondents reported either total or partial reliance on private funding and that 92% of the respondents did not charge user fees.   **(412)**

■ A survey reported in 1978 of the 50 state law libraries (40 or 80% responding) *showed that* the 6 (out of 18) most pressing problems they reported facing, listed in descending order of importance and based on number of libraries reporting the problem and their rating of its severity were:

> increased demands for photocopy service,
> not enough shelf space,
> not enough study space (tables, desks,etc.),
> book budget too low,
> nonprofessional staff too small,
> and theft of materials.   **(358)**

■ A 1978 survey of law school libraries listed in the 1977 *AALS Directory of Law Teachers* (population: 167; responding: 158 or 95%) *showed that* 124 (78%) respondents reported that the law library book budget was not part of the university library's book budget; 22 (14%) reported that it was; and 12 (8%) did not reply. Further, 124 (78%) reported that their library's book budget was allocated as part of the law school's budget.   **(362)**

Ibid. . . . *showed that* of the 22 law school libraries whose book budget was part of the university library's budget the following individuals or groups determined the yearly allocation:

university library director	9 respondents	
law librarian and university library director	7 respondents	
university library director and higher university officials	3 respondents	
higher university officials	1 respondent	
university library committee	1 respondent	
no reply	1 respondent	**(362)**

Ibid. . . . *showed that* 124 (78%) respondents reported that the law school library's personnel budget was allocated as part of the law school's budget rather than as part of the university library's budget; 22 (14%) reported that the personnel budget was part of the university library's budget; and 12 (8%) did not reply. **(362)**

■ A 1980 survey of the private law library and corporate law library membership of the American Association of Law Libraries, excluding part-time librarians (population: 585; responding: 382; usable: 360 or 61%) *showed that* overall, while 75% of the respondents were responsible for planning library acquisitions expenses, only 23% could authorize expenditures over $200. **(377)**

Budget—Materials

Academic

■ An Indiana University survey for the National Science Foundation *showed that* major academic libraries increased their materials budget by an average of 9.4% in the period 1973-76; a 15-18% increase was reported necessary to maintain equivalent coverage. **(016)**

Ibid. . . . *showed that* library administrators reponded to shortages in the library materials serials budget primarily by canceling duplicates and shifting funds from monographic to serials accounts. The third most common tactic was to halt new subscriptions in order to renew old ones. **(016)**

Ibid. . . . *showed that* during the period 1969-76 large academic libraries reduced the percentage of their budget spent on serials or monographs.

In 1969 $2 were spent on serials for every $1 on monographs; by 1976 it had steadily reduced to $1.23 for serials for each $1 spent on monographs.　　　　　　　　　　　　　　　　　　　　　　　　　　　　　**(016)**

■ A study of 1977 survey information gathered by the National Center for Educational Statistics (U.S. Office of Education) concerning the degree to which 1,146 college and university libraries (Liberal Arts Colleges I and II; Comprehensive Universities and Colleges I and II) met the 1975 Standards for College Libraries (ACRL) *showed that* the annual (1977) average operating budget for reporting libraries was $364,000 with a median of $200,000; that the average salaries and wage budget was $188,000 with a median of $103,000; and that the materials budget averaged $124,000 with a median of $64,000.　　　　　　　**(486)**

■ A 1978 survey of law school libraries listed in the 1977 AALS *Directory of Law Teachers* (population: 167; responding: 158 or 95%) *showed that* 124 (78%) respondents reported that the law library book budget was not part of the university library's book budget; 22 (14%) reported that it was; and 12 (8%) did not reply. Further, 124 (78%) reported that their library's book budget was allocated as part of the law school's budget.　　　**(362)**

Ibid. . . . *showed that* of the 22 law school libraries whose book budget was part of the university library's budget the following individuals or groups determined the yearly allocation:

university library director	9 respondents
law librarian and university library director	7 respondents
university library director and higher university officials	3 respondents
higher university officials	1 respondent
university library committee	1 respondent
no reply	1 respondent　　**(362)**

■ A study reported in 1981 of data on 1,146 2-year colleges as reported in the 1977 Higher Education General Information Surveys and compared to the 1979 Association of College and Research Libraries standards *showed that* overall the average library operating expenditures totaled $166,000 with median expenditures totaling $102,000, including average expenditures for privately supported schools (235 reporting) of $42,000 and average expenditures for publicly supported schools (911 reporting) of $198,000;

that overall the average library materials budget was $39,000 with a median of $27,000, including average expenditures for privately supported schools (235 reporting) of $11,000 and average expenditures for publicly supported schools (911 reporting) of $46,000;

that overall the average library salaries and wages budget was $99,000 with a median of $55,000, including average salaries and wages budgets in privately supported schools (235 reporting) of $23,000 and average salaries and wages budgets in publicly supported schools (911 reporting) of $118,000. **(500)**

Special

■ A 1978 survey of law school libraries listed in the 1977 AALS *Directory of Law Teachers* (population: 167; responding: 158 or 95%) *showed that* 124 (78%) respondents reported that the law library book budget was not part of the university library's book budget; 22 (14%) reported that it was; and 12 (8%) did not reply. Further, 124 (78%) reported that their library's book budget was allocated as part of the law school's budget. **(362)**

Ibid. . . . *showed that* of the 22 law school libraries whose book budget was part of the university library's budget the following individuals or groups determined the yearly allocation:

university library director	9 respondents
law librarian and university library director	7 respondents
university library director and higher university officials	3 respondents
higher university officials	1 respondent
university library committee	1 respondent
no reply	1 respondent **(362)**

Budget—Salaries

Academic

■ An Indiana University survey for the National Science Foundation *showed that* in large academic libraries for the period 1967-76 the percentage of the total library budget spent on salaries rose from 56.9% to 61%. **(016)**

■ A study of 1977 survey information gathered by the National Center for Educational Statistics (U.S. Office of Education) concerning the degree to which 1,146 college and university libraries (Liberal Arts Colleges I and II; Comprehensive Universities and Colleges I and II) met the 1975 Standards for College Libraries (ACRL) *showed that* the annual (1977) average operating budget for reporting libraries was $364,000 with a median of $200,000; that the average salaries and wage budget was $188,000 with a median of $103,000; and that the materials budget averaged $124,000 with a median of $64,000.   **(486)**

■ A 1978 survey of law school libraries listed in the 1977 AALS *Directory of Law Teachers* (population: 167; responding: 158 or 95%) *showed that* 124 (78%) respondents reported that the law school library's personnel budget was allocated as part of the law school's budget rather than as part of the university library's budget; 22 (14%) reported that the personnel budget was part of the university library's budget; and 12 (8%) did not reply.
(362)

■ A study reported in 1981 of data on 1,146 2-year colleges as reported in the 1977 Higher Education General Information Surveys and compared to the 1979 Association of College and Research Libraries standards *showed that* overall the average library operating expenditures totaled $166,000 with median expenditures totaling $102,000, including average expenditures for privately supported schools (235 reporting) of $42,000 and average expenditures for publicly supported schools (911 reporting) of $198,000;

> that overall the average library materials budget was $39,000 with a median of $27,000, including average expenditures for privately supported schools (235 reporting) of $11,000 and average expenditures for publicly supported schools (911 reporting) of $46,000;

> that overall the average library salaries and wages budget was $99,000 with a median of $55,000, including average salaries and wages budgets in privately supported schools (235 reporting) of $23,000 and average salaries and wages budgets in publicly supported schools (911 reporting) of $118,000.   **(500)**

■ A study reported in 1983 concerning costs among academic libraries based on data gathered by the National Center for Education Statistics for the year 1977 and various sources of institutional data (involving 3,057 institutions, including 2-year public, 2-year private, 4-year public, and 4-year private schools) *showed that*, when the average expenditures for library salaries were divided by average library operating expenditures, the proportion of money spent on salaries was as follows:

4-year public college and university libraries	47% budget for salaries
4-year private college and university libraries	48% budget for salaries

continued

2-year private college libraries 52% budget for salaries
2-year public college libraries · 56% budget for salaries **(797)**

Public

■ A survey of 53 U.S. public libraries (all responding) reported in 1983 concerning circulation and expenditures *showed that*, using 1980 as a base year (index value = 100), expenditures rose 10% by 1981 (index value 110), while expenditures had risen a further 11% by 1982 (index value 121). However, when expenditures were adjusted for inflation using the Consumer Price Index, there was no increase in real expenditures in 1981 (index value = 100), although there was a 4% real increase in expenditures the following year, in 1982 (index value = 104). Further, between 1980-82 the amount of expenditures spent on salaries rose from 63% to 64%, while the amount of expenditures spent on materials dropped from 16% to 15%. The amount spent on "other" remained constant at 21%. **(791)**

Special

■ A study of 1977 survey information gathered by the National Center for Educational Statistics (U.S. Office of Education) concerning the degree to which 1,146 college and university libraries (Liberal Arts Colleges I and II; Comprehensive Universities and Colleges I and II) met the 1975 Standards for College Libraries (ACRL) *showed that* the annual (1977) average operating budget for reporting libraries was $364,000 with a median of $200,000; that the average salaries and wage budget was $188,000 with a median of $103,000; and that the materials budget averaged $124,000 with a median of $64,000. **(486)**

■ A 1978 survey of law school libraries listed in the 1977 AALS *Directory of Law Teachers* (population: 167; responding: 158 or 95%) *showed that* 124 (78%) respondents reported that the law school library's personnel budget was allocated as part of the law school's budget rather than as part of the university library's budget; 22 (14%) reported that the personnel budget was part of the university library's budget; and 12 (8%) did not reply. **(362)**

Certification

Special

■ A 1980 survey of the private law library and corporate law library membership of the American Association of Law Libraries, excluding part-time librarians (population: 585; responding: 382; usable: 360 or

61%) *showed that*, of 342 respondents, the average salary of 59 respondents with American Association of Law Libraries certification was $23,503, while the average salary for 283 respondents without such certification was $19,660.   **(377)**

Communication

Academic

■ A study of all professional librarians (sample size 57; 56 responding) in 4 medium-sized academic libraries in the northeastern U.S. *showed that* those librarians who had direct responsibility for the operation of the library contacted a substantially larger quantity of factual information sources than other librarians in the organization. Furthermore, the librarians on whom these administrators relied for information also have more faculty information sources than the typical librarian.   **(028)**

Ibid. . . . administrators tended to rely on 2 or 3 selected individuals in the organization for all information regardless of the nature of the decision or of the individual's competence regarding that decision.   **(028)**

Ibid. . . . *showed that* information seeking followed the formal lines of authority. There was little cross-departmental information seeking; e.g., a public service librarian would seek information from the head of public service rather than a colleague in technical services.   **(028)**

Ibid. . . . *showed that* there was a statistically significant relationship at the .08 level between job type/organizational position and contacts with information sources. Administrators had the most contact, followed by public service librarians, followed by technical service librarians.   **(028)**

Ibid. . . . *showed that* all librarians who were identified as involved in decision making were "information rich" (those scoring in the top 50% of total contacts with information sources); the reverse, however, was not true. "Information richness" appeared to be a necessary but not sufficient cause for involvement in library decision making.   **(028)**

Ibid. . . . *showed that* there was a statistically significant relationship at the .01 level between those librarians defined as "information rich" (those scoring in the top 50% of total contacts with information sources) and involvement in decision making. **(028)**

■ A survey reported in 1976 of the libraries in the largest private and largest public college/university in each state of the continental U.S. (sample size: 100 [sic]; responding: 79 or 79%) *showed that* 94% of the respondents conduct [professional] staff meetings, although only 52% of the respondents conduct such meetings regularly. **(413)**

Public

■ A study reported in 1979 assessing organizational climate in public libraries using a modified version of Educational Testing Service's Institutional Functioning Inventory (survey size: professional staff in 16 public libraries with a response rate of 50-100% per library) *showed that* libraries that had some kind of shared decision making were also characterized by a high degree of mutually supporting relationships among professional staff. Specifically, the scale intercorrelation between "democratic governance" and "support" was .85 (no significance level given). **(565)**

Ibid. . . . *showed that* libraries that had some kind of shared decision making were also characterized by a high degree of morale and the feeling that one could speak one's own mind and exercise one's own judgment when the occasion demanded. Specifically, the scale intercorrelation between "democratic governance" and "espirit" was .94 and between "democratic governance" and "freedom" was .79 (no significance level given). **(565)**

Contracts and Policies, Nonprofessional

Academic

■ A survey of academic libraries reported in 1970 (sample size: 120; responding: 65) concerning fringe benefits in academic libraries *showed that* nonprofessionals were given paid vacation in the amount of 2 weeks in 69% of responding institutions; 3 weeks in 12%; 1 month in 12%; and 5 weeks in 7%. **(200)**

Ibid. . . . *showed that* nonprofessionals were granted time off for funerals for relatives in the following amounts: 1-4 days in 37% of responding institutions; week plus in 3%; as needed in 8%; and no policy in 45%.

Time off for friends' funerals was 1 hour to 1/2 day in 12% of cases; 1-4
days in 8% of cases; as needed in 5% of cases; and no policy in 74% of
cases.   **(200)**

Ibid. . . . *showed that* time allotted for jury duty and voting was the same
for both professional and nonprofessional staff in responding libraries with
"as needed" or "no policy" reported by 95% and 90% of responding
institutions, respectively.   **(200)**

Contracts and Policies, Professional—Appointments

Academic

■ A survey reported in 1983 of the U.S. academic members of the
Association of Research Libraries concerning faculty status for professionals (population: 89 libraries; responding: 89 or 100%, including 57 state
and 32 private institutions) *showed that* the types of final appointments that
could be achieved by a majority of the professional staff were as follows:

> indefinite tenure was the practice in 34 (59.7%) of the state
> and 4 (12.5%) of the private institutions;

> continuing appointments were the practice in 19 (33.3%) of the
> state and 22 (68.8%) of the private institutions;

> and term appointments were the practice in 4 (7.0%) of the
> state and 6 (18.7%) of the private institutions.

Further, indefinite tenure and continuing appointments were "perceived
by respondents as nearly identical."   **(788)**

Contracts and Policies, Professional—Length of Contract

Academic

■ A 1967 survey of 4-year state colleges and universities (sample size:
321; responding: 200 or 62.3%; usable: 183 or 57%) *showed that* faculty
and librarians were most likely to be treated alike with regard to fringe
benefits (89.6% institutions), tenure criteria (77.6% institutions), sabbatical leave (74.3% institutions), participation in faculty government (71.0%

institutions), and use of academic titles (65.0% institutions). They were least likely to be treated alike in rate of pay (29.0% institutions), academic vacations (33.9% institutions), and promotion policies (49.7% institutions). **(186)**

■ A 1970 survey of Canadian community college libraries concerning academic status, salaries, and fringe benefits (sample size: 108; responding: 49; usable: 43 or 39.8%) *showed that* 93% of the libraries reported that professionals work for a full year while 7% reported that professionals work on a 10-month basis. **(537)**

■ A survey reported in 1978 of academic librarians at 6 comparable libraries *showed that* librarians in a bargaining unit were more likely to have an academic-year contract (67.3% respondents), whereas librarians without a bargaining unit were more likely to have a calendar-year contract (66.7% respondents). **(008)**

■ A 1980 survey of academic librarians in Alabama, Georgia, and Mississippi concerning faculty status (sample size: 416; responding: 271; usable: 267 or 64.2%) *showed that* 91.8% reported 12-month contracts, 3.0% reported 9-month contracts, 4.9% reported "other," and .3% did not respond. **(502)**

■ A survey reported in 1981 of library directors in 4-year colleges and universities in 7 Rocky Mountain states (survey size: 76; responding: 64 or 84%) concerning faculty status of librarians *showed that* only 2 (5%) respondents reported 9-month contracts for librarians, while 7 (18%) respondents reported that the publishing requirements were the same for the librarians as for the teaching faculty. **(492)**

■ A survey reported in 1983 of the U.S. academic members of the Association of Research Libraries concerning faculty status for professionals (population: 89 libraries; responding: 89 or 100%, including 57 state and 32 private institutions) *showed that* the benefits and privileges given librarians in state institutions versus private institutions were as follows:

faculty rank	20 (35.1%) state;	1 (3.1%) private
indefinite tenure	34 (59.6%) state;	4 (12.5%) private
research funds	51 (89.5%) state;	13 (40.6%) private
travel funds	all libraries	

continued

research leave 47 (82.5%) state; 25 (78.1%) private
sabbatical leave 35 (61.4%) state; 10 (31.3%) private
tuition break 41 (71.9%) state; 28 (87.5%) private
option of 9-month
appointment 15 (26.3%) state; 7 (21.9%) private **(788)**

Ibid. . . . *showed that* the types of final appointments that could be achieved by a majority of the professional staff were as follows:

indefinite tenure was the practice in 34 (59.7%) of the state and 4 (12.5%) of the private institutions;

continuing appointments were the practice in 19 (33.3%) of the state and 22 (68.8%) of the private institutions;

and term appointments were the practice in 4 (7.0%) of the state and 6 (18.7%) of the private institutions.

Further, indefinite tenure and continuing appointments were "perceived by respondents as nearly identical." **(788)**

Ibid. . . . *showed that* the types of rank assigned the majority of librarians were as follows)

faculty rank was assigned by 20 (35.1%) of the state and 1 (3.1%) of the private institutions;

equivalent rank was assigned by 21 (36.8%) of the state and 7 (21.9%) of the private institutions;

numerical rank was assigned by 13 (22.8%) of the state and 20 (62.5%) of the private institutions;

"other" was used in 3 (5.3%) of the state and 4 (12.5%) of the private institutions. **(788)**

■ A survey reported in 1983 of head librarians of accredited institutions of higher education in New York state including 2-year colleges, 4-year colleges, universities, and graduate/professional schools (survey size: 264; responding: 188 or 71%) concerning faculty status for librarians *showed that*, of the total respondents, librarians had the following academic rights (multiple responses allowed):

eligible to serve on the campus
governing board 76% of total
eligible for release time for
professional activities 68% of total
eligible for sabbatical and
other professional leaves 64% of total
eligible for tenure 58% of total

continued

eligible for research funds   55% of total
given professorial titles   30% of total
given release time for research   20% of total
academic-year appointment   16% of total   **(516)**

Contracts and Policies, Professional—Overtime

Academic

■ A survey reported in 1966 of 93 accredited 4-year colleges and universities in New York state concerning overtime policies for professionals *showed that* 36 libraries (47%) reported official policies on overtime, while 38 (50%) reported having no official policy on overtime.   **(175)**

Ibid. . . . *showed that* of the 36 libraries with official policies for professional overtime, when it is required, 10 compensate with wages, 24 compensate with time off, and one does not compensate; when the overtime is voluntary, 2 compensate with wages, 23 compensate with time, and 8 do not compensate.   **(175)**

Ibid. . . . *showed that* of the 38 libraries without an official policy on professional overtime, 23 compensate with time, 11 do not compensate, and none compensate with wages.   **(175)**

Contracts and Policies, Professional—Sick Leave and Vacation

Academic

■ A survey of academic libraries reported in 1970 (sample size: 120; responding: 65) concerning fringe benefits in academic libraries *showed that* professionals were given 10-15 days sick leave in 38% of responding libraries; 1 month in 19%; 60-90 days in 2%; as needed in 23%; and there was no policy in 17%. 62% of responding libraries cumulate sick leave.   **(200)**

Ibid. . . . *showed that* professionals were given paid vacation in the amount of 2 weeks in 10% of responding institutions; 3 weeks in 6%; 1 month in 65%; and 5 weeks in 19%.   **(200)**

Ibid. . . . *showed that* professionals were granted time off for funerals for relatives in the following amounts: 1-4 days in 34% of responding institutions; week plus in 4%; as needed in 10%; and no policy in 51%. Time off for friends' funerals was 1 hour to 1/2 day in 12% of responding institutions; 1-4 days in 8% of cases; as needed in 6% of cases; and no policy in 73% of cases. **(200)**

Ibid. . . . *showed that* time allotted for jury duty and voting was the same for both professional and nonprofessional staff in responding libraries with "as needed" or "no policy" reported by 95% and 90% of responding institutions, respectively. **(200)**

Copyright

Academic

■ A 1979 survey of 3 types of health sciences libraries (U.S. academic medical libraries, special health science libraries, and hospital libraries) concerning compliance with the copyright law (survey size: 273 libraries; responding: 157 or 57%) *showed that* 87% of the respondents reported that they were "familiar" or "very familiar" with the law. Further, 82% reported that they had the MLA guide *The Copyright Law and the Health Sciences Librarian* available for patrons and staff to read, while "nearly 60%" reported that they had an extensive collection of printed materials explaining the law for patrons and staff. **(736)**

Ibid. . . . *showed that* only 12 (7.6%) libraries (10 academic, 1 hospital, and 1 special) reported they were registered with the Copyright Clearance Center, Inc., and only 6 reported ever using its services. **(736)**

Ibid. . . . *showed that* the number of libraries by library type that reported that the copyright law had had no effect on collection maintenance was as follows:

academic libraries	73 (82%)	libraries
hospital libraries	35 (83%)	libraries
special libraries	13 (87%)	libraries

The number of libraries by library type that reported that the copyright law had had no effect on library service was as follows:

academic libraries	58 (65%)	libraries
hospital libraries	28 (65%)	libraries
special libraries	12 (80%)	libraries

(736)

Ibid. . . . *showed that* only 68% of the respondents had AV collections and the facilities to make copies, while only 39% had actually used their facilities to copy or reformat AV programs. Of those who had copied AV materials, 93% reported they seek permission from the copyright owner, while 7% reported they never seek permission to copy AV material. Of those seeking permission, "about 20%" handle the permission "by placing conditional language on their purchase orders or by including a request to copy with the purchase order." **(736)**

Special

■ A 1979 survey of 3 types of health sciences libraries (U.S. academic medical libraries, special health science libraries, and hospital libraries) concerning compliance with the copyright law (survey size: 273 libraries; responding: 157 or 57%) *showed that* 87% of the respondents reported that they were "familiar" or "very familiar" with the law. Further, 82% reported that they had the MLA guide *The Copyright Law and the Health Sciences Librarian* available for patrons and staff to read, while "nearly 60%" reported that they had an extensive collection of printed materials explaining the law for patrons and staff. **(736)**

Ibid. . . . *showed that* only 12 (7.6%) libraries (10 academic, 1 hospital and 1 special) reported they were registered with the Copyright Clearance Center, Inc., and only 6 reported ever using its services. **(736)**

Ibid. . . . *showed that* the number of libraries by library type that reported that the copyright law had had no effect on collection maintenance was as follows:

academic libraries	73 (82%)	libraries
hospital libraries	35 (83%)	libraries
special libraries	13 (87%)	libraries

The number of libraries by library type that reported that the copyright law had had no effect on library service was as follows:

academic libraries	58 (65%)	libraries
hospital libraries	28 (65%)	libraries
special libraries	12 (80%)	libraries **(736)**

Ibid. . . . *showed that* only 68% of the respondents had AV collections and the facilities to make copies, while only 39% had actually used their facilities to copy or reformat AV programs. Of those who had copied AV materials, 93% reported they seek permission from the copyright owner, while 7% reported they never seek permission to copy AV material. Of those seeking permission, "about 20%" handle the permission "by placing conditional language on their purchase orders or by including a request to copy with the purchase order."   **(736)**

Directors—General

General

■ A study reported in 1981 of information on chief librarians generated in a 1975-76 survey of Canadian librarians in public, special, and academic libraries (study size: 96 chief librarians, including 49 females and 47 males) *showed that* female chief librarians reported working an average of 44.4 hours weekly, while men reported working 43.2 hours weekly.   **(557)**

Academic

■ A 1966 survey of Catholic college and university libraries in institutions with at least 1,000 full-time students (sample size: 70; responding: 56 or 80%) *showed that* of the library directors 5 (9%) hold rank of dean or equivalent, 44 (78%) hold faculty rank, 2 (3%) hold faculty status, and 5 (9%) hold no rank. In 39 libraries (70%) librarians hold faculty rank; in 7 (12%) they hold faculty status; and in 9 (16%) they hold no rank. **(187)**

■ A 1972 survey of chief library administrators in public comprehensive community colleges (population: 586; usable responses: 75.9% [no raw number given]) *showed that* 86.2% of the respondents reported primary responsibility for selecting new staff members; 91.3% reported primary responsibility for the library budget; and 71.4% reported responsibility for the audiovisual budget.   **(452)**

Ibid. . . . *showed that* directors were represented on curriculum committees either personally or by staff in 71.6% of the institutions.   **(452)**

Ibid. . . . *showed that* 58.7% of the respondents report to the dean of instruction, 13.3% report to the vice-president, 11.5% report to the president, 10% report to other deans, and 6.5% have other reporting arrangements.   **(452)**

■ A random sample of directors of academic libraries in the U.S. undertaken in 1976 (sample size: 266; response: 215 or 80.8%) *showed that* the median tenure of directors was 6 years, with the average tenure 8.1 years. **(121)**

■ A survey reported in 1977 of moderate-sized (120,000-500,000 volumes) U.S. academic libraries listed in the 1972-73 *American Library Directory* (survey size: 200; responding: 147 or 74%) *showed that* faculty participated in the periodical selection process in 95% of the responding libraries, while students actively participated in only 9% of the libraries. Further, the library administrator was responsible for final approval of selections in 49% of the libraries; the serials librarian was responsible for final approval in 29% of the libraries; and in 17 (12%) of the libraries teaching faculty were responsible for final selection. **(454)**

■ A survey reported in 1977 of 20 library directors of college and university libraries in the northeastern U.S. in institutions with enrollments ranging from 2,000 to 21,000 students *showed that* response to the question of frequency of work-related contacts beyond the library was as follows: "nearly all the time" (15%), "rather often" (60%), "sometimes" (20%), and "rarely" (5%). **(457)**

Ibid. . . . *showed that* the degree to which respondents reported that their performance depended on the behavior of people outside the library was as follows: "very great extent" (30%), "considerable extent" (45%), "some extent" (15%), and "very little" (10%). **(457)**

Ibid. . . . *showed that* the degree to which their job placed them "in the middle" between 2 groups of people was reported as follows: "nearly all the time" (10%), "rather often" (60%), "sometimes" (25%), and "rarely" (5%). **(457)**

■ A 1978 survey of law school libraries listed in the 1977 *AALS Directory of Law Teachers* (population: 167; responding: 158 or 95%) *showed that* the full official title of the head law librarian was as follows: law librarian (117 or 74%), director of the law library (33 or 21%), other (2%), and no reply (3%). **(362)**

Ibid. . . . *showed that* 151 respondents reported that the head law school librarian attended faculty meetings in the law school, while 32 attended faculty meetings, in the library system; 141 voted in law school faculty meetings, while 28 voted in library faculty meetings; and 143 were voting members of faculty committees in the law school, while 29 were voting members of faculty committees in the library. **(362)**

■ A survey reported in 1980 of newly appointed library directors of 4-year colleges and universities (positions announced in library journals between June 1977 and February 1979 and excluding law, medical, and service academy appointments) (survey size: 66; responding: 54 or 81.8%) *showed that* search committees were used in 50 cases, with the chief academic officer conducting the search in 4 cases—all at small private colleges. **(482)**

Ibid. . . . *showed that* 16 (29.6%) respondents reported that they had fewer than 2 library employees on their search committee while only 4 (7.4%) reported that more than half of the the search committee consisted of library employees. No respondents reported a search committee of only library employees. In only 7 (13.0%) cases was the search committee chaired by a library employee. **(482)**

Ibid. . . . *showed that* only 4 (7.4%) respondents reported that the search committee or hiring officers made an on-site visit to their former library as part of the search process. **(482)**

Ibid. . . . *showed that* during the interview "almost all" respondents reported meeting with the president, the chief academic officer, and the professional library staff; 43 (79.6%) respondents reported meeting with the nonprofessional library staff; 40 (74.1%) reported meeting with the faculty library committee; 33 (61.1%) reported meeting with the academic dean; 32 (59.3%) reported meeting the previous library director; and 29 (53.7%) reported meeting students. **(482)**

Ibid. . . . *showed that* "most" of the respondents reported meeting with 6-10 individuals and groups, while 6 (11.1%) reported meeting with 4-5 individuals and groups, and 6 (11.1%) reported meeting with 11-16 individuals and groups. **(482)**

Ibid. . . . *showed that* 18 (33.3%) of the respondents reported being invited back for a second visit. Further, 21 (38.9%) reported spending less than 2 days on the interview visit; 16 (29.6%) reported spending 2 days on the interview visit; and 14 (25.9%) reported interview visits longer than 2 days. **(482)**

Public

■ A survey reported in 1980 of the values of 44 directors of large U.S. public libraries (response: 25 or 57%), 60 full-time faculty in ALA accredited library school programs (response: 35 or 58%), and 175 students in accredited library school programs (response: 128 or 73%) as measured by the Rokeach Value Survey *showed that* all three groups ranked highly: self-respect, wisdom, freedom, inner harmony, and family security. All placed a low value on salvation, national security, social recognition, pleasure, and comfortable life.   **(290)**

Ibid. . . . .*showed that* the top 3 values for library directors were: sense of accomplishment (lasting contribution), exciting life (a stimulating, active life), and family security (taking care of loved ones).

The top 3 values for library school faculty were: sense of accomplishment (lasting contribution), self respect (self-esteem), and wisdom (a mature understanding of life).

The top 3 values for library school students were: self- respect (self-esteem), wisdom (a mature understanding of life), and freedom (independent, free choice).   **(290)**

Special

■ A 1976 survey of head law librarians in North American schools (sample size: 178; responding: 154 or 86.7%) *showed that* 49 (32%) law school library directors taught law school legal bibliography courses only; 35 (23%) taught both legal bibliography and substantive courses in the law school; 16 (10%) taught courses in both the law school and library school; 13 (8%) taught substantive courses only in the law school; 2 (1%) taught library school legal bibliography courses only; 2 (1%) taught legal research courses outside of the law or library school; and 37 (24%) taught no courses.   **(357)**

Ibid. . . . *showed that* the numbers of class hours taught per academic year by 105 law school library directors were as follows:

26 (25%) law library directors	0-10 hours/year
15 (14%) law library directors	11-20 hours/year
9 (9%) law library directors	21-30 hours/year
14 (13%) law library directors	31-40 hours/year
17 (16%) law library directors	41-50 hours/year
24 (23%) law library directors	51+ hours/year
12 (11%) law library directors	no response **(357)**

Ibid. . . . *showed that* the amount of time spent in class and in class preparation by the 105 law school library directors who taught classes was as follows:

25 (24%) law library directors	0-10% time
26 (25%) law library directors	11-20% time

continued

32 (30%) law library directors 21-30% time
9 (8%) law library directors 31-40% time
13 (12%) law library directors 41-50% time
1 (1%) law library director 51+% time **(357)**

Ibid. . . . *showed that* of 115 law school library directors who teach 52 (45%) of the directors considered themselves librarians, 64 (55%) considered themselves both teachers and librarians, and none considered themselves teachers only. **(357)**

■ A survey of private law firm libraries (sample size: 278; responding: 141 or 51%) concerning budgeting practices *showed that* 87% of the librarians reported to an attorney in charge of the library or a library committee, while 23% were accountable to an office administrator. **(361)**

■ A 1978 survey of law school libraries listed in the 1977 *AALS Directory of Law Teachers* (population: 167; responding: 158 or 95%) *showed that* the full official title of the head law librarian was as follows: law librarian (117 or 74%), director of the law library (33 or 21%), other (2%), and no reply (3%). **(362)**

Ibid. . . . *showed that* 151 respondents reported that the head law school librarian attended faculty meetings in the law school, while 32 attended faculty meetings in the library system; 141 voted in law school faculty meetings, while 28 voted in library faculty meetings; and 143 were voting members of faculty committees in the law school, while 29 were voting members of faculty committees in the library. **(362)**

Ibid. . . . *showed that* 82 (52%) respondents felt it desirable that head law school librarians carry teaching responsibilities; 15 (10%) felt that head law school librarians should teach but only legal bibliography; 21 (13%) reported mixed feelings; and 40 (25%) felt that head law school librarians should not teach. **(362)**

■ A preliminary analysis reported in 1976 of a survey of American Association of Law Library members (survey size: "approximately 2,000" individuals; responding: "approximately 1,400" or 70%, of which responses from 888 respondents were analyzed at the time of the report) *showed that* 50% of the men and 50% of the women respondents were head librarians. This compares to an earlier survey of AALL members in 1970, when 58% of the men were head librarians. **(793)**

Directors—Accredited Library Degree Programs

Academic

■ A study reported in 1978 of 23 middle managers and 11 administrators in 5 Association of Research Libraries libraries, as well as a review of ads for 82 middle managerial positions in academic libraries posted in 1975, *showed that* 43 (52.4%) of the ads listed an ALA-accredited library master's degree as a qualification; 37 (45.1%) listed library master's degree without specifying ALA-accredited; 30 (36.6%) listed second master's degree; 4 (4.9%) listed Ph.D.; 1 (1.2%) listed an other professional degree; and 1 stated that a master's degree was not required. **(423)**

Ibid. . . . *showed that*, of 23 middle managers, 21 (91.3%) had ALA-accredited master's degrees; none had unaccredited library master's degrees; 13 (56.5%) had second master's degrees; 1 (4.3%) had a Ph.D.; and 2 (8.7%) had an other professional degree. **(423)**

Directors—Age

General

■ A study reported in 1981 of information on chief librarians generated in a 1975-76 survey of Canadian librarians in public, special, and academic libraries (study size: 96 chief librarians including 49 females and 47 males) *showed that* women chief librarians tend to be younger than males. For example, the average age of female chief librarians was 44.5 years, compared to 46.4 years for males. Further, 17 (34.7%) of the women were in their 30s compared to 12 (25.5%) of the males, while 13 (27.7%) of the males and 9 (18.4%) of the females were in their 40s. **(557)**

Academic

■ A survey reported in 1967 of selected head college librarians in the U.S. (sample size: 660; responding: 414 or 62.7%) *showed that* men tended to become head librarians at an earlier age than women librarians. Of the

85 librarians who were under 40 years of age, 65 (74.46%) were men. Only in the 50+-years-old category do women have a higher percentage of head positions, 130 (68.42%) compared to 60 (31.58%) for men.   **(177)**

■ A 1972 survey of chief library administrators in public comprehensive community colleges (population: 586; usable responses: 75.9% [no raw number given]) *showed that* 62.6% of the chief library learning resource administrators were male, and 37.4% were female. Further, the modal age bracket of respondents was 40-49 years of age.   **(452)**

■ A 1972 study of U.S. medical school libraries and other large biomedical libraries (collection of 35,000+ volumes and staff of 3 or more) concerning the status of women professionals (survey size: 160 libraries; responding: 143; usable: 140 or 87.5%) *showed that*, of 37 women and 64 men in the sample whose age was known, men became head medical librarians at a younger age than women. The age at which these librarians became heads follows:

under 30 years old	5 (13.5%) women;	8 (12.5%) men
30-34 years old	4 (10.8%) women;	24 (37.5%) men
35-39 years old	9 (24.3%) women;	11 (17.2%) men
40-44 years old	7 (18.9%) women;	16 (25.0%) men
45-49 years old	6 (16.2%) women;	4 (6.3%) men
50 and older	6 (16.2%) women;	1 (1.6%) men **(709)**

■ A 1980 survey of first-time-appointed academic library directors during the period 1970-80 (survey size: 230 directors; responding: 141 or 61.3%, including 98 males and 43 females) *showed that* for all directors at the time of appointment the average age was 40.4 years, and the median age was 39 years. For males the average age was 39.4 years with a median of 39 years, while for females the average age was 42.7 years with a median of 42 years.   **(785)**

■ A study reported in 1983 of data compiled on 153 Association of Research Libraries and major public library directors *showed that* public librarians obtained their first directorship at an average age of 35.9 years, while academic librarians obtained their first directorship at an average age of 39.3 years. 27% of the public library directors got their first directorship while in their 20s and 71% had their first directorship before they reached 40, compared to 7% of the academic directors who received their first directorship during their 20s, and 49% had their directorships before age 40.   **(275)**

Ibid. . . . *showed that* 65% of the library directors who majored in fields outside the liberal arts had their first directorship before age 40, compared to 59% of the liberal arts majors. **(275)**

Public

■ A study reported in 1983 of data compiled on 153 Association of Research Libraries and major public library directors *showed that* public librarians obtained their first directorship at an average age of 35.9 years, while academic librarians obtained their first directorship at an average age of 39.3 years. 27% of the public library directors got their first directorship while in their 20s and 71% had their first directorship before they reached 40, compared to 7% of the academic directors who received their first directorship during their 20s and 49% had their directorships before age 40. **(275)**

Ibid. . . . *showed that* 65% of the library directors who majored in fields outside the liberal arts had their first directorship before age 40, compared to 59% of the liberal arts majors. **(275)**

Special

■ A survey reported in 1971 of the professional law librarians listed as members of the American Association of Law Libraries (population not given; response: "approximately 50%," no number given) *showed that*, of 286 female and 138 male head law librarians, 22% of the women and 8% of the men were under 30 years of age; 26% of the women and 30% of the men were between 30 and 45 years of age; and 42% of the women and 57% of the men were over 45 years of age. 10% of the women and 5% of the men did not respond. **(383)**

■ A 1972 study of U.S. medical school libraries and other large biomedical libraries (collection of 35,000+ volumes and staff of 3 or more) concerning the status of women professionals (survey size: 160 libraries; responding: 143; usable: 140 or 87.5%) *showed that*, of 37 women and 64 men in the sample whose age was known, men became head medical librarians at a younger age than women. The age at which these librarians became heads follows:

under 30 years old	5 (13.5%) women;	8 (12.5%) men
30-34 years old	4 (10.8%) women;	24 (37.5%) men
35-39 years old	9 (24.3%) women;	11 (17.2%) men
40-44 years old	7 (18.9%) women;	16 (25.0%) men

continued

45-49 years old   6 (16.2%) women;   4 (6.3%) men
50 and older   6 (16.2%) women;   1 (1.6%) men **(709)**

Directors—Career Patterns

General

■ A study reported in 1981 of information on chief librarians generated in a 1975-76 survey of Canadian librarians in public, special, and academic libraries (study size: 96 chief librarians including 49 females and 47 males) *showed that* 3 (6.3%) of the women and 13 (28.9%) of the men were chief librarians in their first job, while 6 (12.5%) of the women and 2 (4.4%) of the men were department heads as their first job.   **(557)**

Ibid. . . . *showed that* career pattern for chief librarians was as follows:

started in their 20s and took no breaks (24 or 53.3% women; 22 or 56.4% men);

started in their 20s and took a break of less than 5 years (7 or 15.6% women; 0 men);

started in their 20s and took a break of more than 5 years (2 or 4.4% women; 1 or 2.6% men);

started in their 30s (12 or 26.7% women; 16 or 41% men).   **(557)**

■ A study reported in 1981 of a portion of the COSWL data, involving the responses of 739 personal members (195 men; 544 women) of the American Library Association who were at the time of the study employed in libraries and who had received their professional library degree prior to 1971, *showed that* 64.7% of the male library directors, 45.6% of male middle managers, and 32.6% of male librarians/other reported a career pattern involving different positions in different libraries, compared to 45.8% of female library directors, 44.9% of female middle managers, and 35.3% of female librarians/other. This was the most common career pattern for both groups.   **(241)**

Academic

■ A survey reported in 1967 of selected head college librarians in the U.S. (sample size: 660; responding: 414 or 62.7%) *showed that* men were more likely to be heads of tax-supported college libraries, while women were more likely to be heads of privately supported college libraries. Out of 143 head librarians in tax-supported colleges 82 (57.34%) were men, while out of 271 head librarians in privately supported schools 152 (56.09%) were women. **(177)**

Ibid. . . . *showed that* men are more likely than women to be head librarians of larger colleges. Out of 114 head librarians of colleges with enrollments ranging from 1,500 to 5,000 (the largest category in the study) 72 (63.15%) were men. The percentage of male head librarians decreased as college size decreased to the smallest category of colleges (less than 500 students), where 46 (63.89%) of the head librarians were women and 26 (36.11%) were men. **(177)**

Ibid. . . . *showed that* women head librarians tended to change positions less often than men. Of 173 head librarians who had been in their present positions for over 10 years, 112 (64.80%) were women. Of 82 head librarians who had been in their present positions for over 16 years, 60 (73.17%) were women. **(177)**

Ibid. . . . *showed that* men tended to become head librarians at an earlier age than women librarians. Of the 85 librarians who were under 40 years of age, 65 (74.46%) were men. Only in the 50+-years-old category do women have a higher percentage of head positions, 130 (68.42%) compared to 60 (31.58%) for men. **(177)**

■ A 1972 survey of chief library administrators in public comprehensive community colleges (population: 586; usable responses: 75.9% [no raw number given]), *showed that* prior to their present position 69.7% had been librarians (3% of these had had audiovisual responsibilities as well), 7.9% had been working in a learning resource center, 5% had been audiovisual or media specialists, "fewer than 10%" had been teachers, and 8% reported "other." **(452)**

■ A 1972 study of U.S. medical school libraries and other large biomedical libraries (collection of 35,000+ volumes and staff of 3 or more) concerning the status of women professionals (survey size: 160 libraries; responding: 143; usable: 140 or 87.5%) *showed that*, in a comparison of the 25 largest and 25 smallest medical libraries in the total sample, women were more likely to be head of the smaller libraries while men were more likely to be head of the larger libraries. Specifically, although women librarians constituted 75.2% of the professional staff in the larger libraries (305 women to 101 men), women held only 25% of the head positions in these libraries (out of 24 filled positions, 6 heads were women, and 18 were men). In the smaller libraries, where women constituted 83.7% of the professional staff (82 women to 16 men), women held 70.8% of the head positions (out of 24 filled positions, 17 heads were women, and 7 were men).   **(709)**

Ibid. . . . *showed that* since 1950 the biggest gender change had taken place in the head positions of the larger medical libraries. In the 25 largest libraries women held 25% of the filled top positions in 1972, while in 1950 women held 57.1% of the top positions in these libraries. In the smallest libraries women held 70.8% of the filled positions in 1972, while in 1950 women held 89.5% of the top positions in these libraries.   **(709)**

■ A random sample of directors or academic libraries in the U.S. undertaken in 1976 (sample size: 266; response 215 or 80.8%) *showed that*, contrary to earlier findings, there was no statistically significant relationship between organizational size of library and internal succession. In fact, the data suggested that larger libraries were more likely to hire from the outside. 32.2% of the smaller libraries hired internal candidates, compared to 22.3% of the larger libraries (6 or more professionals).   **(121)**

Ibid. . . . *showed that* of present directors 28% had been internal candidates, 56% had been external candidates from another library, 7% had come from a nonlibrary position, 7% from school, and 2% had been unemployed.   **(121)**

Ibid. . . . *showed that* there was a statistically significant tendency for women library directors to have been hired internally in both public and private institutions regardless of organizational size (significance level of .01). In private institutions 55.6% of the women had been internal candidates, compared to 21.8% men; in public institutions 44.4% of the women candidates had been internal, compared to 11.7% of the men.
                                                                      (121)

■ A 1977 survey of all libraries in U.S. medical schools and U.S. health science libraries holding over 40,000 volumes with staffs of 3 or more (survey size: 149 libraries; responding: 126 or 84.6%) *showed that* of 28 female heads, 26 (92.9%) had only female associate librarians, and 2

(7.1%) had only male associate librarians; while, of 53 male heads, 37 (69.8%) had only female associate librarians, 10 (18.9%) had only male associate librarians, and 6 (11.3%) had 1 male and 1 female as associate librarians. **(727)**

Ibid. . . . *showed that* female head librarians tended to be concentrated in the smaller libraries, while male head librarians tended to be concentrated in larger libraries. Nevertheless, in both types of libraries men held head librarian positions in higher proportion than their overall numbers in the workforce in both types of libraries would suggest. For example, in the 25 largest libraries by collection size women constituted 75% of the professional workforce but held only 30.4% of 23 filled head librarian positions, while in the 25 smallest libraries by collection size, where women constituted 76% of the professional workforce, they still held only 56.5% of filled head librarian positions. **(727)**

Ibid. . . . *showed that* a higher proportion of female head librarians was appointed' from within. For example, 20 (27.8%) of the males and 21 (45.7%) of the females who were head librarians at the time of the survey were appointed to the head librarian position from within. **(727)**

Ibid. . . . *showed that* overall men tended to head larger libraries both in terms of collection and in terms of staff. For example, for a male head librarian (excluding the National Library of Medicine) the average collection size was 138,696 volumes and 29.9 staff members, while for female head librarians the average collection size was 111,299 volumes and 24.2 staff members. **(727)**

■ A review of 122 newly hired library directors of accredited U.S. 4-year colleges and universities during 1977-79 *showed that* new directors whose previous institution was a low prestige institution tended to go to low prestige institutions (83%), where new directors whose previous institution was high prestige tended to split evenly between high and low prestige institutions. In 90% of the cases where new directors of low prestige institutions came from high prestige institutions, "unambiguous career advancement in terms of position level or size of library or institution was evident." **(044)**

Ibid. . . . *showed that* the highest proportion of new female directors (50-51%) tended to be in small private and public institutions and medium-sized private institutions, that women were more likely than men to be internal appointees (30% vs. 9%) and to be hired from positions outside academic libraries (33% vs. 11%). **(044)**

Ibid. . . . *showed that* 83% (101) had previous positions in academic libraries, and 93% (114) had previous positions in some type of library or library-related organization. **(044)**

Ibid. . . . *showed that* of the 101 library directors whose previous position was in an academic library, 46 came from large libraries as opposed to 29 from medium-sized and 26 from small libraries. **(044)**

Ibid. . . . *showed that* previous experience in a library of comparable or larger size was important for gaining director positions in medium and large libraries. The breakdown of new directors' previous library's affiliation was as follows:

NEW DIRECTORS OF	FROM
small libraries (62)	21 small libraries
	14 medium libraries
	11 large libraries
	16 other
medium libraries (24)	5 small libraries
	10 medium libraries
	11 large libraries
	3 other
large libraries (31)	5 medium libraries
	24 large libraries
	2 other **(044)**

■ A 1980 survey of first-time-appointed academic library directors during the period 1970-80 (survey size: 230 directors; responding: 141 or 61.3%, including 98 males and 43 females) *showed that*, of 122 respondents, the position from which they were appointed to a directorship was as follows:

77 (63.1%) respondents, including 59 (69.4%) males and 18 (48.6%) females, held top management positions (second in command to the director or head of collection development, reader/public services, technical services) at the time of their appointment to the director position;

19 (15.6%) respondents, including 12 (14.1%) males and 7 (18.9%) females, held middle management positions (e.g. department heads, undergraduate library heads, etc.) at the time of their appointment to the director position;

26 (21.3%) respondents, including 14 (16.5%) males and 12 (32.4%) females, held other positions at the time of their appointment to the director position. **(785)**

Ibid. . . . *showed that*, of 77 respondents moving into a directorship from a top management position, 31 (40.3%) came from a general administration position, 25 (32.5%) came from a technical services position, 17 (22.1%) came from a reader/public services position, and 4 (5.2%) came from a collection development position. **(785)**

Ibid. . . . *showed that* of 19 respondents moving into a directorship from a middle management position, 6 (31.6%) came from a general administration position, none came from a technical services position, and 13 (68.4%) came from a public services position. **(785)**

Ibid. . . . *showed that*, of 114 respondents, newly appointed directors came from the following types of institutions:

research universities (public and private)	46.5% respondents
comprehensive colleges and universities	24.4% respondents
doctorate-granting universities	15.8% respondents
private liberal arts colleges	13.1% respondents

while newly appointed directors went to the following types of institutions:

comprehensive colleges and universities	39.5% respondents
private liberal arts colleges	25.4% respondents
public research universities	19.3% respondents
doctorate-granting universities	15.0% respondents

Further, public comprehensive colleges appointed the largest percentage of females to library directorships, with 15 (48.4%) females appointed out of 31 positions filled. **(785)**

■ A study reported in 1983 of data compiled on 153 Association of Research Libraries and major public library directors *showed that*, where the first professional position was known, 77% of the public library directors began in public libraries, while 80% of the academic library directors

began in academic libraries. Only 16% of the public library directors began
in academic libraries, while only 11% of the academic library directors
began in public libraries.   **(275)**

Ibid. . . . *showed that* public librarians obtained their first directorship at
an average age of 35.9 years, while academic librarians obtained their first
directorship at an average age of 39.3 years. 27% of the public library
directors got their first directorship while in their 20s, and 71% had their
first directorship before they reached 40, compared to 7% of the academic
directors who received their first directorship during their 20s and 49% had
their directorships before age 40.   **(275)**

Public

■ A study reported in 1983 of data compiled on 153 Association of
Research Libraries and major public library directors *showed that*,
where the first professional position was known, 77% of the public
library directors began in public libraries, while 80% of the academic
library directors began in academic libraries. Only 16% of the public library directors began in academic libraries, while only 11% of the
academic library directors began in public libraries.   **(275)**

Ibid. . . . *showed that* public librarians obtained their first directorship at
an average age of 35.9 years, while academic librarians obtained their first
directorship at an average age of 39.3 years. 27% of the public library
directors got their first directorship while in their 20s and 71% had their
first directorship before they reached 40, compared to 7% of the academic
directors who received their first directorship during their 20s and 49% had
their directorships before age 40.   **(275)**

Ibid. . . . *showed that* of 114 respondents, newly appointed directors came
from the following types of institutions:

research universities (public and private)	46.5% respondents
comprehensive colleges and universities	24.4% respondents
doctorate-granting universities	15.8% respondents
private liberal arts colleges	13.1% respondents

while newly appointed directors went to the following types of institutions:

comprehensive colleges and universities	39.5% respondents

continued

private liberal arts colleges	25.4% respondents
public research universities	19.3% respondents
doctorate-granting universities	15.0% respondents

Further, public comprehensive colleges appointed the largest percentage of females to library directorships, with 15 (48.4%) females appointed out of 31 positions filled.   **(785)**

Special

A 1972 study of U.S. medical school libraries and other large biomedical libraries (collection of 35,000+ volumes and staff of 3 or more) concerning the status of women professionals (survey size: 160 libraries; responding: 143; usable: 140 or 87.5%) *showed that*, in a comparison of the 25 largest and 25 smallest medical libraries in the total sample, women were more likely to be head of the smaller libraries, while men were more likely to be head of the larger libraries. Specifically, although women librarians constituted 75.2% of the professional staff in the larger libraries (305 women to 101 men), women held only 25% of the head positions in these libraries (out of 24 filled positions, 6 heads were women, and 18 were men). In the smaller libraries, where women constituted 83.7% of the professional staff (82 women to 16 men), women held 70.8% of the head positions (out of 24 filled positions, 17 heads were women, and 7 were men).   **(709)**

Ibid. . . . *showed that* since 1950 the biggest gender change had taken place in the head positions of the larger medical libraries. In the 25 largest libraries women held 25% of the filled top positions in 1972, while in 1950 women held 57.1% of the top positions in these libraries. In the 25 smallest libraries women held 70.8% of the filled positions in 1972, while in 1950 women held 89.5% of the top positions in these libraries.   **(709)**

■ A 1977 survey of all libraries in U.S. medical schools and U.S. health science libraries holding over 40,000 volumes with staffs of 3 or more (survey size: 149 libraries; responding: 126 or 84.6%) *showed that* women head librarians tended to be concentrated in the smaller libraries, while male head librarians tended to be concentrated in larger libraries. Nevertheless, in both types of libraries men held head librarian positions in higher proportion than their overall numbers in the workforce in both types of libraries would suggest. For example, in the 25 largest libraries by collection size, women constituted 75% of the professional workforce but held only 30.4% of 23 filled head librarian positions, while in the 25 smallest libraries by collection size, where women constituted 76% of the professional workforce, they still held only 56.5% of filled head librarian positions.   **(727)**

Ibid. . . . *showed that* a higher proportion of female head librarians was appointed from within. For example, 20 (27.8%) of the males and 21 (45.7%) of the females who were head librarians at the time of the survey were appointed to the head librarian position from within.   **(727)**

Ibid. . . . *showed that* overall men tended to head larger libraries both in terms of collection and in terms of staff. For example, for a male head librarian (excluding the National Library of Medicine) the average collection size was 138,696 volumes and 29.9 staff members, while for female head librarians the average collection size was 111,299 volumes and 24.2 staff members.   **(727)**

Directors—Education

General

■ A survey reported in 1978 of traceable North American librarians who had earned library doctorates in American Library Association accredited programs between 1930 and 1975 (survey size: 568; responding: 403 or 71%) *showed that*, based on a scoring system where "3" = essential, "2" = important, "1" = useful, and "0" = unimportant, respondents overall rated the library doctorate 2.4 in obtaining their present posts and 1.99 in performing the duties of their present post. Specifically:

> library educators rated the library doctorate 2.81 in obtaining their present posts and 2.33 in performing their duties;

> library administrators ranked the library doctorate 2.06 in obtaining their present position and 1.73 in performing their duties;

> library researchers ranked the library doctorate 1.86 in obtaining their present position and 1.51 in performing their duties;

> individuals in library operations ranked the library doctorate 1.20 in obtaining their present position and 1.07 in performing their duties.   **(463)**

Academic

■ A 1972 study of U.S. medical school libraries and other large biomedical libraries (collection of 35,000+ volumes and staff of 3 or more) concerning the status of women professionals (survey size: 160 libraries;

responding: 143; usable: 140 or 87.5%) *showed that*, overall, 16 (11.4%) of the 140 head medical librarians held doctorates. Of the female head librarians 3 (5.5%) held doctorates, while 13 (16.6%) of the male head librarians held doctorates. **(709)**

■ A 1974-75 study of university libraries including all Association of Research Libraries libraries (sample size: 92; responding: 72 or 78%) and all library schools with ALA-accredited programs (sample size: not given; responding: 44 or 80%) *showed that*, of 72 responding library directors and 44 responding library school deans, the numbers who felt it was desirable to hire subject Ph.D.'s in the following positions were as follows: administration (50% library directors; 74.2% deans), reference (70.8% library directors; 83.9% deans), bibliography (87.5% library directors; 93.6% deans), archives (86.1% library directors; 87.1% deans), and technical services (34.7% library directors; 3.2% deans). **(445)**

■ A study reported in 1975 of the degree to which 2-year college libraries (sample size 26; responding, 23) in the state of Ohio conformed to the "Guidelines for Two-Year College Learning Resources Programs" established by the ACRL Board of Directors in 1972 *showed that* 16 of the LRCs required the M.L.S. degree and 1 either an M.L.S. or the M.S. in audiovisual education for the head of the unit, while only 3 did not require a master's degree of some kind. **(127)**

■ A 1976 survey of head law librarians in North American schools (sample size: 178; responding: 154 or 86.7%) *showed that* 18 (12%) of the library directors held an M.L.S. only, that 30 (19%) held a J.D. or LL.B. only; and that 104 (68%) held both an M.L.S. and J.D. or LL.B. degree. 2 (1%) held other degrees. **(357)**

■ A 1977 survey of all libraries in U.S. medical schools and U.S. health science libraries holding over 40,000 volumes with staffs of 3 or more (survey size: 149 libraries; responding: 126 or 84.6%) *showed that*, of the 72 male head librarians, 10 (13.9%) held doctorates, while of 46 female head librarians, 3 (6.5%) held doctorates. **(727)**

■ A study reported in 1978 of 23 middle managers and 11 administrators in 5 Association of Research Libraries libraries as well as a review of ads for 82 middle managerial positions in academic libraries posted in 1975 *showed that* 43 (52.4%) of the ads listed an ALA-accredited library master's degree as a qualification; 37 (45.1%) listed library master's degree without specifying ALA-accredited; 30 (36.6%) listed second master's degree; 4 (4.9%) listed Ph.D.; 1 (1.2%) listed an other professional degree; and 1 stated that a master's degree was not required.   **(423)**

■ A 1978 survey of law school libraries listed in the 1977 *AALS Directory of Law Teachers* (population: 167; responding: 158 or 95%) *showed that* the degrees held by the head law librarian were as follows:

undergraduate degree only	1 (0.6%) respondent
undergraduate and library science degrees	12 (07.6%) respondents
undergraduate and law degrees	20 (12.7%) respondents
all three degrees	121 (76.6%) respondents
no degree	1 (0.6%) respondent
no response	3 (1.9%) respondents **(362)**

■ A survey reported in 1978 of the degree to which library doctorates were required in advertisements appearing over a 6-month period (June 1976 through December 1976) in a wide range of publications for professional positions in library schools and head administrative posts in academic libraries (46 ads for library school positions; 53 ads for head administrators in academic libraries) *showed that* 5 (9.4%) of the 53 positions in academic libraries required a doctorate, with 4 of the positions requiring subject, not library doctorates. A further 21 (39.6%) positions indicated a preference for a doctorate, with 5 preferring a library doctorate, 6 preferring a subject doctorate, and 11 accepting either. 27 (50.9%) positions did not mention the need for a doctorate in the ads.   **(463)**

Ibid. . . . *showed that*, of the library school ads, 39 (84.8%) required a doctorate of some kind with 23 (50%) requiring a library doctorate and 16 (34.8%) indicating that a subject doctorate was also acceptable.   **(463)**

■ A survey reported in 1978 of traceable North American librarians who had earned library doctorates in American Library Association accredited programs between 1930 and 1975 (survey size: 568; responding: 403 or 71%) *showed that* 51.3% reported being in library education; 33.8% reported being in the field of library administration; 11.1% reported library research (as distinct from any other categories); and 3.8% reported being in library operations.   **(463)**

■ A 1980 survey of first-time-appointed academic library directors during the period 1970-80 (survey size: 230 directors; responding: 141 or 61.3%, including 98 males and 43 females) *showed that* the U.S. library degrees held by respondents were as follows (multiple responses allowed):

bachelor's degree (undergraduate minor in library science) was held by 3 (2.1%) of the directors, including none of the males and 3 (7.0%) of the females;

5th-year bachelor's degree in library science was held by 6 (4.3%) of the directors, including 1 (1.0%) of the males and 5 (11.6%) of the females;

master's in library science was held by 132 (93.6%) of the directors, including 92 (93.9%) of the males and 40 (93.0%) of the females;

certificates of advanced study (or equivalent) were held by 7 (5.0%) of the directors, including 5 (5.1%) of the males and 2 (4.7%) of the females;

doctorate in library science was held by 14 (9.9%) of the directors, including 10 (10.2%) of the males and 4 (9.3%) of the females. **(785)**

Ibid. . . . *showed that*, of 122 respondents, the position from which they were appointed to a directorship was as follows:

77 (63.1%) respondents, including 59 (69.4%) males and 18 (48.6%) females, held top management positions (second in command to the director or head of collection development, reader/public services, technical services) at the time of their appointment to the director position;

19 (15.6%) respondents, including 12 (14.1%) males and 7 (18.9%) females, held middle management positions (e.g., department heads, undergraduate library heads, etc.) at the time of their appointment to the director position;

26 (21.3%) respondents, including 14 (16.5%) males and 12 (32.4%) females, held other positions at the time of their appointment to the director position. **(785)**

Ibid. . . . *showed that*, of 77 respondents moving into a directorship from a top management position, 31 (40.3%) came from a general administration position, 25 (32.5%) came from a technical services position, 17 (22.1%) came from a reader/public services position, and 4 (5.2%) came from a collection development position. **(785)**

Ibid. . . . *showed that* of 19 respondents moving into a directorship from a middle management position, 6 (31.6%) came from a general administration position, none came from a technical services position, and 13 (68.4%) came from a public services position. **(785)**

■ A study reported in 1981 of job listings for college and university libraries reported in *Library Journal* and *College and Research Libraries News* during 1970-79 (5,269 job listings) *showed that*, overall for the survey period for director university positions, 39.8% required Ph.D., 12.7% required a second master's, while 47.5% required no additional educational certification. Overall for director college positions, 19.9% required a Ph.D., 16.4% required a second master's, while 63.7% required no additional educational certification. **(494)**

Ibid. . . . *showed that* director positions in both the college and university environments required a statistically significantly higher level of educational requirements than nondirector positions in either colleges or universities. Significant at the .05 level or less. **(494)**

Ibid. . . . *showed that* both director and nondirector positions in the university environment listed statistically significantly higher educational requirements than director and nondirector positions in the college environment. Significant at the .05 level or less. **(494)**

Ibid. . . . *showed that* educational requirements for nondirector positions generally increased from 1970 through 1976, with a peak in the 1974-76 period and decline in educational requirements subsequently. The only exceptions to this pattern were college director positions, whose educational requirements increased throughout the survey period. **(494)**

■ A study reported in 1983 of data compiled on 153 Association of Research Libraries and major public library directors *showed that* all but 1 of the 153 directors graduated from a library school, with the top 7 schools (in terms of graduating major library directors) graduating 50.7% of the directors.

Columbia	19 (12.5%)	directors
Illinois	13 (8.6%)	
Michigan	13 (8.6%)	
Simmons	11 (7.2%)	
Chicago	7 (4.6%)	
Louisiana State	7 (4.6%)	
Wisconsin (Madison)	7 (4.6%)	**(275)**

Ibid. . . . *showed that* 57% of the academic directors held one or more degrees beyond a master's in library science, while 20% of the public library directors held further degrees. 1/3 of the academic directors had doctorates, "mostly in library science." **(275)**

Public

■ A survey reported in 1967 of midwestern librarians (37 men, 408 women, total 445) in small public libraries (i.e., serving populations of 10,000 to 35,000), *showed that*:

of those librarians under 30 years of age, 91.6% had completed 4 years of college;

of librarians in their 30s, 85.0% had completed college;

of librarians in their 40s, 65.3% had completed college;

of librarians in their 50s, 52.0% had completed college;

of librarians in their 60s, 53.1% had completed college;

and of those librarians 70+, 50.0% had completed college. **(282)**

Ibid. . . . *showed that*, of the respondents as a group, 36.0% had no college degree; 26.4% had no more than a college degree; 13.3% had no more than a fifth-year bachelor's degree; and 24.1% had no more than a master's degree. **(282)**

Ibid. . . . *showed that* 54.3% of the librarians with professional degrees worked in communities with median incomes of less than $7,000, while 72.2% of the librarians with less training worked in such communities; 19.4% of the librarians with professional degrees worked in communities with median incomes $10,000+, while only 6.5% of the librarians with less training worked in such communities. A positive correlation (correlation coefficient = .20) between professional training and community income was determined. (No significance level given.) **(282)**

Ibid. . . . *showed that* there was a slight statistical relationship (correlation coefficient = .14) between size of community and professional education of the librarian. 29.4% of the librarians with professional degrees and 40.3% of the librarians with less education worked in libraries serving communities of 10,000 to 14,999, while 16.5% of the librarians with professional degrees and 10.9% of the librarians with less education worked in libraries serving communities of 30,000 to 34,999 (no significance level given). **(282)**

■ A study reported in 1983 of data compiled on 153 Association of Research Libraries and major public library directors *showed that* all but 1 of the 153 directors graduated from a library school,with the top 7 schools (in terms of graduating major library directors) graduating 50.7% of the directors.

Columbia graduated	19 (12.5%) directors	
Illinois	13 (8.6%) directors	
Michigan	13 (8.6%) directors	
Simmons	11 (7.2%) directors	
Chicago	7 (4.6%) directors	
Louisiana State	7 (4.6%) directors	
Wisconsin (Madison)	7 (4.6%) directors	**(275)**

Ibid. . . . *showed that* 57% of the academic directors held one or more degrees beyond a master's in library science, while 20% of the public library directors held further degrees. 1/3 of the academic directors had doctorates, "mostly in library science." **(275)**

Special

■ A survey reported in 1971 of the professional law librarians listed as members of the American Association of Law Libraries (population not given; response: "approximately 50%," no number given) *showed that*, of 286 female and 138 male head law librarians, the [highest] degree achieved was high school diploma for 15% of the women and 3% of the men; was a B.A. or B.S. for 21% of the women and 8% of the men; was M.A. or M.L.S. for 34% of the women and 35% of the men; and was LL.B. or J.D. for 24% of the women and 41% of the men. 2% of the women and 6% of the men did not respond. **(383)**

■ A 1972 study of U.S. medical school libraries and other large biomedical libraries (collection of 35,000+ volumes and staff of 3 or more) concerning the status of women professionals (survey size: 160 libraries; responding: 143; usable: 140 or 87.5%) *showed that*, overall, 16 (11.4%) of the 140 head medical librarians held doctorates. Of the female head librarians 3 (5.5%) held doctorates, while 13 (16.6%) of the male head librarians held doctorates. **(709)**

■ A 1976 survey of head law librarians in North American schools (sample size: 178; responding: 154 or 86.7%) *showed that* 18 (12%) of the library directors held an M.L.S. only; that 30 (19%) held a J.D. or LL.B. only; and that 104 (68%) held both an M.L.S. and J.D. or LL.B. degree. 2 (1%) held other degrees. **(357)**

■ A 1977 survey of all libraries in U.S. medical schools and U.S. health science libraries holding over 40,000 volumes with staffs of 3 or more (survey size: 149 libraries; responding: 126 or 84.6%) *showed that* of the 72 male head librarians, 10 (13.9%) held doctorates, while of 46 female head librarians, 3 (6.5%) held doctorates. **(727)**

■ A 1978 survey of law school libraries listed in the 1977 *AALS Directory of Law Teachers* (population: 167; responding: 158 or 95%) *showed that* the degrees held by the head law librarian were as follows:

undergraduate degree only	1 (0.6%)	respondent
undergraduate and library science degrees	12 (07.6%)	respondents
undergraduate and law degrees	20 (12.7%)	respondents
all three degrees	121 (76.6%)	respondents
no degree	1 (0.6%)	respondent
no response	3 (1.9%)	respondents **(362)**

■ An annual survey reported in 1981 of state law libraries in North America (no population given; no response given) *showed that* the highest degree held by 23 head librarians in state law libraries was as follows: M.L.S. (13 head librarians), law degree (2), both M.L.S. and law degree (5), other master's (1), bachelor's (1), and high school (1). **(380)**

Directors—Internal Succession

Academic

■ A random sample of directors of academic libraries in the U.S. undertaken in 1976 (sample size: 266; response: 215 or 80.8%) *showed that*, contrary to earlier findings, there was no statistically significant relationship between organizational size of library and internal succession. In fact, the data suggested that larger libraries were more likely to hire from the outside. Specifically, 32.2% of the smaller libraries hired internal candidates compared to 22.3% of the larger libraries (6 or more professionals). **(121)**

Ibid. . . . *showed that* of present directors 28% had been internal candidates, 56% had been external candidates from another library, 7% had come from a nonlibrary position, 7% from school, and 2% had been unemployed.   **(121)**

Ibid. . . . *showed that* there was a statistically significant tendency for women library directors to have been hired internally in both public and private institutions regardless of organizational size (significance level of .01). In private institutions 55.6% of the women had been internal candidates compared to 21.8% men; in public institutions 44.4% of the women candidates had been internal compared to 11.7% of the men.

(121)

■ A 1977 survey of all libraries in U.S. medical schools and U.S. health science libraries holding over 40,000 volumes with staffs of 3 or more (survey size: 149 libraries; responding: 126 or 84.6%) *showed that* a higher proportion of female head librarians was appointed from within. For example, 20 (27.8%) of the males and 21 (45.7%) of the females who were head librarians at the time of the survey were appointed to the head librarian position from within.   **(727)**

Special

■ A 1977 survey of all libraries in U.S. medical schools and U.S. health science libraries holding over 40,000 volumes with staffs of 3 or more (survey size: 149 libraries; responding: 126 or 84.6%) *showed that* a higher proportion of female head librarians were appointed from within. For example, 20 (27.8%) of the males and 21 (45.7%) of the females who were head librarians at the time of the survey were appointed to the head librarian position from within.   **(727)**

Directors—Job Interviews

Academic

■ A survey reported in 1980 of newly appointed library directors of 4-year colleges and universities (positions announced in library journals between June 1977 and February 1979 and excluding law, medical, and service acadamy appointments) (survey size: 66; responding: 54 or 81.8%) *showed that* search committees were used in 50 cases, with the chief academic officer conducting the search in 4 cases—all at small private colleges.   **(482)**

Ibid. . . . *showed that* 16 (29.6%) respondents reported that their search committee had fewer than 2 library employees on their committees, while only 4 (7.4%) reported that more than half of the the search committee consisted of library employees. No respondents reported a search committee of only library employees. In only 7 (13.0%) cases was the search committee chaired by a library employee. **(482)**

Ibid. . . . *showed that* only 4 (7.4%) respondents reported that the search committee or hiring officers made an on-site visit to their former library as part of the search process. **(482)**

Ibid. . . . *showed that* during the interview "almost all" respondents reported meeting with the president, the chief academic officer, and the professional library staff; 43 (79.6%) respondents reported meeting with the nonprofessional library staff; 40 (74.1%) reported meeting with the faculty library committee; 33 (61.1%) reported meeting with the academic dean; 32 (59.3%) reported meeting the previous library director; and 29 (53.7%) reported meeting students. **(482)**

Ibid. . . . *showed that* "most" of the respondents reported meeting with 6-10 individuals and groups, while 6 (11.1%) reported meeting with 4-5 individuals and groups, and 6 (11.1%) reported meeting with 11-16 individuals and groups. **(482)**

Ibid. . . . *showed that* 18 (33.3%) of the respondents reported being invited back for a second visit. Further, 21 (38.9%) reported spending less than 2 days on the interview visit; 16 (29.6%) reported spending 2 days on the interview visit; and 14 (25.9%) reported interview visits longer than 2 days. **(482)**

Directors—Job Satisfaction

General

■ A survey reported in 1978 of traceable North American librarians who had earned library doctorates in American Library Association accredited programs between 1930 and 1975 (survey size: 568; responding: 403 or 71%) *showed that* respondents were generally happy with the type of work they were doing. Specifically:

of library administrators 76.1% reported that they preferred administration to other type of work, while only 10.9% reported that they preferred education;

of individuals in library operations, 53.3% preferred this type of work, while 26.7% reported they would prefer library administration;

of library educators 86.7% preferred this type of work, while only 7.1% reported they would prefer library administration;

of library researchers 67.6% preferred this type of work [no information is given on those preferring alternative types of work]. **(463)**

Academic

■ A 1972 survey of chief library administrators in public comprehensive community colleges (population: 586; usable responses: 75.9% [no raw number given]) *showed that* 94.3% reported that the position was satisfying with "less than 6%" reporting dissatisfaction. **(452)**

Directors—Length of Service

General

■ A study reported in 1981 of information on chief librarians generated in a 1975-76 survey of Canadian librarians in public, special, and academic libraries (study size: 96 chief librarians including 49 females and 47 males) *showed that* length of career of chief librarians was as follows:

less than 10 years	15 (31.3%) women;	11 (23.4%) men
10-19 years	14 (29.2%) women;	21 (44.7%) men
20-29 years	10 (20.8%) women;	11 (23.4%) men
30 or more years	9 (18.7%) women;	4 (8.5%) men **(557)**

Academic

■ A survey reported in 1967 of selected head college librarians in the U.S. (sample size: 660; responding: 414 or 62.7%) *showed that* women head librarians tended to change positions less often than men. Of 173 head librarians who had been in their present positions for over 10 years, 112 (64.80%) were women. Of 82 head librarians who had been in their present positions for over 16 years, 60 (73.17%) were women. **(177)**

■ A 1972 survey of chief library administrators in public comprehensive community colleges (population: 586; usable responses: 75.9% [no raw number given]) *showed that* respondents had served the following length of time in their present positions: 1 year or less ("slightly less than 10%" respondents), 2-5 years (47.9% respondents), 6-10 years (25.5% respondents), 10+ years (16% respondents). **(452)**

■ A random sample of directors of academic libraries in the U.S. undertaken in 1976 (sample size: 266; response: 215 or 80.8%) *showed that* the median tenure of directors was 6 years with the average tenure 8.1 years. **(121)**

School

■ A 1983 survey of a systematic sample of school library media centers concerning data for fiscal year 1982-83 (survey size: 2,000 centers; responding: 1,297; usable: 1,251 or 62%) *showed that* a comparison of privately supported (72) and publicly supported (1,179) school library media centers revealed that media specialists in private schools served fewer students, had more money to spend on resources, administered smaller collections, and earned more modest salaries. Specifically:

enrollment averaged 460 students for private schools and 669 for public schools;

total materials expenditure per student averaged $12.55 for private schools and $9.62 for public schools;

the number of books per student averaged 27.08 for private schools and 18.44 for public schools;

the number of AV items per student averaged 3.2 for private schools and 3.26 for public schools;

in private schools the media specialist averaged 8.92 years of experience with a salary of $13,880, while in public schools the media specialists averaged 11.08 years of experience with a salary of $20,389. **(56)**

Special

■ A survey reported in 1971 of the professional law librarians listed as members of the American Association of Law Libraries (population not given; response: "approximately 50%," no number given) *showed that* of 286 female and 138 male head law librarians, the length of time in the profession was as follows: 1-5 years (31% women; 22% men); 6-10 years (18% women; 12% men); 11-15 years (16% women; 12% men); 16+ years (33% women; 40% men). 2% of the women and 6% of the men did not respond. **(383)**

Directors—Library Advisory Committee

Academic

■ A 1967 survey of the 64 ARL library directors (56 responding; 54 with library advisory committees) concerning library advisory committees *showed that* the average number of members on a library advisory committee was 13 with a range from 6 to 66.   **(181)**

Ibid. . . . *showed that* approximately 2/3 of the respondents reported that the library director was consulted on appointments made to the library advisory committee. The actual appointments were made in 20 cases by the university administration, in 17 cases by the teaching faculty, in 13 cases by the administration and faculty jointly, and by the governing board of the university in 4 cases.   **(181)**

Ibid. . . . *showed that* the library director was an ex officio member of 43 library advisory committees, chair of 6, and served in miscellaneous capacities in the remaining 5 instances. Further, in 43 library advisory committees the library director was the only person officially representing the library, while in 11 cases from 1 to 13 staff members other than the director served as members of the committee.   **(181)**

Ibid. . . . *showed that* the library advisory committee functions largely in an advisory capacity (45 instances), concerned largely with establishment of policies in the operation of the library (a "major activity" or "active" in 28 libraries), and involved in the maintenance of liaison among faculty, library, and administration ("active role" 22 libraries), while the committee's role in selecting new key library staff is quite small (none in 44 libraries) as is also its role in book selection (none in 30 libraries). **(181)**

Directors—Management Style and Attitudes

Academic

■ A survey of all ARL directors plus all other state university library directors reported in 1968 concerning the degree to which librarians participate in traditional faculty activities (72 responding) *showed that* library directors strongly favored or encouraged: writing and publication

(100%), campus committee and similar assignments (100%), professsional service on local, state, and national basis (100%), consulting work (99%), research (97%), surveys (96%), leaves of absence (92%), participation in nonlibrary professional association work (92%), participation in nonprofessional local activities (89%), and teaching (71%). **(182)**

Ibid. . . . *showed that* 76% of respondents reported allowing time for research, and 83% provided some sort of financial assistance. About 60% reported that the research need not be related to library operations or problems. **(182)**

Ibid. . . . *showed that* 86% of respondents reported giving time off for free consulting, while 74% would give the time when the consultant was paid. For surveys, 83% of respondents reported giving time off for free surveys, while 72% would give the time when the surveyor was paid. **(182)**

Ibid. . . . *showed that* all respondents reported giving time for professional activities, and 99% said they pay [some] expenses. 78% of respondents said they paid some expenses to national meetings for staff not on programs or committees. **(182)**

Ibid. . . . *showed that* respondents from 43% of the institutions reported that librarians have been given leave for study or foreign assignments within the last 3 years. **(182)**

Ibid. . . . *showed that*, for participation in nonlibrary professional work, time off is given by 85% of the institutions but expenses are paid "probably to a very limited extent" by only 47%. **(182)**

Ibid. . . . *showed that*, for participation in nonprofessional local activities, 39% of respondents reported that they neither gave time nor any expenses. In terms of time alone, 59% of respondents give it, while 39% do not. **(182)**

■ A survey reported in 1976 of the libraries in the largest private and largest public college/university in each state of the continental U.S.

(sample size: 100 [sic]; responding: 79 or 79%) *showed that* 94% of the respondents conduct [professional] staff meetings, although only 52% of the respondents conduct such meetings regularly. **(413)**

■ A survey conducted in 1976 of heads of American academic libraries (215 responses; 80.8% response rate) *showed that* directors of public academic libraries (in contrast to directors of private academic libraries) dealt less with students (r = −.24) and private donors (r = −.24) and were more extensively involved in dealing with the administration (r = .20), attending professional meetings (r = .20), and obtaining financial resources (r = .28). (All correlations significant at the .01 level.) **(021)**

Ibid. . . . *showed that* library directors spent the following percentage of their time with others as follows: library staff 48%, faculty 15%, administration 13%, students 13%, foundations and donors 3%, other librarians 5%, other persons 3%. **(021)**

Ibid. . . . *showed that* library directors spent the single greatest part of their energy on internal library affairs, above all the library budget. **(021)**

Ibid. . . . *showed that*, although female library directors were more heavily involved in their libraries' internal affairs than male library directors, this was a function not of gender but of their greater representation in small, private institutions. Male directors in this kind of library exhibited the same administrative orientation. **(021)**

Ibid. . . . *showed that* the larger the library the greater involvement the director was likely to have in the external environment, e.g., fund raising (.40 zero-order correlation), professional activities (r = .15), and representing the library to the public (r = .15). **(021)**

■ A study reported in 1980 of all professional librarians (sample size 57; responding: 56) in 4 medium-sized academic libraries in the northeastern U.S. *showed that* administrators tended to rely on 2 or 3 selected individuals in the organization for all information regardless of the nature of the decision or of the individual's competence regarding that decision. **(028)**

Ibid. . . . *showed that* there was a statistically significant relationship at the .01 level between those librarians defined as "information rich" (those scoring in the top 50% of total contacts with information sources) and involvement in decision making. **(028)**

Ibid. . . . *showed that* those librarians who had direct responsibility for the operation of the library contacted a substantially larger quantity of factual information sources than other librarians in the organization. Furthermore, the librarians on whom these administrators relied for information also had more factual information sources than the typical librarian.

(028)

■ A survey reported in 1983 of directors of Association for Research Libraries concerning their attitudes toward joint degree programs (resulting in both a library degree and a degree in some other field) (population surveyed: 111 directors; responding: 93 or 84%) *showed that* only 9 (9.7%) respondents opposed joint degree programs while 38 (40.9%) felt that "most academic disciplines" were suitable for joint programs. The 2 disciplines most frequently mentioned as desirable for joint programs were computer science (47 or 50.3% respondents) and management or business (47 or 50.3% respondents). **(800)**

Ibid. . . . *showed that*, in considering applicants for jobs, directors reported they would consider the joint degree as follows:

asset	70 (75.3%)	respondents
irrelevant	12 (12.9%)	respondents
liability	2 (2.2%)	respondents
no response	9 (9.7%)	respondents **(800)**

Ibid. . . . *showed that* 54 (58.1%) respondents felt that joint graduate degrees were equal to the same degrees earned independently; 27 (29.0%) felt they were not equal; and 12 (12.9%) did not respond. **(800)**

Ibid. . . . *showed that* directors' responses to hiring job applicants with joint graduate degrees compared to hiring applicants with just the M.L.S. degree were as follows:

6 (6.5%) respondents reported that there would be no preference between the candidates;

65 (69.9%) reported they would be more likely to hire the candidate with the joint degrees, while 2 (2.2%) reported they would be more likely to hire the candidate with the M.L.S. only;

47 (50.5%) reported they would pay more to a candidate with the joint degrees, while 20 (21.5%) reported they would not pay more;

43 (46.2%) reported they felt 2 graduate degrees were desirable for nearly all professional positions, 3 (3.2%) reported that they felt 2 graduate degrees were undesirable for most positions, 54 (58.1%) reported they felt 2 graduate degrees were desirable for specialist positions, and 30 (32.3%) reported they felt 2 graduate degrees were desirable for administrative positions. **(800)**

Directors—Mentoring

Academic

■ A survey of ARL Directors in 1980 (sample 111; responding 81, including 70 male and 11 female directors) *showed that* 77% indicated they had had a mentor during their career, including 76% of the males and 82% of the females. **(043)**

Ibid. . . . *showed that* they reported the following number of mentors during their career:

1 mentor	25%
2 mentors	8%
3 mentors	18%
4 mentors	11%
5 mentors	13%
more than 5	24%

There was little difference between male and female responses to this question. **(043)**

Ibid. . . . *showed that*, while the highest number of both men and women reporting mentors indicated they had them during the first 5 years of professional life (78 and 8 respectively), the number of male directors reporting mentors after 10 years of professional work dropped by more than half (to 36) while the number of women reporting mentors after this time tended to remain relatively high (6). **(043)**

Ibid. . . . *showed that* 84% considered mentoring "significant" or "very significant" to their success as compared to luck, which 45% reported as "significant" or "very significant." · **(043)**

Ibid. . . . *showed that*, of the 196 librarians being mentored at the time of the study, 109 (54%) were female and 87 (44%) were male. Female directors were mentoring 21 librarians (76% female; 24% male), while male directors were mentoring 175 librarians (53% female; 47% male). The percentage of women librarians in ARL libraries was 62%. **(043)**

Ibid. . . . *showed that* there were the following numbers of proteges per director)

1 protege	4%
2 proteges	34%
3 proteges	12%
4 proteges	18%
5 proteges	12%
over 5 proteges	20% **(043)**

Ibid. . . . *showed that* over 60% of the directors who had had mentors had proteges, while only 5% of those who had not had mentors had proteges. 19% of the directors (all male) reported having neither mentors nor proteges. **(043)**

Directors—Minorities

Academic

■ A 1980 survey of first-time-appointed academic library directors during the period 1970-80 (survey size: 230 directors; responding: 141 or 61.3%, including 98 males and 43 females) *showed that* ethnic background was as follows:

Asian-Americans accounted for 2 (1.4%) of the directors, including 2 (2.0%) of the males and none of the females;

Hispanics accounted for 2 (1.4%) of the directors, including 2 (2.0%) of the males and none of the females;

blacks accounted for 14 (10.0%) of the directors, including 7 (7.2%) of the males and 7 (9.3%) of the females;

whites accounted for 120 (85.1%) of the directors, including 85 (86.8%) of the males and 35 (81.4%) of the females;

3 individuals did not reply to the question. **(785)**

Directors—Mobility

General

■ A study reported in 1981 of a portion of the COSWL data, involving the responses of 739 personal members (195 men; 544 women) of the American Library Association who were at the time of the study employed in libraries and who had received their professional library degree prior to 1971, *showed that* fewer males than females reported limits to their mobility in terms of job seeking. 69.6% of male directors reported no mobility limits; 54.4% of male middle managers and 57.1% of male librarians/other reported no mobility limits compared to 47.3% of female directors; 42.4% of female middle managers and 42.5% of female librarians/other reported no mobility limits.   **(241)**

Academic

■ A 1977 survey of all libraries in U.S. medical schools and U.S. health science libraries holding over 40,000 volumes with staffs of 3 or more (survey size: 149 libraries; responding: 126 or 84.6%) *showed that*, in order to accept the head librarian position held at the time of the survey, 43 (59.7%) men and 19 (41.3%) women had to relocate. Of those head librarians who did not have to relocate, 6 (20.7%) of the males and 11 (40.7%) of the females would not have accepted had taking the position required a relocation.   **(727)**

Special

■ A 1977 survey of all libraries in U.S. medical schools and U.S. health science libraries holding over 40,000 volumes with staffs of 3 or more (survey size: 149 libraries; responding: 126 or 84.6%) *showed that*, in order to accept the head librarian position held at the time of the survey, 43 (59.7%) men and 19 (41.3%) women had to relocate. Of those head librarians who did not have to relocate, 6 (20.7%) of the males and 11 (40.7%) of the females would not have accepted had taking the position required a relocation.   **(727)**

Directors—Personal Life

General

■ A study reported in 1981 of a portion of the COSWL data, involving the responses of 739 personal members (195 men; 544 women) of the American Library Association who were at the time of the study employed in libraries and who had received their professional library degree prior to

1971, *showed that* 85.5% of male library directors, 66.2% of male middle managers, and 56.1% of male librarians/other were married, compared to 52.6% of female library directors, 47.9% of female middle managers, and 45.7% of female librarians/other. **(241)**

Ibid. . . . *showed that* 4.3% of male library directors, 11.8% of male middle managers, and 7.0% of male librarians/other were divorced, compared to 17.1% of female directors, 19.3% of female middle managers, and 18.1% of female librarians/other. Also showed that 7.2% of male library directors, 19.1% of male middle managers, and 35.1% of male librarians/other had never married, compared to 30.3% of female library directors, 31.4% of female middle managers, and 34.7% of female librarians/other. **(241)**

■ A study reported in 1981 of information on chief librarians generated in a 1975-76 survey of Canadian librarians in public, special, and academic libraries (study size: 96 chief librarians including 49 females and 47 males) *showed that*, among currently or previously married librarians, 25 (78.1%) of the men reported children, while 15 (53.6%) of the females reported children. **(557)**

Ibid. . . . *showed that* the marital status of 95 chief librarians was as follows: currently married (22 or 44.9% women; 31 or 67.4% men), previously married (7 or 14.3% women; 3 or 6.5% men), and single (20 or 40.8% women; 12 or 26.1% men). **(557)**

Academic

■ A 1980 survey of first-time-appointed academic library directors during the period 1970-80 (survey size: 230 directors; responding: 141 or 61.3%, including 98 males and 43 females) *showed that* marital status at the time of the appointment was as follows:

single individuals accounted for 24 (17.0%) of the directors, including 11 (11.2%) of the males and 13 (30.2%) of the females;

married individuals accounted for 96 (68.1%) of the directors, including 78 (79.6%) of the males and 18 (41.9%) of the females;

divorced individuals accounted for 16 (11.3%) of the directors, including 8 (8.2%) of the males and 8 (18.6%) of the females;

widowed individuals accounted for 3 (2.1%) of the directors, including none of the males and 3 (7.0%) of the females;

2 individuals did not reply to the question.   **(785)**

Special

■ A survey reported in 1971 of the professional law librarians listed as members of the American Association of Law Libraries (population not given; response: "approximately 50%," no number given) *showed that* of 286 women head law librarians 43% were married and 57% were single, compared to 138 men head law librarians of whom 83% were married and 17% were single.   **(383)**

Directors—Professional Organizations

Academic

■ A 1980 survey of first-time-appointed academic library directors during the period 1970-80 (survey size: 230 directors; responding: 141 or 61.3%, including 98 males and 43 females) *showed that*, of 134 respondents, 91 (67.9%) respondents, including 58 (61.7%) males and 33 (82.5%) females, reported holding no offices (including committee chairs) in national library organizations in the 5 years prior to appointment to a directorship, while 43 (32.1%) reported holding 1-15 offices.   **(785)**

Directors—Professional Service

Academic

■ A 1980 survey of first-time-appointed academic library directors during the period 1970-80 (survey size: 230 directors; responding: 141 or 61.3%, including 98 males and 43 females) *showed that*, of 134 respondents, 91 (67.9%) respondents, including 58 (61.7%) males and 33 (82.5%) females, reported holding no offices (including committee chairs) in national library organizations in the 5 years prior to appointment to a directorship, while 43 (32.1%) reported holding 1-15 offices.   **(785)**

Directors—Research and Publication

Academic

■ A 1980 survey of first-time-appointed academic library directors during the period 1970-80 (survey size: 230 directors; responding: 141 or 61.3%, including 98 males and 43 females) *showed that*, of 77 respondents moving into a directorship from a top management position, 31 (40.3%) came from a general administration position, 25 (32.5%) came from a technical services position, 17 (22.1%) came from a reader/public services position, and 4 (5.2%) came from a collection development position. **(785)**

Ibid. . . . *showed that*, of 19 respondents moving into a directorship from a middle management position, 6 (31.6%) came from a general administration position, none came from a technical services position, and 13 (68.4%) came from a public services position. **(785)**

Ibid. . . . *showed that* the numbers of publications in the 10 years prior to appointment of a directorship were as follows:

> Books (141 respondents): 109 (77.3%) respondents reported no books published, including 74 (75.5%) males and 35 (81.4%) females; 22 (15.6%) respondents reported publishing 1 book, including 17 (17.3%) males and 5 (11.6%) females; and 10 (7.1%) respondents reported publishing 2 or more books, including 7 (7.1%) males and 3 (7.0%) females.

> Chapters in books (136 respondents): 108 (79.4%) respondents reported no chapters in books published, including 74 (77.9%) males and 34 (82.9%) females, while 28 (20.6%) respondents reported publishing from 1 to 10 chapters.

> Articles (137 respondents): 62 (45.3%) respondents reported publishing no articles, including 40 (41.7%) males and 22 (53.7%) females; 44 (32.1%) respondents reported publishing from 1-5 articles, including 33 (34.4%) males and 11 (26.8%) females; and 27 (19.7%) respondents reported 6-80 articles published, including 19 (19.8%) males and 8 (19.5%) females.

> Book reviews (132 respondents): 73 (55.3%) respondents reported publishing no book reviews, including 47 (52.8%) males and 26 (60.5%) females; 44 (25.8%) respondents reported publishing 1-10 reviews, including 21 (23.6%) males and 13 (30.2%) females; and 25 (18.9%) respondents reported publishing 11-500+ reviews, including 21 (23.6%) males and 4 (9.3%) females. **(785)**

Directors—Salaries

General

■ A study reported in 1981 of information on chief librarians generated in a 1975-76 survey of Canadian librarians in public, special, and academic libraries (study size: 96 chief librarians including 49 females and 47 males) *showed that* females earned an average of $16,444, while males earned an average of $20,896. Further, higher male salaries held true for each library type (small public, medium public, large public, special library, small university library, and college library) except large university library, where no women chiefs were represented.   (557)

Academic

■ A 1978 survey of law school libraries listed in the 1977 *AALS Directory of Law Teachers* (population: 167; responding: 158 or 95%) *showed that* the source of the head law librarian's salary was as follows:

law school	127
university library	6
both	12
other	1
no reply	12

(362)

■ A 1979 survey of libraries in accredited North American veterinary schools (population: 25 libraries; responding: 23 or 92%) *showed that,* of the 18 veterinary libraries housed separately, the salaries of the head librarian ranged from $14,125 to $21,853, with an average salary of $17,275 and a median salary of $17,300. Of all 23 respondents, the average salary of the head veterinary librarian was $18,192.   (740)

■ The annual survey of law school libraries and librarians conducted in 1980 by the American Bar Association, American Association of Law Libraries, and Association of American Law Schools (population not given; response: 168 libraries) *showed that* the median salary of U.S. head law school librarians was overall $37,000, while by size of library it was as follows:

small (under 70,000 vols.)	$39,200
medium (70,000-99,999 vols.)	$29,830
medium-large (100,000-199,999 vols.)	$35,448
large (200,000+ vols.)	$43,519

(382)

Special

■ A survey reported in 1971 of the professional law librarians listed as members of the American Association of Law Libraries (population not given; response: "approximately 50%," no number given) *showed that* of 286 female and 138 male head law librarians, the salary range was as follows:

25% of the women and 9% of the men reported salaries under $7,599;

26% of the women and 7% of the men reported salaries between $7,600 and $9,999;

22% of the women and 10% of the men reported salaries between $10,000 and $12,499;

26% of the women and 46% of the men reported salaries between $12,500 and $19,999;

and 1% of the women and 22% of the men reported salaries over $20,000. **(383)**

■ A survey of 1976 data on U.S. law libraries serving a local bar (survey size: not given; responding: 74 libraries) *showed that* salaries for head librarians by size of library (in volumes) averaged as follows:

small library (5,000-15,000 volumes): salary averaged $8,200 with a range of $5,000 to $17,000;

medium-small library (15,001-30,000 volumes): salary averaged $11,045 with a range of $5,640 to $21,600;

medium library (30,001-60,000 volumes): salary averaged $17,362 with a range of $10,200 to $27,220;

medium-large library (60,001-100,000 volumes): salary averaged $21,210 with a range of $14,658 to $30,045;

large library (100,001-150,000 volumes): salary averaged $22,814 with a range of $17,581 to $33,408;

very large library (150,001 or more volumes): salary averaged $31,202 with a range of $20,000 to $46,968. **(648)**

Ibid. . . . *showed that* the average salary for professional librarians (excluding head librarians) was $15,396, with a median of $15,156 and a range from $5,595 to $41,112. Further, the starting salaries for professional librarians averaged $9,757, with a median of $9,000 and a range from $5,564 to $14,292. **(648)**

■ A 1978 survey of law school libraries listed in the 1977 *AALS Directory of Law Teachers* (population: 167; responding: 158 or 95%) *showed that* for head law school librarians their faculty status/rank and/or tenure was or would be held in the following bodies:

law school	130 respondents
law library faculty (3 joint with law school)	8 respondents
both law school and university library	8 respondents

continued

university library   4 respondents
university general faculty   1 respondent
none   3 respondents
no reply   4 respondents   (362)

■ A 1979 survey of libraries in accredited North American veterinary schools (population: 25 libraries; responding: 23 or 92%) *showed that*, of the 18 veterinary libraries housed separately, the salaries of the head librarian ranged from $14,125 to $21,853, with an average salary of $17,275 and a median salary of $17,300. Of all 23 respondents, the average salary of the head veterinary librarian was $18,192.   **(740)**

■ The annual survey of law school libraries and librarians conducted in 1980 by the American Bar Association, American Association of Law Libraries, and Association of American Law Schools (population not given; response: 168 libraries) *showed that* the median salary of U.S. head law school librarians was overall $37,000, while by size of library it was as follows:

small (under 70,000 vols.) $39,200
medium (70,000-99,999 vols.) $29,830
medium-large (100,000-199,999 vols.) $35,448
large (200,000+ vols.) $43,519   **(382)**

Ibid. . . . *showed that* the median dollar amount of fringe benefits received by U.S. head law school librarians was overall $6,160, while by size of library it was as follows:

small (under 70,000 vols.) $7,789
medium (70,000-99,999 vols.) $5,054
medium-large (100,000-199,999 vols.) $6,030
large (200,000+ vols.) $7,623   **(382)**

■ An annual survey reported in 1981 of state law libraries in North America (no population given; no response given) *showed that* average salaries of head librarians for state law libraries was:

small (70,000 or less vols.) $26,789
medium (70,001-100,000 vols.) $25,534
large (100,000+ vols.) $28,950   **(380)**

Ibid. . . . *showed that* the highest degree held by 23 head librarians in state law libraries was as follows: M.L.S. (13 head librarians), law degree (2), both M.L.S. and law degree (5), other master's (1), bachelor's (1), and high school (1). **(380)**

■ An annual survey reported in 1981 of U.S. and Puerto Rican court law libraries (no population given; no response given) *showed that* for FY 1980-81 the average salaries for head librarians (professional and nonprofessional) in court law libraries of the following sizes were:

small (under 20,000 vols.)	$16,381
medium (20,001-60,000 vols.)	$23,116
large (60,001-100,000 vols.)	$26,746
very large (100,000+ vols.)	$36,400 **(381)**

■ An annual survey reported in 1981 of North American county law libraries (population not given; respondents not given) showed that the average salary in FY 1980-81 for head librarians was:

small (5,000-15,000 vols.)	$12,900
medium-small (15,001-30,000 vols.)	$14,362
medium (30,001-60,000 vols.)	$21,636
medium-large (60,001-100,000 vols.)	$26,146
large (100,001-150,000 vols.)	$37,320
very large (150,001+ vols.)	$36,301 **(379)**

Directors—Teaching

Academic

■ A 1972 survey of chief library administrators in public comprehensive community colleges (population: 586; usable responses: 75.9% [no raw number given]) *showed that* respondents reported that 6.7% of their time was devoted to teaching (4.5% informal instruction; 2.2% formal course work). Further, 78% reported they they did not wish to devote any time to formal teaching, while 95% reported they would prefer to spend less than 10% of their time on course work. **(452)**

■ A 1976 survey of head law librarians in North American schools (sample size: 178; responding: 154 or 86.7%) *showed that* 49 (32%) law school library directors taught law school legal bibliography courses only; 35 (23%) taught both legal bibliography and substantive courses in the law school; 16 (10%) taught courses in both the law school and library school; 13 (8%) taught substantive courses only in the law school; 2 (1%) taught library school legal bibliography courses only; 2(1%) taught legal research courses outside of the law or library school; and 37 (24%) taught no courses. **(357)**

Ibid. . . . *showed that* the numbers of class hours taught per academic year
by 105 law school library directors were as follows:

26 (25%)	law library directors	0-10 hours/year
15 (14%)	law library directors	11-20 hours/year
9 (9%)	law library directors	21-30 hours/year
14 (13%)	law library directors	31-40 hours/year
17 (16%)	law library directors	41-50 hours/year
24 (23%)	law library directors	51+ hours/year
12 (11%)	law library directors	no response **(357)**

Ibid. . . . *showed that* the amount of time spent in class and in class
preparation by the 105 law school library directors who taught classes was
as follows:

25 (24%)	law library directors	0-10% time
26 (25%)	law library directors	11-20% time
32 (30%)	law library directors	21-30% time
9 (8%)	law library directors	31-40% time
13 (12%)	law library directors	41-50% time
1 (1%)	law library director	51+% time **(357)**

Ibid. . . . *showed that*, of 115 law school library directors who teach,
52 (45%) of the directors considered themselves librarians, 64 (55%)
considered themselves both teachers and librarians, and none considered
themselves teachers only.   ·   **(357)**

■ A 1978 survey of law school libraries listed in the 1977 *AALS Directory
of Law Teachers* (population: 167; responding: 158 or 95%) *showed that* 82
(52%) respondents felt it desirable that head law school librarians carry
teaching responsibilities; 15 (10%) felt that head law school librarians
should teach but only legal bibliography; 21 (13%) reported mixed
feelings; and 40 (25%) felt that head law school librarians should not teach.
(362)

Special

■ A 1976 survey of head law librarians in North American schools
(sample size: 178; responding: 154 or 86.7%) *showed that* 49 (32%) law
school library directors taught law school legal bibliography courses only;
35 (23%) taught both legal bibliography and substantive courses in the law
school; 16 (10%) taught courses in both the law school and library school;
13 (8%) taught substantive courses only in the law school; 2 (1%) taught
library school legal bibliography courses only; 2(1%) taught legal research
courses outside of the law or library school; and 37 (24%) taught no
courses.   **(357)**

Ibid. . . . *showed that* the numbers of class hours taught per academic year by 105 law school library directors were as follows:

26 (25%) law library directors   0-10 hours/year
15 (14%) law library directors   11-20 hours/year
9 (9%) law library directors   21-30 hours/year ·
14 (13%) law library directors   31-40 hours/year
17 (16%) law library directors   41-50 hours/year
24 (23%) law library directors   51+ hours/year
12 (11%) law library directors   no response   **(357)**

Ibid. . . . *showed that* the amount of time spent in class and in class preparation by the 105 law school library directors who taught classes was as follows:

25 (24%) law library directors   0-10% time
26 (25%) law library directors   11-20% time
32 (30%) law library directors   21-30% time
9 (8%) law library directors   31-40% time
13 (12%) law library directors   41-50% time
·1 (1%) law library director   51+% time   **(357)**

Ibid. . . . *showed that*, of 115 law school library directors who teach, 52 (45%) of the directors considered themselves librarians, 64 (55%) considered themselves both teachers and librarians, and none considered themselves teachers only.   **(357)**

■ A 1978 survey of law school libraries listed in the 1977 *AALS Directory of Law Teachers* (population: 167; responding: 158 or 95%) *showed that* 82 (52%) respondents felt it desirable that head law school librarians carry teaching responsibilities; 15 (10%) felt that head law school librarians should teach but only legal bibliography; 21 (13%) reported mixed feelings; and 40 (25%) felt that head law school librarians should not teach.
                                               (362)

Grants

General

■ A 1978 study undertaken by the National Library of Medicine to investigate patterns and methods of communicating results of grant activities during the period 1970-77 (population: 344 grantees, including 35 library research grantees, 130 library project grantees, and 179 library improvement grantees; responding: 222 or 65%) *showed that*, based on a total of 783 communications reported, the average number of communications (both written and oral presentations) per grantee by type of grant was as follows:

library research grant	9.6 communications per grantee
library resource project	4.2 communications per grantee
library resource improvement	.4 communications per grantee **(728)**

Ibid. . . . *showed that* the distribution of type of communication was as follows:

audiovisual	7 (.9%)	communications
book	20 (2.6%)	communications
chapter in book	25 (3.2%)	communications
thesis	30 (3.8%)	communications
newsletter or in-house report	99 (12.6%)	communications
report or proceeding	107 (13.7%)	communications
journal article	175 (22.3%)	communications
oral presentation	320 (40.9%)	communications **(728)**

Academic

■ A review reported in 1980 of public library research reported in the 1970s that involved at least 1 person-year of effort (193 studies considered, consisting of 90 doctoral dissertations, 40 HEA Title II-B projects, and 63 other reports, monographs, or studies) *showed that*:

universities were the facilitating agency for 90 dissertations, 21 Title II-B projects, and 16 other projects;

professional associations were the facilitating agency for 4 Title II-B projects;

R and D firms were the facilitating agency for 7 Title II B projects and 22 other projects;

municipal, state, or regional agencies were the facilitating agency for 8 Title II-B projects and 11 other projects;

and individuals were the facilitating agency for 14 projects.   **(364)**

■ A survey reported in 1980 of Association of Research Libraries Directors in academic libraries (population: 94; responding: 68 or 72%) concerning publication requirements for professional library staff *showed that* (multiple responses allowed): 18 (23%) institutions provide funding for research within the library; 40 (51%) reported research funding is available from the university; and 20 (26%) reported that research funding is not available.   **(480)**

■ A review reported in 1982 of Title II-C funds awarded during the period FY 1978-79 through FY 1981-82 *showed that* 74.9% ($17,187,252) went to academic institutions and 25.1% ($5,767,495) went to public and independent research libraries. Of the academic awards, bibliographic control and access projects accounted for $12,511,014, collection development for $2,076,327, and preservation for $2,599,884. Of the independent and public research library awards, $2,932,639 went to bibliographic control and access, $2,221,332 went to preservation, and $613,524 for collection development. A total of 60 institutions received 98 grants, including 47 academic libraries, 3 public libraries, and 10 independent research libraries. **(040)**

Public

■ A review reported in 1980 of public library research reported in the 1970s that involved at least 1 person-year of effort (193 studies considered, consisting of 90 doctoral dissertations, 40 HEA Title II-B projects, and 63 other reports, monographs, or studies) *showed that*:

universities were the facilitating agency for 90 dissertations, 21 Title II-B projects, and 16 other projects;

professional associations were the facilitating agency for 4 Title II-B projects;

R and D firms were the facilitating agency for 7 Title II B projects and 22 other projects;

municipal, state or regional agencies were the facilitating agency for 8 Title II-B projects and 11 other projects;

and individuals were the facilitating agency for 14 projects. **(364)**

Ibid. . . . *showed that* the 6 most popular areas for public library research were:

public services	43 projects
user studies	37 projects
management	33 projects
funding	21 projects
cooperation	20 projects
history	20 projects **(364)**

Special

■ A 1978 study undertaken by the National Library of Medicine to investigate patterns and methods of communicating results of grant activities during the period 1970-77 (population: 344 grantees, including 35 library research grantees, 130 library project grantees, and 179 library improvement grantees; responding: 222 or 65%) *showed that* based on a total of 783 communications reported, the average number of communications (both written and oral presentations) per grantee by type of grant was as follows:

library research grant   9.6 communications per grantee
library resource project   4.2 communications per grantee
library resource improvement   .4 communications per grantee **(728)**

Ibid. . . . *showed that* the distribution of type of communication was as follows:

audiovisual   7 (.9%) communications
book   20 (2.6%) communications
chapter in book   25 (3.2%) communications
thesis   30 (3.8%) communications
newsletter or in-house
  report   99 (12.6%) communications
report or proceeding   107 (13.7%) communications
journal article   175 (22.3%) communications
oral presentation   320 (40.9%) communications   **(728)**

Hours

Academic

■ A 1967 survey of medical school libraries concerning reference services (survey size: 93 libraries; responding: 85 or 91.4%) *showed that* the libraries were open an average of 87.9 hours per week and provided reference services an average of 53.8 hours per week.   **(682)**

■ An hourly room count at the University of Denver's late study area in 1972 at the beginning, middle, and end of winter quarter (January 1, January 30, and March 8) *showed that* use is heaviest during exam periods with head counts for the period from midnight to 8 a.m. totaling 26, 48, and 254 respectively.   **(095)**

■ A random sampling of 196 public and private academic libraries in 4-year institutions (response rate 169) reported in 1974 *showed that* responding libraries were open an average of 90.3 hours a week, with a range of 114 hours to 56 hours a week. Of 159 responses to the question of evening professional staffing, 120 libraries (75%) reported professional staff were on duty until 10:00 p.m., while 25 libraries (16%) reported professional staff were on duty until 11:00 p.m.   **(095)**

Ibid. . . . *showed that* 30 libraries (18%) reported having some form of late-study facility. Of these 30, 11 were operated from 1 to 2 hours after regular library closing, 8 were open 3-4 hours after regular library closing, and 9 were operated on an around-the-clock basis. A total of 9 of these 30 (30%) were unstaffed. **(095)**

Ibid. . . . *showed that* during exam week 87 (52%) of responding libraries reported minor extensions of hours to accommodate increased library use. **(095)**

■ A study of 1977 survey information gathered by the National Center for Educational Statistics (U.S. Office of Education) concerning the degree to which 1,146 college and university libraries (Liberal Arts Colleges I and II; Comprehensive Universities and Colleges I and II) met the 1975 Standards for College Libraries (ACRL) *showed that* both the average and median number of hours open per week was 82 hours, with a range of 9 to 168 hours. **(486)**

■ A study reported in 1981 of data on 1,146 2-year colleges as reported in the 1977 Higher Education General Information Surveys and compared to the 1979 Association of College and Research Libraries standards *showed that* overall the hours open per week ranged from 10 to 168, with an average and median of 64 hours per week. **(500)**

Special

■ A 1967 survey of medical school libraries concerning reference services (survey size: 93 libraries; responding: 85 or 91.4%) *showed that* the libraries were open an average of 87.9 hours per week and provided reference services an average of 53.8 hours per week. **(682)**

■ A 1972 survey of prison law libraries (sample size: 90; responding: 68% [no number given, 62 assumed]) *showed that* 7 (11.3%) of the prison law libraries were open 11 to 30 hours per week; 15 (24.2%) were open 31 to 40 hours per week; and 16 (25.8%) were open longer than 40 hours per week. **(389)**

■ A 1974 survey of a random sample of U.S. museum libraries (including history, art, and science museums) listed in the 1973 *Official Museum Directory* (population: 2,556; sample size: 856; responding: 374 or 43.7%) *showed that* hours open per week ranged from 0 to 88, with an average of 35 and a median of 40. **(412)**

■ A survey of 1976 data on U.S. law libraries serving a local bar (survey size: not given; responding: 74 libraries) *showed that*, of 72 respondents, the numbers of regular hours the libraries were open were as follows:

20 hours/week	2 (2.8%) libraries	
35-39 hours/week	9 (12.5%) libraries	
40-59 hours/week	44 (61.1%) libraries	
60-79 hours/week	14 (19.4%) libraries	
over 80 hours/week	3 (4.2%) libraries	**(648)**

Institutional Comparisons and Rankings

General

■ A 1980 survey of randomly selected American Library Association personal members (sample size: 3,000 members; responding: 1,987 or 67.1%, including 1,583 full-time members employed at the time of the survey that provided the subsample analyzed here) *showed that*, in academic, public, and school libraries, the average annual salary for women was less than that for men. Specifically:

average academic library salary	$14,850 women; $20,520 men
average public library salary	$14,236 women; $19,319 men
average school library salary	$14,725 women; $18,692 men **(668)**

Academic

■ A survey reported in 1978 of academic music librarians and members of the American Musicological Society (sample size: 320; usable responses: 156 or 49%), concerning the perception of quality of music libraries at academic institutions offering graduate degrees in music *showed that*, when respondents were asked to name the top 5 academic music libraries in the U.S., the 6 most frequently mentioned music libraries were (multiple responses allowed):

Berkeley	74.3% respondents	
Eastman	70.5% respondents	
Harvard	66.6% respondents	
Yale	64.1% respondents	
Illinois	38.4% respondents	
Indiana	32.6% respondents	**(465)**

Ibid. . . . *showed that*, of the 15 top-ranked academic music libraries as rated by music librarians and members of the American Musicological Society, 14 were in schools also on the Roose-Anderson list of the top 17 schools in terms of quality of graduate faculty; 13 were on the Roose-Anderson list of the top 14 schools in terms of effectiveness of doctoral programs; and 4 were on the Blau-Margulies list of 8 top academic professional music libraries.　　　　**(465)**

■　A study reported in 1983 of 3 surveys made by the American Medical Association's Division of Library and Archival Services in 1969, 1973, and 1979 concerning the status of health sciences libraries in the U.S.(survey size for each survey ran between 12,000-14,000 health-related organizations, with a response rate for each survey around 95%) *showed that* the rank order of the 9 states with the largest number of health sciences libraries did not change between 1969 and 1979 (although the number of libraries changed in every case). The rank order with the 1979 number of health sciences libraries reported was as follows:

1. New York	251 libraries
2. California	248 libraries
3. Pennsylvania	197 libraries
4. Illinois	177 libraries
5. Ohio	138 libraries
6. Massachusetts	119 libraries
7. Michigan	118 libraries
8. Texas	112 libraries
9. New Jersey/Wisconsin	84 libraries

(745)

School

■　A 1983 survey of a systematic sample of school library media centers concerning data for fiscal year 1982-83 (survey size: 2,000 centers; responding: 1,297; usable: 1,251 or 62%) *showed that* a comparison of schools with (666 schools) and without (597 schools) district-level library media coordinators revealed that schools without district coordinators spent more money per student on resources and had more books per student than schools with district coordinators. However, schools with district coordinators paid media specialists higher salaries, had more AV items per student, had more clerical assistance, and used more adult volunteers than schools without district coordinators. Specifically:

total materials expenditure per student in schools with coordinators averaged $8.80, and in schools without coordinators averaged $10.92;

average books per student in schools with coordinators averaged 18, and in schools without coordinators averaged 20;

number of AV items per student in schools with coordinators averaged 3.45, and in schools without coordinators averaged 3.03;

media specialist salary in schools with coordinators averaged $20,699, and in schools without coordinators averaged $19,354;

the number of clerical assistants and adult volunteers in schools with coordinators averaged .83 and 2.46, respectively, and in schools without coordinators averaged .77 and 1.85, respectively.   **(056)**

Special

■ A survey reported in 1978 of academic music librarians and members of the American Musicological Society (sample size: 320; usable responses: 156 or 49%) concerning the perception of quality of music libraries at academic institutions offering graduate degrees in music *showed that*, when respondents were asked to name the top 5 academic music libraries in the U.S. the 6 most frequently mentioned music libraries were (multiple responses allowed):

Berkeley	74.3% respondents
Eastman	70.5% respondents
Harvard	66.6% respondents
Yale	64.1% respondents
Illinois	38.4% respondents
Indiana	32.6% respondents **(465)**

Ibid. . . . *showed that*, of the 15 top-ranked academic music libraries as rated by music librarians and members of the American Musicological Society, 14 were in schools also on the Roose-Anderson list of the top 17 schools in terms of quality of graduate faculty; 13 were on the Roose-Anderson list of the top 14 schools in terms of effectiveness of doctoral programs; and 4 were on the Blau-Margulies list of 8 top academic professional music libraries.   **(465)**

■ A study reported in 1983 of 3 surveys made by the American Medical Association's Division of Library and Archival Services in 1969, 1973, and 1979 concerning the status of health sciences libraries in the U.S.(survey size for each survey ran between 12,000-14,000 health-related organizations, with a response rate for each survey around 95%) *showed that* the rank order of the 9 states with the largest number of health sciences libraries did not change between 1969 and 1979 (although the number of libraries changed in every case). The rank order with the 1979 number of health sciences libraries reported was as follows:

1. New York	251 libraries	
2. California	248 libraries	
3. Pennsylvania	197 libraries	
4. Illinois	177 libraries	
5. Ohio	138 libraries	
6. Massachusetts	119 libraries	
7. Michigan	118 libraries	
8. Texas	112 libraries	
9. New Jersey/Wisconsin	84 libraries	**(745)**

Institutional Demographics

Academic

■ A study reported in 1975 of the degree to which 2-year college libraries (sample size, 26; responding, 23) in the state of Ohio conformed to the "Guidelines for Two-Year College Learning Resources Programs" established by the ACRL Board of Directors in 1972 *showed that* most of the learning resource centers were not directly involved in curriculum planning, selection of the appropriate media for instruction, or presentation of independent study programs. **(127)**

Ibid. . . . *showed that* half of the Learning Resource Centers provided autotutorial carrels of some sort, a third had learning laboratory services and telecommunication production, but almost none provided computer services, campus duplicating (other than library photocopying), printing services, or dial access services. **(127)**

Ibid. . . . *showed that* more than a third did not have control or records for the location of learning equipment; however, most did control and keep catalogs of all learning materials. **(127)**

■ A 1979 survey of libraries in accredited North American veterinary schools (population: 25 libraries; responding: 23 or 92%) *showed that,* of the 18 separately housed veterinary libraries, the average potential veterinary populations served in 1977-78 were:

number of faculty	87.9 individuals
number of interns and residents	13.4 individuals

continued

                    number of professional
                    veterinary students   316.4 individuals
                    number of graduate students   59.1 individuals   **(740)**

Ibid. . . . *showed that*, of the 18 veterinary libraries housed separately, the
physical size of the library ranged from 2,163 square feet at Tuskegee to
15,437 square feet at Kansas State University, with the average veterinary
library occupying 5,785 square feet of space. The number of reader
stations available ranged from 33 at Washington State University to 225 at
Iowa State University, with the average veterinary library providing 120
reader stations.   **(740)**

■ A study reported in 1981 of data on 1,146 2-year colleges as reported in
the 1977 Higher Education General Information Surveys and compared to
the 1979 Association of College and Research Libraries standards *showed
that* FTE student enrollments were as follows:

                    less than 1,000   32% of total
                    1,000 to 2,999   34% of total
                    3,000 to 4,999   11% of total
                    5,000 to 6,999   7% of total
                    7,000 to 8,999   5% of total
                    9,000 or more   10% of total

Further, 82% of the private 2-year colleges had enrollments of less than
1,000 FTE students, while only 19% of the public 2-year colleges had
enrollments that small.   **(500)**

■ A survey reported in 1983 of Medical Library Association institutional
members concerning their use of audiovisual materials (survey size:
300; responding: 201; usable: 198 or 66%) *showed that* 65 (33%) respondents reported providing no AV services of any kind, while 143 (77%)
respondents did provide some sort of AV service.   **(750)**

Public

■ A study reported in 1980-81 comparing level of public library development (a composite factor made up of staff size, expenditures, total books
in the collection, and circulation) with 9 community characteristics
(e.g., education, per capita income, occupational prestige, etc.) *showed
that*, based on 1,441 libraries and communities nationwide, median

education (of adults) was most strongly associated with public library development. Specifically, the relationship was positive with an r2 = .564. (The relationship was significant at the .05 level.) **(568)**

Ibid. . . . *showed that* for the northeastern region and the southern region of the U.S., based on 401 and 296 libraries and communities, respectively, median education (of adults) was the factor most strongly associated with public library development. In both cases the relationship was positive with an r2 = .459 and r2 = .421, respectively. (The relationships were significant at the .05 level.) **(568)**

Ibid. . . . *showed that* for the midwestern region of the U.S., based on 466 libraries and communities, occupational prestige index was the factor most strongly associated with public library development. The relationship was positive with an r2 = .583. (The relationship was significant at the .05 level.) **(568)**

Ibid. . . . *showed that* for the western region of the U.S., based on 278 libraries and communities, income per capita was the factor most strongly associated with public library development. The relationship was positive with an r2 = .537. (The relationship was significant at the .05 level.) **(568)**

School

■ A 1983 survey of a systematic sample of school library media centers concerning data for fiscal year 1982-83 (survey size: 2,000 centers; responding: 1,297; usable: 1,251 or 62%) *showed that* a comparison of privately supported (72) and publicly supported (1,179) school library media centers revealed that media specialists in private schools served fewer students, had more money to spend on resources, administered smaller collections, and earned more modest salaries. Specifically:

enrollment averaged 460 students for private schools and 669 for public schools;

total materials expenditure per student averaged $12.55 for private schools and $9.62 for public schools;

the number of books per student averaged $27.08 for private schools and $18.44 for public schools;

the number of AV items per student averaged $3.2 for private schools and $3.26 for public schools;

in private schools the media specialist averaged 8.92 years of experience with a salary of $13,880, while in public schools the

media specialist averaged 11.08 years of experience with a
salary of $20,389. **(056)**

Special

■ A preliminary analysis reported in 1976 of a survey of American
Association of Law Library members (survey size: "approximately 2,000"
individuals; responding: "approximately 1,400" or 70%, of which responses from 888 respondents were analyzed at the time of the report)
showed that the library size (in volumes) in which respondents worked was
as follows:

small (50,000 volumes or less)	41% respondents
medium (50-100,000 volumes)	22% respondents
large (100-200,000 volumes)	22% respondents
very large (200,000 volumes or more)	15% respondents **(793)**

Ibid. . . . *showed that* the type of library in which respondents worked was
as follows:

law school libraries	45% respondents
bar or lawyer association libraries	5% respondents
law firm libraries	21% respondents
nonlaw firm libraries	6% respondents
government libraries	23% respondents

This represented a 10% drop in members employed in law school libraries
and a 13% increase in members employed in law firms [from the earlier
1970 survey of AALL members]. **(793)**

■ A 1979 survey of libraries in accredited North American veterinary
schools (population: 25 libraries; responding: 23 or 92%) *showed that*, of
the 18 veterinary libraries housed separately, the physical size of the
library ranged from 2,163 square feet at Tuskegee to 15,437 square feet at
Kansas State University, with the average veterinary library occupying
5,785 square feet of space. The number of reader stations available ranged
from 33 at Washington State University to 225 at Iowa State University,
with the average veterinary library providing 120 reader stations. **(740)**

Ibid. . . . *showed that*, of the 18 separately housed veterinary libraries, the
average potential veterinary populations served in 1977-78 were:

number of faculty	87.9 individuals
number of interns and residents	13.4 individuals
number of professional	
veterinary students	316.4 individuals
number of graduate students	59.1 individuals (740)

■ A survey reported in 1980 of the largest medical library in each state (sample size: 51; responding: 37) *showed that* 26 (91%) reported that they were open to the public; 8 (22%) reported they were partly open to the public; and 3 (8%) reported they were not open to the public. **(236)**

Ibid. . . . *showed that*, in terms of providing medical information to nonmedical or nonallied health professionals, patients, or laymen, 7 (20%) reported a completely open policy; 24 (65%) reported they were open to the public with limited services; 1 (3%) reported open to some of the public; 1 (3%) reported open to the public through the public library; and 3 (8%) reported not being open to the public at all. **(236)**

Ibid. . . . *showed that* 12 (32%) reported they would like to serve the public extensively; 7 (19%) reported they would perhaps like to serve the public extensively; and 10 (27%) reported they would not like to serve the public extensively. **(236)**

Ibid. . . . *showed that* in order to provide priority service to the public, 20 (54%) libraries reported the need for additional personnel; 22 (59%) reported the need for additional materials such as patient education books; 7 (19%) reported the need for malpractice insurance; and 17 (46%) reported the need for additional building size, space, and facilities.
(236)

Ibid. . . . *showed that* 21 (57%) respondents referred questions from the public to public libraries; 8 (22%) referred questions to the local medical association; 10 (27%) referred questions to a physician; and 3 (8%) referred questions to other libraries. **(236)**

■ A study reported in 1983 of 3 surveys made by the American Medical Association's Division of Library and Archival Services in 1969, 1973, and 1979 concerning the status of health sciences libraries in the U.S.(survey size for each survey ran between 12,000-14,000 health-related organizations, with a response rate for each survey around 95%) *showed that* between 1969 and 1979 the number of health sciences libraries had decreased. The number of health science libraries in each of the 3 years was as follows:

1969   3,155 health sciences libraries
1973   2,984 health sciences libraries
1979   2,775 health sciences libraries

This represented a 5.4% decline between 1969-73 and a 7.0% decline between 1973-79. **(745)**

Ibid. . . . *showed that* the overall 10-year decline between 1969 and 1979 in number of health sciences libraries was not uniform by specific type of library. For example:

hospital libraries increased from 1,727 in 1969 to 1,949 in 1979 for a net increase of 222 (13%) libraries;

medical school libraries increased from 101 in 1969 to 126 in 1979 for a net increase of 25 (25%) libraries;

medical society libraries decreased from 39 in 1969 to 16 in 1979 for a net decrease of 23 (59%) libraries;

while all other health sciences libraries decreased from 1,288 in 1969 to 684 in 1979 for a net decrease of 604 (47%) libraries. **(745)**

Ibid. . . . *showed that* the overall 10-year decline between 1969 and 1979 in number of health sciences libraries was not uniform by geographic region. For example, of the 11 National Library of Medicine regions, 8 regions decreased while 3 regions (Mid-atlantic, Southeastern, and Pacific southwest) increased their number of health sciences libraries. **(745)**

■ A study reported in 1983 of surveys of medical school libraries for the period 1960-61 through 1980-81, made by the American Medical Association, the Medical Library Assoication, the Association of Academic Health Sciences Library Directors, and the National Library of Medicine, *showed that* between 1960-61 and 1980-81 the number of medical school libraries increased from 86 to 126 (a 46.5% increase). **(746)**

■ A study reported in 1983 of 3 surveys made by the American Medical Association's Division of Library and Archival Services in 1969, 1973, and 1979 concerning the status of health sciences libraries in the U.S.(survey size for each survey ran between 12,000-14,000 health-related organizations, with a response rate for each survey around 95%) *showed that*, while the number of hospitals declined by 2.4% (from 7,167 hospitals to 6,988 hospitals) during the period 1969 through 1979, the number of hospital libraries increased by 12.8% (from 1,727 hospital libraries to 1,949 hospital libraries, an increase of 222 libraries) during the same period.   **(747)**

■ A survey reported in 1983 of Medical Library Association institutional members concerning their use of audiovisual materials (survey size: 300; responding: 201; usable: 198 or 66%) *showed that* 65 (33%) respondents reported providing no AV services of any kind, while 143 (77%) respondents did provide some sort of AV service.   **(750)**

Insurance

General

■ A 1966 survey of library insurance in 13,500 libraries (1,369 [10.4%] responding) by the Library Technology Project and the Insurance for Libraries Committee (ALA, Library Administration Division) *showed that* of the responding libraries only 299 (21.8%) indicated that they had bought or were about to buy an all-risk insurance policy.   **(079)**

Job Hunting

General

■ A study reported in 1976 of the experience of an individual 1976 library school graduate without previous library experience in the 1976 job market applying for 206 specifically advertised professional-level library openings by submitting a job-specific cover letter and resume *showed that* responses were as follows:

TYPE OF LIBRARY	# LIBRARIES	# RESPONDING	(%)
Academic	106	87	(82)
Public	48	35	(73)
Special	34	24	(71)
Federal	7	4	(57)
State	6	5	(83)
Cooperative	5	5	(100)
TOTAL	206	160	(78 avg.)

TYPE OF POSITION	# LIBRARIES	# RESPONDING	(%)
Administrative	80	65	(81)
Reference	66	50	(75)
Acquisition/Technical Services	30	22	(73)
Circulation	22	17	(77)
Cataloging	5	3	(60)
Media/Microforms	3	3	(100)
TOTAL	206	160	(78 avg.)
			(109)

Ibid. . . . *showed that* the average wait for a response was as follows:

TYPE OF LIBRARY	# LIBRARIES	AVG. WAIT (DAYS)
Academic	87	17
Public	35	17
Special	24	14
Federal	4	45
State	5	10
Cooperative	5	12
TOTAL	160	17 total avg.

TYPE OF POSITION		
Administrative	65	18
Reference	50	19
Acquistions/Technical Services	22	14
Circulation	17	14
Cataloging	3	7
Media/Microforms	3	17
TOTAL	160	17 total avg. **(109)**

Ibid. . . . *showed that*, of the 160 libraries requesting further information, 33 (21%) requested formal applications, 24 (15%) requested reference, and 19 (12%) requested transcripts. However, almost all the employers offering extensive consideration did ask for references.   **(109)**

Ibid. . . . *showed that*, of the 106 positions for which responses were received, the average wait between formal application and notification of final decision was as follows:

TYPE OF LIBRARY	# LIBRARIES	AVG. WAIT (DAYS)
Academic	52	44
Public	26	37
Special	18	25
Federal	4	45
State	3	47
Cooperative	3	26
TOTAL	106	39 total avg.

TYPE OF POSITION		
Administrative	44	42
Reference	33	40
Acquisitions/Technical Services	17	35
Circulation	8	31
Cataloging	2	31
Media/Microforms	2	21
TOTAL	106	39 total avg. **(109)**

■ A survey reported in 1977 of the larger employers of librarians in the state of Indiana and including academic, public, special, and school libraries (31 institutions or systems queried; 30 responding) *showed that* the top-ranked criteria for hiring (ranked #1 by 20 respondents) was how the candidate handled the personal interview; 18 ranked work experience second or third; and 20 ranked recommendations from former employers second or third. 27 ranked library school grades as fourth, fifth, or sixth in importance. **(285)**

■ A study of reopened, extended, or second searches in 110 North American libraries as revealed through job notices during the period 1975-80 *showed that* there were 0 in 1975, 3 in 1976, 11 in 1977, 53 in 1978, 67 in 1979, and 34 in the first half of 1980. **(312)**

Ibid. . . . *showed that,* based on a follow-up survey of acquisitions positions that had been reopened, extended, or searched a second time (responses received for 9 out of the 14 acquisitions positions so identified), the applicant pool was slightly larger the second time around, rising from an average of 19 applications per position to 23 applications per position. **(312)**

Ibid. . . . *showed that,* based on a follow-up survey of acquisitions positions that had been reopened, extended, or searched a second time (responses received for 6 out of the 14 acquisitions positions so identified), only 5% of the applicants for the 6 positions were "repeat" applicants, with 4 of the 6 positions having no "repeat" applicants.   **(312)**

■ A review reported in 1981 of the help-wanted ads in *American Libraries* and *Library Journal* for odd-numbered years from 1961 through 1979 plus 1980, for all aspects of librarianship at all levels, *showed that* from 1967 on, the number of M.L.S.'s granted exceeded jobs advertised as follows:

YEAR	TOTAL ADS IN AL & LJ	INDEX	M.L.S. DEGREES GRANTED	INDEX
1961	2,826	100	1,931	100
1963	3,159	112	2,363	122
1965	3,673	130	3,211	166
1967	4,401	156	4,489	233
1969	3,171	112	5,932	307
1971	1,505	53	7,001	363
1973	1,071	38	7,696	393
1975	1,105	39	8,091	419
1977	1,215	43	7,572	392
1979	1,384	49	5,906	306
1980	1,508	53	5,374	278

(110)

Academic

■ A survey reported in 1978 of 407 academic and public libraries who had filled professional positions (61% [no number given] responding with 233 or 57% usable responses) *showed that* there was an average of 73 applicants for each academic library position and 47 for each public library position. Broken down by level: entry level averaged 92 applicants per position for academic libraries and 65 for public libraries; departmental level averaged 58 applicants per academic library position and 36 per public library position; administrative level averaged 73 applicants per academic position and 50 per public position.   **(227)**

■ A study reported in 1978, of 23 middle managers and 11 administrators in 5 Association of Research Libraries libraries as well as a review of ads for 82 middle managerial positions in academic libraries posted in 1975, *showed that* 43 (52.4%) of the ads listed an ALA-accredited library master's degree as a qualification; 37 (45.1%) listed library master's degree without specifying ALA-accredited; 30 (36.6%) listed second master's degree; 4 (4.9%) listed Ph.D.; 1 (1.2%) listed an other professional degree; and 1 stated that a master's degree was not required.   **(423)**

■ A survey of the 50 largest ARL libraries (30 responding) in 1979 regarding filling middle- and upper-level research manager positions during the period July 1976-November 1979 *showed that* the 3 most common qualities sought were:

administration/management skills/experience	24 responses
relative experience and understanding of large libraries	15 responses
interpersonal skills	15 responses

The quality most lacking in recent applications was managerial ability/experience (19 responses). **(046)**

Ibid. . . . *showed that* the three most common reasons for reopening a search were:

finalist unacceptable after personal interviews	18 responses
total applicant pool not acceptable	10 responses
failure to negotiate terms of employment with successful candidate	9 responses **(046)**

Ibid. . . . *showed that* 17 of the libraries had reopened a search at least once, which involved 32 of the 186 positions opened. In 4 cases there was a third search. The reopened searches were in public services (13), technical services (13), and other (10). **(046)**

■ A survey reported in 1980 of newly appointed library directors of 4-year colleges and universities (positions announced in library journals between June 1977 and February 1979 and excluding law, medical, and service academy appointments) (survey size: 66; responding: 54 or 81.8%) *showed that* search committees were used in 50 cases, with the chief academic officer conducting the search in 4 cases—all at small private colleges. **(482)**

Ibid. . . . *showed that* 16 (29.6%) respondents reported that their search committee had fewer than 2 library employees, while only 4 (7.4%) reported that more than half of the the search committee consisted of library employees. No respondents reported a search committee of only library employees. In only 7 (13.0%) cases was the search committee chaired by a library employee. **(482)**

Ibid. . . . *showed that* only 4 (7.4%) respondents reported that the search committee or hiring officers made an on-site visit to their former library as part of the search process.   **(482)**

Ibid. . . . *showed that* during the interview "almost all" respondents reported meeting with the president, the chief academic officer, and the professional library staff; 43 (79.6%) respondents reported meeting with the nonprofessional library staff; 40 (74.1%) reported meeting with the faculty library committee; 33 (61.1%) reported meeting with the academic dean; 32 (59.3%) reported meeting the previous library director; and 29 (53.7%) reported meeting students.   **(482)**

Ibid. . . . *showed that* "most" of the respondents reported meeting with 6-10 individuals and groups, while 6 (11.1%) reported meeting with 4-5 individuals and groups, and 6 (11.1%) reported meeting with 11-16 individuals and groups.   **(482)**

Ibid. . . . *showed that* 18 (33.3%) of the respondents reported being invited back for a second visit. Further, 21 (38.9%) reported spending less than 2 days on the interview visit; 16 (29.6%) reported spending 2 days on the interview visit; and 14 (25.9%) reported interview visits longer than 2 days.   **(482)**

Level of Work

Academic

■ A survey reported in 1965 of 163 professional librarians in academic and public libraries in Michigan who indicated which of 50 professional and 50 nonprofessional tasks (from the *ALA Descriptive List of Professional and Non-Professional Duties in Libraries*) they did *showed that* of the total sample 64.97% of all tasks reported were professional. 72.04% of the tasks reported by academic librarians were professional compared to 62.93 % of nonacademic librarians' tasks; 64.28% of the public service librarians' tasks were reported as professional compared to 70.14% of nonpublic service librarians'; and 58.89% of the junior librarians' tasks were professional compared to 65.98% of the senior librarians' tasks.   **(174)**

Public

■ A survey reported in 1965 of 163 professional librarians in academic and public libraries in Michigan who indicated which of 50 professional and 50 nonprofessional tasks (from the *ALA Descriptive List of Professional* and *Non-Professional Duties in Libraries*) they did *showed that* of the total sample 64.97% of all tasks reported were professional. 72.04% of the tasks reported by academic librarians were professional compared to 62.93 % of nonacademic librarians' tasks; 64.28% of the public service librarians' tasks were reported as professional compared to 70.14% of nonpublic service librarians'; and 58.89% of the junior librarians' tasks were professional compared to 65.98% of the senior librarians' tasks.   **(174)**

Library Cooperation

General

■ A survey reported in 1982 of the directors of 20 (19 or 95% responding) OCLC distributing networks (e.g., ILLINET, SOLINET, FEDLINK, etc.) *showed that* the 2 top areas in which 17 respondents desired or anticipated further growth for their networks were (multiple responses allowed): more OCLC members (12 respondents ranking first or second choice) and other contracting activity, processing/delivery (8 respondents ranking first or second choice).   **(343)**

Ibid. . . . *showed that* the 4 most common non-OCLC-related information retrieval services contracted through the networks (either being offered as of May 1980 or planned for offering by mid-1981) reported by 12 respondents were (multiple responses allowed):

BRS (8 respondents offering; 2 planning),
Lockheed DIALOG (7 respondents offering; 2 planning),
SDC ORBIT (6 offering; 2 planning),
New York Times Information Service (5 offering; 4 planning). **(343)**

Ibid. . . . *showed that* the 5 most commonly reported current or planned uses of members' records supplied through OCLC reported by 14 respondents were (multiple responses allowed):

union list (11 respondents),
circulation control (11 respondents),
subject access (10 respondents),
management information (8 respondents),
interlibrary loan (6 respondents).   **(343)**

Ibid. . . . *showed that* the number of professional employees employed per network rose from 3.5 in 1977 to "approximately" 5 in 1980, while the number of clerical employees rose from between 4.5 to 5 per network in 1977 to 6+ in 1980. **(343)**

Ibid. . . . *showed that* of 17 respondents 6 reported that 75% or more of their funding came from a surcharge to members on services obtained from vendors; 4 reported that 75% or more of their funding came from member fees; and 4 reported that 75% or more of their funding came from state funds. **(343)**

Academic

■ A survey reported in 1972 of 2,600 U.S. colleges and universities (usable responses: 1,516) *showed that* 698 (46%) participated in some form of cooperative activity. A follow-up study reported at the same time subsequently identified 125 organizations as meeting a strict 6-point definition of academic library consortia. **(212)**

Ibid. . . . *showed that* the 4 activities common to at least half of the academic library consortia were as follows: reciprocal borrowing privileges, 78% (97 consortia); expanded interlibrary loan service, 64% (80); union catalogs or lists, 62% (78); and photocopying services, 58% (72). **(212)**

Ibid. . . . *showed that* the 2 most common techniques for evaluating consortia effectiveness were informal feedback from library personnel participating in consortium activities, 66% (82 consortia) and informal feedback from the ultimate users of service, 49% (61 consortia). **(212)**

Ibid. . . . *showed that* 96 of the 125 consortia identified had been established between 1966 and 1970. **(212)**

■ A 1978-79 study underwritten by the NSF Division of Information Science and Technology of academic and research journal subscription and cancellation for both individuals and libraries (individual questionnaires: 2,817; usable responses, 1,190; library questionnaires: 4,997; usable responses: 1,905) of journals at least 5 years old *showed that*, of 358 libraries, 329 (91.9%) reported that journal subscription cancellations were not due in any degree to membership in a consortium or network whose policies formally encouraged cancellation of titles elsewhere, while 29 (8.1%) reported that such membership did play a role in the cancellation decision. **(264)**

■ A study reported in 1982 at the Paul Klapper Library in Queens College, CUNY, comparing ILL requests for off-campus material requested during a 3-month period in Fall 1979 (200 requests) and a 3-month period during Spring 1981 (333 requests), *showed that* the success rate in 1979 and 1981, respectively, for TWX requests from other CUNY units was 100% (for 11 requests) and 94% (for 36 requests), for OCLC was 100% (for 79 requests) and 95% (for 130 requests), for the New York State ILL system was 86% (for 35 requests) and 84% (for 57 requests), and for the ALA procedure and form was 74% (for 75 requests) and 76% (for 110 requests). **(346)**

Public

■ An informal survey in 1962 of the 50 state library extension agencies (38 responding) to assess trends of library service since 1954 *showed that* the one trend to which all respondents agreed was a movement away from the traditional emphasis on recreational reading to an increasing recognition of the importance of reference and informational services. The next highest rated trend was movement away from dependence on a limited library staff to provide all programming toward involving more community people in the library's program. The third highest was a trend away from local self-sufficiency toward greater intrastate library cooperation. **(063)**

■ A 1976 study that identified 55 combined school and public library arrangements across the U.S. *showed that* 44 (80%) were in communities with less than 10,000 residents; 9 (16%) were in communities of 10-20,000 residents; 1 (2%) in a community of 60,000; and 1 (2%) in a community of 500,000. (This largest community was in the process of phasing out their combined arrangement, however.) **(226)**

Ibid. . . . *showed that* combined libraries are most often located in school attendance centers. Only 4 of the 55 arrangements surveyed were housed in buildings separate from schools. **(226)**

Ibid. . . . *showed that*, in 23 (42%) of the surveyed combined arrangements, libraries were staffed with 2 or more professionals, with at least 1 being a certified teacher/librarian and another trained in public librarianship; 23 (42%) were staffed with either school or public librarians; 2 (4%) were staffed by professionals with training in both areas. (No information was given on the remaining 5 arrangements.) **(226)**

Ibid. . . . *showed that* in 26 (47%) of the combined arrangements public library personnel operate the libraries during summers and vacation periods when school is not in session; in 17 (31%) staffing responsibility is shared with school librarians during these times; in 5 (9%) paraprofessionals operate the libraries; and in 3 (5%) volunteers handle library duties during these periods.   **(226)**

Ibid. . . . *showed that* the 2 main benefits of merging were providing a better selection of print and nonprint materials (cited by 34 or 62% of respondents) and making public library service available to their communities for the first time (cited by 18 or 33% of respondents).   **(226)**

Ibid. . . . *showed that* the most frequently mentioned problem with merging was governance and management (cited by 17 or 31% of respondents).
(226)

■ A 1978 survey of cooperation and attitudes toward cooperation between public and school libraries at the state level in Iowa involving elementary schools, secondary schools, and public libraries (sample size: 360; responding: 250; usable: 230 or 63.9%) *showed that* the top 7 desirable cooperative activites reported were (multiple responses allowed):

planning of peak research paper periods	55% respondents
joint book selection meetings	50% respondents
joint publicity efforts	46% respondents
coordinated acquisition of some materials	45% respondents
joint catalog of holdings	44% respondents
joint summer reading program	44% respondents
shared storytelling/book talks	42% respondents

(365)

Ibid. . . . *showed that* the top 7 cooperative activities in which schools and public libraries were actually involved were (multiple responses allowed):

planning of peak research paper periods	4.3% respondents
shared film rentals	3.5% respondents
joint summer reading program	3.5% respondents
shared storytelling/book talks	3.0% respondents
use of school library materials in public library during summer	3.0% respondents
joint publicity efforts	3.0% respondents
coordinated acquisition of some materials	2.6% respondents

(365)

Special

■ A survey reported in 1980 of the largest medical library in each state (sample size: 51; responding: 37) *showed that* 21 (57%) respondents referred questions from the public to public libraries; 8 (22%) referred questions to the local medical association; 10 (27%) referred questions to a physician; and 3 (8%) referred questions to other libraries. **(236)**

Library Cooperation—Combined School and Public Libraries

Public

■ A 1976 study that identified 55 combined school and public library arrangements across the U.S. *showed that* 44 (80%) were in communities with less than 10,000 residents; 9 (16%) were in communities of 10-20,000 residents; 1 (2%) in a community of 60,000; and 1 (2%) in a community of 500,000. (This largest community was in the process of phasing out their combined arrangement, however.) **(226)**

Ibid. . . . *showed that* combined libraries are most often located in school attendance centers. Only 4 of the 55 arrangements surveyed were housed in buildings separate from schools. **(226)**

Ibid. . . . *showed that*, in 23 (42%) of the surveyed combined arrangements, libraries were staffed with 2 or more professionals, with at least 1 being a certified teacher/librarian and another trained in public librarianship; 23 (42%) were staffed with either school or public librarians; 2 (4%) were staffed by professionals with training in both areas. (No information was given on the remaining 5 arrangements.) **(226)**

Ibid. . . . *showed that* in 26 (47%) of the combined arrangements public library personnel operate the libraries during summers and vacation periods when school is not in session; in 17 (31%) staffing responsibility is shared with school librarians during these times; in 5 (9%) paraprofessionals operate the libraries; and in 3 (5%) volunteers handle library duties during these periods. **(226)**

Ibid. . . . *showed that* the 2 main benefits of merging were providing a better selection of print and nonprint materials (cited by 34 or 62% of respondents) and making public library service available to their communities for the first time (cited by 18 or 33% of respondents). **(226)**

Ibid. . . . *showed that* the most frequently mentioned problem with merging was governance and management (cited by 17 or 31% of respondents).
(226)

■ A study reported in 1976 comparing the attitudes of high school and public librarians in the Toronto (Canada) metropolitan area toward combining school and public libraries (survey size: 100 school librarians and 73 public librarians; responding: 75 or 75% of the school librarians and 38 or 52.1% of the public librarians) *showed that* 32% of the school librarians versus 19% of the public librarians agreed or strongly agreed that combination school/public libraries would generally be "geographically inconvenient for the general public." **(543)**

Ibid. . . . *showed that* school and public librarians revealed substantial differences in their views of how comfortable various patron groups would be in using combined school/public libraries. For example:

28% of the school librarians versus 59% of the public librarians agreed or strongly agreed that students from other schools would be reluctant to use the combined libraries;

42% of the school librarians versus 76% of the public librarians agreed or strongly agreed that adults, due to a fear of intruding, would hesitate to enter a branch library located in a school;

60% of the school librarians versus 86% of the public librarians agreed or strongly agreed that the general public would be reluctant to enter the library through the school buildings. **(543)**

Ibid. . . . *showed that*, while school and public librarians revealed little difference in attitudes concerning the potential for tax savings that combining the libraries would bring about, substantial differences were revealed between the 2 groups concerning reductions of staff and collection duplication. For example:

55% of the school librarians versus 51% of the public librarians disagreed or strongly disagreed that tax dollars would be saved by combining school and public libraries;

79% of the school librarians versus 68% of the public librarians disagreed or strongly disagreed that fewer staff would be needed to run combined libraries;

44% of the school librarians versus 62% of the public librarians disagreed or strongly disagreed that combined libraries would require less duplication of collections. **(543)**

Ibid. . . . *showed that* there were substantial differences between the 2 groups in their expectations of how collections would be affected. For example:

> 40% of the school librarians versus 62% of the public librarians disagreed or strongly disagreed that a combined library would offer patrons a better collection;

> 63% of the school librarians versus 73% of the public librarians agreed or strongly agreed that "some materials considered suitable for a public library would be considered controversal in a [combined library]";

> 45% of the school librarians versus 54% of the public librarians agreed or strongly agreed that combined libraries would "be less likely to purchase certain materials, e.g. adult fiction." **(543)**

Ibid. . . . *showed that* both groups were generally in agreement that separate administrative control was necessary if combined libraries were to run well, while there was substantial disagreement between the 2 groups concerning the importance of 2 separate budgets. For example, 53% of the school librarians versus 49% of the public librarians agreed or strongly agreed that separate administrative control was necessary for combined libraries to be a success, while 73% of the school librarians versus 59% of the public librarians agreed or strongly agreed that combined libraries should have separate budgets. **(543)**

Ibid. . . . *showed that* there were substantial differences between the 2 groups as to whether combined libraries would provide better-trained staff and particularly whether public library staff could meet the needs of school staff and students. For example, 40% of the school librarians versus 59% of the public librarians disagreed or strongly disagreed that a combined library would provide a better-trained staff. Further, 68% of the school librarians versus 21% of the public librarians agreed or strongly agreed that "public librarians would be unable to deal with the needs of the staff and students with respect to the school program." **(543)**

Ibid. . . . *showed that* there were substantial differences between the 2 groups in their attitudes toward patron circulation policy. For example:

> 73% of the school librarians versus 32% of the public librarians disagreed or strongly disagreed with the idea that "materials required by students for school work should circulate freely to the general public and the students";

> 48% of the school librarians versus 24% of the public librarians

disagreed or disagreed strongly with the idea that all
audiovisual materials in a combined library "should circulate
freely to the general public and the students."   **(543)**

Ibid. . . . *showed that* there was little difference between the 2 groups in
their perception of a basic difference of purpose between school and public
libraries. For example, 97% of the school librarians and 95% of the public
librarians agreed or strongly agreed that such a difference of purpose
between the 2 types of libraries existed.   **(543)**

Ibid. . . . *showed that* there were substantial differences between the 2
groups concerning their perception of the importance of the educational
role versus the recreational role in public libraries. For example, 73% of
the school librarians versus 27% of the public librarians agreed or strongly
agreed that the "public library places a greater emphasis upon its recreational role than upon its educational role." The 2 groups showed less
difference in their perception of the importance of the educational role
versus the recreational role in school libraries. For example, 97% of the
school librarians versus 81% of the public librarians agreed or strongly
agreed that the "school library places greater emphasis upon its educational role than upon its recreational role."   **(543)**

Ibid. . . . *showed that* 65% of the school librarians versus 78% of the
public librarians disagreed or strongly disagreed that the general public
would receive better library service from a combined library, while 64% of
the school librarians versus 43% of the public librarians disagreed or
strongly disagreed that students would receive better library service from a
combined library.   **(543)**

■ A 1978 survey of cooperation and attitudes toward cooperation
between public and school libraries at the state level in Iowa involving
elementary schools, secondary schools, and public libraries (sample size:
360; responding: 250; usable: 230 or 63.9%) *showed that* the top 7 desirable
cooperative activities reported were (multiple responses allowed):

planning of peak research paper periods	55% respondents
joint book selection meetings	50% respondents
joint publicity efforts	46% respondents
coordinated acquisition of some materials	45% respondents
joint catalog of holdings	44% respondents
joint summer reading program	44% respondents
shared storytelling/book talks	42% respondents

(365)

Ibid. . . . *showed that* the top 7 cooperative activities in which schools and public libraries were actually involved were (multiple responses allowed):

planning of peak research paper periods	4.3% respondents
shared film rentals	3.5% respondents
joint summer reading program	3.5% respondents
shared storytelling/book talks	3.0% respondents
use of school library materials in public library during summer	3.0% respondents
joint publicity efforts	3.0% respondents
coordinated acquisition of some materials	2.6% respondents

(365)

School

■ A study reported in 1976 comparing the attitudes of high school and public librarians in the Toronto (Canada) metropolitan area toward combining school and public libraries (survey size: 100 school librarians and 73 public librarians; responding: 75 or 75% of the school librarians and 38 or 52.1% of the public librarians) *showed that* 32% of the school librarians versus 19% of the public librarians agreed or strongly agreed that combination school/public libraries would generally be "geographically inconvenient for the general public." **(543)**

Ibid. . . . *showed that* school and public librarians revealed substantial differences in their views of how comfortable various patron groups would be in using combined school/public libraries. For example:

28% of the school librarians versus 59% of the public librarians agreed or strongly agreed that students from other schools would be reluctant to use the combined libraries;

42% of the school librarians versus 76% of the public librarians agreed or strongly agreed that adults, due to a fear of intruding, would hesitate to enter a branch library located in a school;

60% of the school librarians versus 86% of the public librarians agreed or strongly agreed that the general public would be reluctant to enter the library through the school buildings. **(543)**

Ibid. . . . *showed that*, while school and public librarians revealed little difference in attitudes concerning the potential for tax savings that combining the libraries would bring about, substantial differences were revealed between the 2 groups concerning reductions of staff and collection duplication. For example:

55% of the school librarians versus 51% of the public librarians

disagreed or strongly disagreed that tax dollars would be saved
by combining school and public libraries;

79% of the school librarians versus 68% of the public librarians
disagreed or strongly disagreed that fewer staff would be
needed to run combined libraries;

44% of the school librarians versus 62% of the public librarians
disagreed or strongly disagreed that combined libraries would
require less duplication of collections.　　　　　　　　　**(543)**

Ibid. . . . *showed that* there were substantial differences between the 2
groups in their expectations of how collections would be affected. For
example:

40% of the school librarians versus 62% of the public librarians
disagreed or strongly disagreed that a combined library would
offer patrons a better collection;

63% of the school librarians versus 73% of the public librarians
agreed or strongly agreed that "some materials considered
suitable for a public library would be considered controversial
in a [combined library]";

45% of the school librarians versus 54% of the public librarians
agreed or strongly agreed that combined libraries would "be
less likely to purchase certain materials, e.g., adult fiction."　**(543)**

Ibid. . . . *showed that* both groups were generally in agreement that
separate administrative control was necessary if combined libraries were to
run well, while there was substantial disagreement between the 2 groups
concerning the importance of 2 separate budgets. For example, 53% of the
school librarians versus 49% of the public librarians agreed or strongly
agreed that separate administrative control was necessary for combined
libraries to be a success, while 73% of the school librarians versus 59% of
the public librarians agreed or strongly agreed that combined libraries
should have separate budgets.　　　　　　　　　　　　　**(543)**

Ibid. . . . *showed that* there were substantial differences between the 2
groups as to whether combined libraries would provide better-trained staff
and particularly whether public library staff could meet the needs of school
staff and students. For example, 40% of the school librarians versus 59% of
the public librarians disagreed or strongly disagreed that a combined
library would provide a better-trained staff. Further, 68% of the school
librarians versus 21% of the public librarians agreed or strongly agreed that
"public librarians would be unable to deal with the needs of the staff and
students with respect to the school program."　　　　　　**(543)**

Ibid. . . . *showed that* there were substantial differences between the 2 groups in their attitudes toward patron circulation policy. For example:

73% of the school librarians versus 32% of the public librarians disagreed or strongly disagreed with the idea that "materials required by students for school work should circulate freely to the general public and the students;"

48% of the school librarians versus 24% of the public librarians disagreed or disagreed strongly with the idea that all audiovisual materials in a combined library "should circulate freely to the general public and the students." **(543)**

Ibid. . . . *showed that* there was little difference between the 2 groups in their perception of a basic difference of purpose between school and public libraries. For example, 97% of the school librarians and 95% of the public librarians agreed or strongly agreed that such a difference of purpose between the 2 types of libraries existed. **(543)**

Ibid. . . . *showed that* there were substantial differences between the 2 groups concerning their perception of the importance of the educational role versus the recreational role in public libraries. For example, 73% of the school librarians versus 27% of the public librarians agreed or strongly agreed that the "public library places a greater emphasis upon its recrea-tional role than upon its educational role." The 2 groups showed less difference in their perception of the importance of the educational role versus the recreational role in school libraries. For example, 97% of the school librarians versus 81% of the public librarians agreed or strongly agreed that the "school library places greater emphasis upon its education-al role than upon its recreational role." **(543)**

Ibid. . . . *showed that* 65% of the school librarians versus 78% of the public librarians disagreed or strongly disagreed that the general public would receive better library service from a combined library, while 64% of the school librarians versus 43% of the public librarians disagreed or strongly disagreed that students would receive better library service from a combined library. **(543)**

■ A 1976 study that identified 55 combined school and public library arrangements across the U.S. *showed that* 44 (80%) were in communities with less than 10,000 residents; 9 (16%) were in communities of 10-20,000 residents; 1 (2%) in a community of 60,000; and 1 (2%) in a community of 500,000. (This largest community was in the process of phasing out their combined arrangement, however.) **(226)**

Ibid. . . . *showed that* combined libraries are most often located in school attendance centers. Only 4 of the 55 arrangements surveyed were housed in buildings separate from schools.   **(226)**

Ibid. . . . *showed that*, in 23 (42%) of the surveyed combined arrangements, libraries were staffed with 2 or more professionals, with at least 1 being a certified teacher/librarian and another trained in public librarianship; 23 (42%) were staffed with either school or public librarians; 2 (4%) were staffed by professionals with training in both areas. (No information was given on the remaining 5 arrangements.)   **(226)**

Ibid. . . . *showed that* in 26 (47%) of the combined arrangements public library personnel operate the libraries during summers and vacation periods when school is not in session; in 17 (31%) staffing responsibility is shared with school librarians during these times; in 5 (9%) paraprofessionals operate the libraries; and in 3 (5%) volunteers handle library duties during these periods.   **(226)**

Ibid. . . . *showed that* the 2 main benefits of merging were providing a better selection of print and nonprint materials (cited by 34 or 62% of respondents) and making public library service available to their communities for the first time (cited by 18 or 33% of respondents).   **(226)**

Ibid. . . . *showed that* the most frequently mentioned problem with merging was governance and management (cited by 17 or 31% of respondents).
                                                                             (226)

■ A 1978 survey of cooperation and attitudes toward cooperation between public and school libraries at the state level in Iowa involving elementary schools, secondary schools, and public libraries (sample size: 360; responding: 250; usable: 230 or 63.9%) *showed that* the top 7 desirable cooperative activities reported were (multiple responses allowed):

planning of peak research paper periods	55% respondents
joint book selection meetings	50% respondents
joint publicity efforts	46% respondents
coordinated acquisition of some materials	45% respondents
joint catalog of holdings	44% respondents
joint summer reading program	44% respondents
shared storytelling/book talks	42% respondents

                                                                             (365)

Ibid. . . . *showed that* the top 7 cooperative activities in which schools and public libraries were actually involved were (multiple responses allowed):

planning of peak research paper periods	4.3% respondents
shared film rentals	3.5% respondents
joint summer reading program	3.5% respondents
shared storytelling/book talks	3.0% respondents
use of school library materials in public library during summer	3.0% respondents
joint publicity efforts	3.0% respondents
coordinated acquisition of some materials	2.6% respondents

(365)

Library Efficiency

Academic

■ A study reported in 1983 concerning costs among academic libraries based on data gathered by the National Center for Education Statistics for the year 1977 and various sources of institutional data (involving 3,057 institutions, including 2-year public, 2-year private, 4-year public, and 4-year private schools) *showed that*, for all types of libraries except for 2-year private college libraries, the larger the library, the less efficiently it could be run. More specifically, the greater the output in terms of volumes added, reference, circulation, hours open, and interlibrary loan the greater the per unit costs.   **(797)**

Library Friends

General

■ A 1974 survey of 88 SPEC member libraries, 43 public libraries, 15 small university libraries, and 13 special libraries involving Friends of the Library groups (129 responding of which 64 [57%] reported having a library Friends group) *showed that* 55% of the libraries surveyed were themselves involved in starting their own library Friends group. 16% of these groups were started entirely by library staff and 39% begun jointly by the library and other interested people from outside the library.   **(125)**

Ibid. . . . *showed that* in university library Friends groups the main participants by far were a mixture of faculty and alumni with book collectors running a poor third, whereas in public library Friends groups the majority were civic leaders with business people, book collectors, and women's clubs following some distance behind.   **(125)**

Ibid. . . . *showed that*, of 62 libraries responding to the question of goals, 40 (55%) reported that both fund raising and developing support for the library were their purposes, whereas 23% reported that general support of the library was their sole objective, and 3 (5%) reported fund raising as their sole objective.   **(125)**

Ibid. . . . *showed that* 83% of the libraries gave administrative support to their Friends groups (typically a liaison officer from the library), that 78% gave clerical assistance to their Friends groups, and 60% provided office space within the library to their Friends groups.   **(125)**

Ibid. . . . *showed that* by inspection there was no strong relationship between size of library and library Friends membership or size of academic institution and size of membership. For example, average Friends membership for small libraries (under 500,000 volumes) was 588, for medium libraries (500,000-1 million volumes) was 288, for large libraries (1 to 2 million volumes) was 620, and for the extra large libraries (over 2 million volumes) was 748; while average Friends membership for small institutions (enrollment under 10,000) was 504, for medium institutions (10,000-20,000 enrollment) was 342, for large institutions (20-30,000 enrollment) was 527, and for extra large institutions (30,000+ enrollment) was 596.   **(125)**

Ibid. . . . *showed that* 21% of responding libraries reported spending their entire Friends' income, after operating expenses, on special collections; 32% included special collections in their expenditures; and 41% mentioned special projects ranging from equipment to building a library.   **(125)**

Ibid. . . . *showed that* of responding libraries 15.5% of university Friends groups did not have an official publication, while 20% of public library Friends did not have an official publication, and all responding special libraries had some type of official publication.   **(125)**

Academic

■ A 1977 survey of health sciences libraries concerning Friends of the Library groups (survey size: 105 libraries; responding: 103 or 98%) *showed that* 24 (23.3%) libraries reported Friends groups; 69 (67.0%) reported not having Friends groups; and 10 (9.7%) reported that formation of a Friends group was under consideration. Further, of the libraries with Friends groups, 16 (15.5% of respondents) reported independent Friends groups for the health science library. **(722)**

Ibid. . . . *showed that*, of the 16 libraries with independent Friends groups, the founding dates of Friends groups were as follows:

1950 or before	2 (12.5%)	libraries
1951-1960	4 (25.0%)	libraries
1961-1970	3 (18.7%)	libraries
1971 or after	7 (43.8%)	libraries

(722)

Ibid. . . . *showed that*, of the 16 libraries with independent Friends groups, the number of members of Friends groups ranged from a minimum of 9 members to a maximum of 760 members. The average number of members was 237, and the median was 113 members. **(722)**

Ibid. . . . *showed that*, of the 16 libraries with independent Friends groups, the groups instrumental in founding the Friends groups were the library, 3 (18.7%) libraries; outside individuals, 2 (12.5%) libraries; and combined effort of library and outside individuals, 11 (68.8%) libraries. **(722)**

Ibid. . . . *showed that*, of the 16 libraries with independent Friends groups, the purpose of Friends groups was (multiple responses allowed): to raise funds for the library, 15 (93.8%) libraries; to develop support for the library, 7 (43.8%) libraries; and to restore the collection, 1 (6.3%) libraries. **(722)**

Ibid. . . . *showed that*, of the 16 libraries with independent Friends groups, the type of library support provided to Friends groups was as follows: no administrative support, 2 (12.5%) libraries; library reimbursed by Friends group for administrative support, 2 (12.5%) libraries; and library provides support at no charge to Friends group, 12 (75.0%). **(722)**

Ibid. . . . *showed that* of the 16 libraries with independent Friends groups, the annual contributions of Friends groups to the library ranged from a minimum of $500 to a maximum of $12,000. The average contribution was $4,870, while the median contribution was $4,750. Further, the annual contributions of the 7 nonindependent (affiliated with the university library) Friends groups to the health sciences libraries averaged "less than $1,000" per health science library. **(722)**

Ibid. . . . *showed that* of the 16 libraries with independent Friends groups, the 5 most frequently mentioned purposes (out of 12) for which Friends' funds were spent were as follows (multiple responses allowed):

rare books	9 (56.3%) libraries	
working-collection books	7 (43.8%) libraries	
social events	6 (37.5%) libraries	
exhibits, displays, and		
publicity	5 (31.3%) libraries	
publications	5 (31.3%) libraries	**(722)**

■ A 1977 survey of North American medical school libraries with library Friends groups solely for the medical school library rare book collection (only 14 such libraries out of the 132 libraries reported in the 1976-77 edition of *Directory of American Medical Education* were identified) (survey size: 14 libraries; responding: 13 or 92.9%) *showed that* the main reported purpose of the Friends groups was "raise money for purchase of rare books" (11 so reporting of 11 respondents). However, 40% of the respondents reported they received no money from their Friends group for the purchase of rare books, and only 10% of the respondents reported that they received more than 30% of the acquisitions funds from their Friends group.   **(734)**

Ibid. . . . *showed that* visual inspection of the data revealed no relationship between age of the rare book collection and the amount of money received from the Friends group. For example, 4 Friends groups gave $1,000-9,999 to rare book collections more than 21 years old, and 4 Friends groups gave $1,000-9,999 to rare book collections less than 21 years old.   **(734)**

Ibid. . . . *showed that* visual inspection of the data suggested a relationship between the length of time a Friends group had been established and the amount of money it gave to the medical rare book collection. For example, 4 out of 6 Friends groups that had been in existence less than 8 years provided $0-499 to the rare book collection, while all 6 of the Friends groups that had been in existence 8 years or more provided $1,000-9,999 to the rare book collection.   **(734)**

Ibid. . . . *showed that* visual inspection of the data suggested that active participation by the librarian in the formation of a Friends group was related to the amount of money provided by Friends groups. For example, of 3 Friends groups formed without support from the librarian, all contributed in the range of $0-499, while of 9 Friends groups formed with the support of the librarian, 8 contributed in the range of $1,000-9,999.
                                                                                                      (734)

Ibid. . . . *showed that* visual inspection of the data suggested no relation-ship between the number of Friends members and the amount of money contributed. For example, of 6 Friends groups with 100 members or less, 4 contributed in the range of $1,000-9,999, while of 5 Friends groups with 101-300 members, 4 contributed in the range of $1,000-9,999. **(734)**

Ibid. . . . *showed that* the 4 most commonly reported activities of Friends groups were:

social events	91%	Friends groups
speakers	91%	Friends groups
annual reports	65%	Friends groups
business meetings	50%	Friends groups

Visual inspection of the data suggested no relationship between the number of activities and the amount of money contributed. For example, 3 of 4 Friends groups with less than 3 activities contributed $1,000-9,999, while 5 of 8 Friends groups with more than 3 activities contributed $1,000-9,999. **(734)**

Ibid. . . . *showed that* the 5 most frequently reported kinds of support (out of 12) that the library provided to Friends groups were as follows:

providing meeting rooms	99%	libraries
doing correspondence	92%	libraries
keeping mailing lists	83%	libraries
addressing envelopes	77%	libraries
paying postage	73%	libraries

Further, visual inspection of the data suggested a relationship between the amount of support the library provided the Friends groups and the amount of support the Friends groups provided the library. For example, of 7 Friends groups receiving $0-499 in support from the library, only 3 contributed in the $1,000-9,999 range, while of 4 Friends groups receiving $500-2,000 in support from the library, all 4 contributed in the 1,000-9,999 range. **(734)**

Ibid. . . . *showed that* the 4 most frequently reported benefits provided to Friends groups by libraries were:

income tax deduction	85%	libraries
social events	77%	libraries
special borrowing privileges	70%	libraries
lectures	70%	libraries

Further, visual inspection of the data suggested no relationship between the number of benefits available to Friends groups and the amount of money contributed. For example, of 7 groups with 1-4 benefits, 5 contributed in the $1,000-9,999 range while of 5 groups with 5-9 benefits, 3 contributed in the $1,000-9,999 range. **(734)**

Special

■ A 1977 survey of health sciences libraries concerning Friends of the Library groups (survey size: 105 libraries; responding: 103 or 98%) *showed that* 24 (23.3%) libraries reported Friends groups; 69 (67.0%) reported not having Friends groups; and 10 (9.7%) reported that formation of a Friends group was under consideration. Further, of the libraries with Friends groups, 16 (15.5% of respondents) reported indpendent Friends groups for the health science library. **(722)**

Ibid. . . . *showed that* of the 16 libraries with independent Friends groups, the founding dates of Friends groups were as follows:

1950 or before	2 (12.5%)	libraries
1951-1960	4 (25.0%)	libraries
1961-1970	3 (18.7%)	libraries
1971 or after	7 (43.8%)	libraries **(722)**

Ibid. . . . *showed that*, of the 16 libraries with independent Friends groups, the number of members of Friends groups ranged from a minimum of 9 members to a maximum of 760 members. The average number of members was 237, and the median was 113 members. **(722)**

Ibid. . . . *showed that*, of the 16 libraries with independent Friends groups, the groups instrumental in founding the Friends groups were the library, 3 (18.7%) libraries; outside individuals, 2 (12.5%) libraries; and combined effort of library and outside individuals, 11 (68.8%) libraries. **(722)**

Ibid. . . . *showed that* of the 16 libraries with independent Friends groups, the purpose of Friends groups was (multiple responses allowed): to raise funds for the library, 15 (93.8%) libraries; to develop support for the library, 7 (43.8%) libraries; and to restore the collection, 1 (6.3%) libraries. **(722)**

Ibid. . . . *showed that* of the 16 libraries with independent Friends groups, the type of library support provided to Friends groups was as follows: no administrative support, 2 (12.5%) libraries; library reimbursed by Friends group for administrative support, 2 (12.5%) libraries; and library provides support at no charge to Friends group, 12 (75.0%). **(722)**

Ibid. . . . *showed that* of the 16 libraries with independent Friends groups, the annual contributions of Friends groups to the library ranged from a minimum of $500 to a maximum of $12,000. The average contribution was $4,870, while the median contribution was $4,750. Further, the annual contributions of the 7 nonindependent (affiliated with the university library) Friends groups to the health sciences libraries averaged "less than $1,000" per health science library. **(722)**

Ibid. . . . *showed that* of the 16 libraries with independent Friends groups, the 5 most frequently mentioned purposes (out of 12) for which Friends' funds were spent were as follows (multiple responses allowed):

rare books	9 (56.3%)	libraries
working-collection books	7 (43.8%)	libraries
social events	6 (37.5%)	libraries
exhibits, displays, and publicity	5 (31.3%)	libraries
publications	5 (31.3%)	libraries **(722)**

■ A 1977 survey of North American medical school libraries with library Friends groups solely for the medical school library rare book collection (only 14 such libraries out of the 132 libraries reported in the 1976-77 edition of *Directory of American Medical Education* were identified) (survey size: 14 libraries; responding: 13 or 92.9%) *showed that* the main reported purpose of the Friends groups was "raise money for purchase of rare books" (11 so reporting of 11 respondents). However, 40% of the respondents reported they received no money from their Friends group for the purchase of rare books, and only 10% of the respondents reported that they received more than 30% of the acquisitions funds from their Friends group. **(734)**

Ibid. . . . *showed that* visual inspection of the data revealed no relationship between age of the rare book collection and the amount of money received from the Friends group. For example, 4 Friends groups gave $1,000-9,999 to rare book collections more than 21 years old, and 4 Friends groups gave $1,000-9,999 to rare book collections less than 21 years old. **(734)**

Ibid. . . . *showed that* visual inspection of the data suggested a relationship between the length of time a Friends group had been established and the amount of money it gave to the medical rare book collection. For example,

4 out of 6 Friends groups that had been in existence less than 8 years provided $0-499 to the rare book collection, while all 6 of the Friends groups that had been in existence 8 years or more provided $1,000-9,999 to the rare book collection. **(734)**

Ibid. . . . *showed that* visual inspection of the data suggested that active participation by the librarian in the formation of a Friends group was related to the amount of money provided by Friends groups. For example, of 3 Friends groups formed without support from the librarian, all contributed in the range of $0-499, while of 9 Friends groups formed with the support of the librarian, 8 contributed in the range of $1,000-9,999.
(734)

Ibid. . . . *showed that* visual inspection of the data suggested no relation-ship between the number of Friends members and the amount of money contributed. For example, of 6 Friends groups with 100 members or less, 4 contributed in the range of $1,000-9,999, while of 5 Friends groups with 101-300 members, 4 contributed in the range of $1,000-9,999. **(734)**

Ibid. . . . *showed that* the 4 most commonly reported activities of Friends groups were:

social events	91%	Friends groups
speakers	91%	Friends groups
annual reports	65%	Friends groups
business meetings	50%	Friends groups

Visual inspection of the data suggested no relationship between the number of activities and the amount of money contributed. For example, 3 of 4 Friends groups with less than 3 activities contributed $1,000-9,999, while 5 of 8 Friends groups with more than 3 activities contributed $1,000-9,999. **(734)**

Ibid. . . . *showed that* the 5 most frequently reported kinds of support (out of 12) that the library provided to Friends groups were as follows:

providing meeting rooms	99%	libraries
doing correspondence	92%	libraries
keeping mailing lists	83%	libraries
addressing envelopes	77%	libraries
paying postage	73%	libraries

Further, visual inspection of the data suggested a relationship between the amount of support the library provided the Friends groups and the amount of support the Friends groups provided the library. For example, of 7 Friends groups receiving $0-499 in support from the library, only 3 contributed in the $1,000-9,999 range, while of 4 Friends groups receiving $500-2,000 in support from the library, all 4 contributed in the 1,000-9,999 range.   **(734)**

Ibid. . . . *showed that* the 4 most frequently reported benefits provided to Friends groups by libraries were:

income tax deduction	85%	libraries
social events	77%	libraries
special borrowing privileges	70%	libraries
lectures	70%	libraries

Further, visual inspection of the data suggested no relationship between the number of benefits available to Friends groups and the amount of money contributed. For example, of 7 groups with 1-4 benefits, 5 contributed in the $1,000-9,999 range while of 5 groups with 5-9 benefits, 3 contributed in the $1,000-9,999 range.   **(734)**

Long-Range Planning

General

■   A survey reported in 1981 of a random sample of public, academic,and special library directors in the state of Missouri (sample size: 154 directors; responding: 143 or 93.8%) concerning long-range planning *showed that* 48 (37.2%) of the directors reported that their libraries engaged in long-range planning (planning for a 5-year period or more), while 81 (62.8%) reported they did not.   **(572)**

Ibid. . . . *showed that*, of the 48 directors who reported involvement in long-range planning, 56.5% reported that their plans were prepared and implemented "on an informal, unwritten policy basis"; 34.8% reported that their plans were part of a formal, written library policy; and 8.7% reported both formal and informal plans.   **(572)**

Ibid. . . . *showed that* of the 48 directors who reported involvment in long-range planning, the 6 most frequently mentioned purposes of the planning (out of 8) were (multiple responses allowed):

capital budgeting	35 (72.9%)	directors
operational resources	33 (68.8%)	directors

continued

use and benefit as an
administrator   31 (64.6%) directors
library automation projects   26 (55.3%) directors
networking activities   22 (45.8%) directors
providing written long-term
objectives for the
library   20 (41.7%) directors   **(572)**

Ibid. . . . *showed that* of the 81 directors who were not involved in long-range planning, 63% listed the reason as "lack of budget and/or staff resources," while 50.6% listed as the reason that their libraries did not need long-term plans. (Multiple responses were allowed.)   **(572)**

Ibid. . . . *showed that* libraries engaged in long-term planning were more likely to have larger collections, a network affiliation, and a director with a bachelor's degree or a master's degree in library science than libraries not engaged in long-term planning to a statistically significantly higher degree (significant at the .01 level or better).   **(572)**

Middle Manager

Academic

■ A study reported in 1978 of 23 middle managers and 11 administrators in 5 Association of Research Libraries libraries, as well as a review of ads for 82 middle managerial positions in academic libraries posted in 1975, *showed that* of 23 middle managers, 21 (91.3%) had ALA-accredited master's degrees; none had unaccredited library master's degrees; 13 (56.5%) had second master's degrees; 1 (4.3%) had a Ph.D.; and 2 (8.7%) had an other professional degree.   **(423)**

Ibid. . . . *showed that* of the 82 middle management positions, 13.4% were staff specialists (e.g. systems analysts, personnel directors, etc.); 26.8% were in technical services; and 59.8% were in public services.   **(423)**

Ibid. . . . . *showed that* 43 (52.4%) of the ads listed an ALA-accredited library master's degree as a qualification; 37 (45.1%) listed library master's degree without specifying ALA-accredited; 30 (36.6%) listed second master's degree; 4 (4.9%) listed Ph.D.; 1 (1.2%) listed an other professional degree; and 1 stated that a master's degree was not required. **(423)**

Minorities

Academic

■ A survey reported in 1978 of 407 academic and public libraries who had filled professional positions (61% [no number given] responding with 233 or 57% usable responses) *showed that* 71% of the academic libraries reported affirmative action "somewhat" or "considerable" important in the hiring process, compared to 41% of the public libraries so reporting. In both groups 5% of the positions were filled with ethnic minorities, and both groups estimated that about 5% of the applicant pool consisted of ethnic minorities. **(227)**

■ A survey during the 1979-80 academic year of publicly supported, 2-year community colleges in Texas concerning library programs for developmental education students (disadvantaged students) (survey size: 52; responding: 46; usable: 43 or 82.7%) *showed that* of 39 respondents at least 1 member of the following ethnic groups was on the staff of the learning resource center:

Anglo	39 (100.0%)	LRCs
black	25 (64.1%)	LRCs
Mexican-American	23 (59.0%)	LRCs
Oriental	5 (12.8%)	LRCs
other	3 (7.7%)	LRCs **(517)**

■ A 1980 survey of first-time-appointed academic library directors during the period 1970-80 (survey size: 230 directors; responding: 141 or 61.3%, including 98 males and 43 females) *showed that* ethnic background was as follows:

Asian-Americans accounted for 2 (1.4%) of the directors, including 2 (2.0%) of the males and none of the females;

Hispanics accounted for 2 (1.4%) of the directors, including 2 (2.0%) of the males and none of the females;

blacks accounted for 14 (10.0%) of the directors, including 7 (7.2%) of the males and 7 (9.3%) of the females;

whites accounted for 120 (85.1%) of the directors, including 85 (86.8%) of the males and 35 (81.4%) of the females;

3 individuals did not reply to the question. **(785)**

Ibid. . . . *showed that* the 132 respondents with a U.S. master's degree in library science received their degrees from a total of 44 schools. The 3 schools with the most master's degree graduates among the respondents were Michigan (12 or 9.0% respondents), Columbia (10 or 7.6% respondents), and Simmons (10 or 7.6% respondents). Further, of the 14 black respondents, 6 (42.9%) received their M.L.S. from Atlanta.   **(785)**

Public

■ A 1969 survey by the Library Administration Division (LAD) of ALA of the largest public and academic libraries, the state library agencies, and 1 public library system in most states (65%libraries responding) *showed that* 84% of responding libraries had minority employees (either full- or part-time). Overall, the breakdown was as follows:

American Indians	1%	
Spanish-Americans	15+%	
Negroes	73+%	
Oriental-Americans	11%	**(075)**

Ibid. . . . *showed that* the average percentage of minority staff respresentation per respondent was as follows:

RESPONDENTS	TOTAL %	% PROFESSIONAL	% OTHER
state agencies	9+	4+	11+
public libraries	16+	8+	23+
systems	8+	8+	8+
academic	4+	4+	5+
			(075)

Ibid. . . . *showed that*, while 27% of all employees were in professional positions, 14+% of minority group employees were in professional positions.   **(075)**

■ A survey reported in 1978 of 407 academic and public libraries who had filled professional positions (61% [no number given] responding with 233 or 57% usable responses) *showed that* 71% of the academic libraries reported affirmative action "somewhat" or "considerable" important in the hiring process, compared to 41% of the public libraries so reporting. In both groups 5% of the positions were filled with ethnic minorities, and both groups estimated that about 5% of the applicant pool consisted of ethnic minorities.   **(227)**

Special

■ A survey reported in 1972 of black employment in law school libraries (sample size: 136; responding: 95 or 70%) *showed that* responding libraries reported a total of 12 black law librarians out of 346 professional law librarians (3.4% of the professional law librarians). This included 7 black women out of 204 women professionals (2%) and 5 black men out of 123 male professionals (1.4%). **(386)**

Ibid. . . . *showed that* responding libraries reported 69 black subprofessionals out of a total of 552 subprofessionals (12.5% of the subprofessionals). This included 44 black women out of 342 female subprofessionals (12.9%) and 25 black men out of 210 male subprofessionals (11.9%). **(386)**

■ A survey reported in 1980 of 23 special librarians who became officers in their organizations *showed that*, of external factors (those over which the respondent had little control) influencing the appointment to officer rank, the one "most frequently mentioned" was a supportive management. The "next most frequently cited external factor" was the women's movement and affirmative action. **(431)**

Morale

Public

■ A study reported in 1979 assessing organizational climate in public libraries using a modified version of Educational Testing Service's Institutional Functioning Inventory (survey size: professional staff in 16 public libraries with a response rate of 50-100% per library) *showed that* libraries that had some kind of shared decision making were also characterized by a high degree of mutually supporting relationships among professional staff. Specifically, the scale intercorrelation between "democratic governance" and "support" was .85 [no significance level given]. **(565)**

Ibid. . . . *showed that* libraries that had some kind of shared decision making were also characterized by a high degree of morale and the feeling that one could speak one's own mind and exercise one's own judgment when the occasion demanded. Specifically, the scale intercorrelation between "democratic governance" and "espirit" was .94 and between "democratic governance" and "freedom" was .79 [no significance level given]. **(565)**

Ibid. . . . *showed that* libraries characterized by supportive relationships, high morale, and freedom were more likely to be involved in innovative activities than libraries that did not score high in these areas. Specifically, the scale intercorrelation between "innovation" and "support" was .81, between "innovation" and "espirit" was .78, and between "innovation" and "freedom" was .78 [no significance levels given].   **(565)**

Networks—Automation

General

■ A survey reported in 1982 of the directors of 20 (19 or 95% responding) OCLC distributing networks (e.g., ILLINET, SOLINET, FEDLINK, etc.), *showed that* the two top areas in which 17 respondents desired or anticipated further growth for their networks were (multiple responses allowed) more OCLC members (12 respondents ranking first or second choice) and other contracting activity, processing/delivery (8 respondents ranking first or second choice).   **(343)**

Ibid. . . . *showed that* the 4 most common non-OCLC-related information retrieval services contracted through the networks (either being offered as of May 1980 or planned for offering by mid-1981) reported by 12 respondents were (multiple responses allowed): BRS (8 respondents offering; 2 planning), Lockheed DIALOG (7 respondents offering; 2 planning), SDC ORBIT (6 offering; 2 planning), New York Times Information Service (5 offering; 4 planning).   **(343)**

Ibid. . . . *showed that* the 5 most commonly reported current or planned uses of members' records supplied through OCLC reported by 14 respondents were (multiple responses allowed): union list (11 respondents), circulation control (11 respondents), subject access (10 respondents), management information (8 respondents), and interlibrary loan (6 respondents).   **(343)**

Networks—Membership

General

■ A 1980 comparison of OCLC, RLG/RLIN, and WLN current as of December 1980 *showed that* OCLC had 2,392 member libraries, including "about" 1,300 college and university libraries, 330 public libraries, 250 federal libraries, 145 special libraries, 77 law libraries, 71 members of the Association of Research Libraries, 168 medical libraries, 37 state libraries, and "at least" 48 art and architecture libraries.   **(339)**

Ibid. . . . *showed that* RLG/RLIN had 23 owner-member libraries, including 21 university libraries, New York Public Library, and the American Antiquarian Society. In addition there were 2 associate members, 2 affiliate members, several museums, and 3 law library special members. Further, 52 additional libraries use RLIN for online cataloging, and 136 libraries use it on a "search-only basis."   **(339)**

Ibid. . . . *showed that* WLN had 65 members, including 34 college and university libraries, 21 public libraries, 2 special libraries, 3 state libraries, 5 law libraries, and the Pacific Northwest Bibliographic Center.   **(339)**

Noise

Academic

■ A 1964-67 study of northern California university, 4-year college, and 2-year college libraries (including 1 Oregon library) *showed that* the top 6 reasons a sample of 1,563 students at 16 institutions gave for studying in the library were quiet (51%), convenience or proximity (29%), materials (27%), atmosphere conducive to study (21%), few distractions and little movement (20%), and concentrate better (10%).   **(244)**

Ibid. . . . *showed that* the main disadvantage to studying in the library given by "1 out of 8" of a sample of 1,563 students at 16 institutions was noise from other people.   **(244)**

Ibid. . . . *showed that* the top 4 major distractions reported by 279 students at 7 institutions were (multiple responses allowed): people coming in and out (73%), other students talking (65%), thinking of other things (62%), and noises other than talking (41%).   **(244)**

Ibid. . . . *showed that* the 3 aspects of the physical library environment that 1,112 students at 16 institutions most often rated as needing improvements were: snack facilities (53%), number of carrels (44%), and quietness (44%).   **(244)**

■ A 1978 study at the State University of New York College at Cortland concerning seating arrangements and noise levels, as measured by accoustical equipment and survey questionnaires, *showed that* replacing tables and upholstered chairs in the central area with individual study carrels and distributing the tables and upholstered chairs thoughout the floor did not reduce the frequency of bursts of noise over 50 decibels. However, subjective ratings of noise levels by students using the library decreased from an average of 4.38 (scale of 10, with 1 = quiet, 10 = noisy; 438 students sampled) to 3.90 (347 students sampled), while annoyance ratings decreased from an average of 4.13 to 3.61. (Both changes were statistically significant at the .005 level.) **(501)**

Ibid. . . . *showed that* after the furniture had been rearranged [no sample size or raw numbers given] 64% of the students reported that the affected floors were "very much" or "somewhat" quieter, 24% reported "no difference", 4% reported that the floors were "noisier," and 8% did not respond. **(501)**

Ibid. . . . *showed that* after the furniture had been rearranged [no sample size or raw numbers given] 47% of the students reported that they liked the change, 25% were indifferent, and 28% disliked the change. Further, 44% reported being able to accomplish more work; 52% reported no difference in work accomplished; and 4% reported being able to do less work. (Both of these distributions were significantly statistically different from chance at the .001 level.) **(501)**

Public

■ A 1966 survey conducted during a 6-week period of 21,385 adult (12 years old or older) public library users in the Baltimore-Washington metropolitan region of Maryland entering the library (79.1% of patrons approached filled out the survey instrument) *showed that* the top 3 difficulties given by 5,029 respondents in trying to use the library were getting parking space (9.2%), library too noisy (5.4%), and difficult to figure out the library arrangement (4.7%). **(301)**

Special

■ A 1973 survey of all county law libraries listed in the 1972 American Association of Law Libraries *Directory of Law Libraries* (population: 260; responding: 86 or 33.1%) *showed that* of 84 respondents reporting on freedom from noise in their libraries, 23 (27.4%) reported "excellent," 38 (45.2%) reported "good," 18 (21.4%) reported "fair," and 21 (25%) reported "poor." **(392)**

Organization—General

Academic

■ A 1965 survey of U.S. university-connected medical school libraries to determine the degree they operate within the context of the medical school administration (decentralized) versus that of the university library (centralized) (survey size: 70 libraries; responding: 68 or 97.1%) *showed that* the predominant pattern for medical school libraries was decentralized, both in terms of budgets (48 or 71% libraries received their budgets from the medical school) and in terms of operations, e.g., acquisitions, cataloging, processing (54 or 79% libraries operated independently of the university library). **(673)**

■ A 1972 survey of chief library administrators in public comprehensive community colleges (population: 586; usable responses: 75.9% [no raw number given]) *showed that* 72.1% of the respondents indicated that audiovisual production is provided to some degree in their learning resource centers. **(452)**

■ A survey reported in 1977 of moderate-sized (120,000-500,000 volumes) U.S. academic libraries listed in the 1972-73 *American Library Directory* (survey size: 200; responding: 147 or 74%) *showed that* faculty participated in the periodical selection process in 95% of the responding libraries, while students actively participated in only 9% of the libraries. Further, the library administrator was responsible for final approval of selections in 49% of the libraries; the serials librarian was responsible for final approval in 29% of the libraries; and in 17 (12%) of the libraries teaching faculty were responsible for final selection. **(454)**

■ A 1979 survey of libraries in accredited North American veterinary schools (population: 25 libraries; responding: 23 or 92%) *showed that* 18 (78.3%) libraries were housed separately (usually in the veterinary school), while 5 (21.7%) were housed as part of larger library facility (in health sciences or agricultural libraries). **(740)**

Public

■ A 1976 study that identified 55 combined school and public library arrangements across the U.S. *showed that* in 26 (47%) of the combined arrangements public library personnel operate the libraries during summer and vacation periods when school is not in session; in 17 (31%) staffing responsibility is shared with school librarians during these times; in 5 (9%) paraprofessionals operate the libraries; and in 3 (5%) volunteers handle library duties during these periods.   **(226)**

Ibid. . . . *showed that* the most frequently mentioned problem with merging was governance and management (cited by 17 or 31% of respondents).

(226)

■ A study reported in 1979 assessing organizational climate in public libraries using a modified version of Educational Testing Service's Institutional Functioning Inventory (survey size: professional staff in 16 public libraries with a response rate of 50-100% per library) *showed that* libraries that had some kind of shared decision making were also characterized by a high degree of mutually supporting relationships among professional staff. Specifically, the scale intercorrelation between "democratic governance" and "support" was .85 [no significance level given].   **(565)**

Ibid. . . . *showed that* libraries that had some kind of shared decision making were also characterized by a high degree of morale and the feeling that one could speak one's own mind and exercise one's own judgement when the occasion demanded. Specifically, the scale intercorrelation between "democratic governance" and "espirit" was .94 and between "democratic governance" and "freedom" was .79 (no significance level given).   **(565)**

Ibid. . . . *showed that* libraries characterized by supportive relationships, high morale, and freedom were more likely to be involved in innovative activities than libraries that did not score high in these areas. Specifically, the scale intercorrelation between "innovation" and "support" was .81, between "innovation" and "espirit" was .78, and between "innovation" and "freedom" was .78 [no significance levels given].   **(565)**

School

■ A 1976 study that identified 55 combined school and public library arrangements across the U.S. *showed that* in 26 (47%) of the combined arrangements public library personnel operate the libraries during summers and vacation periods when school is not in session; in 17 (31%) staffing responsibility is shared with school librarians during these times; in 5 (9%) paraprofessionals operate the libraries; and in 3 (5%) volunteers handle library duties during these periods.   **(226)**

Ibid. . . . *showed that* the most frequently mentioned problem with merging was governance and management (cited by 17 or 31% of respondents).
(226)

Special

■ A 1965 survey of U.S. university-connected medical school libraries to determine the degree they operate within the context of the medical school administration (decentralized) versus that of the university library (centralized) (survey size: 70 libraries; responding: 68 or 97.1%) *showed that* the predominant pattern for medical school libraries was decentralized, both in terms of budgets (48 or 71% libraries received their budgets from the medical school) and in terms of operations, e.g., acquisitions, cataloging, processing (54 or 79% libraries operated independently of the university library).
(673)

■ A survey reported in 1971 of the professional law librarians listed as members of the American Association of Law Libraries (population not given; response: "approximately 50%," no number given) *showed that*, of 426 female respondents, 286 (67.1%) were head law libarians, 76 (17.8%) were assistant head law librarians, 29 (6.8%) were catalogers, and 35 (8.2%) were "other."
(383)

■ A 1972 survey of prison law libraries (sample size: 90; responding: 68% [no number given, 62 assumed]) *showed that* the type of prison law library staff was as follows (multiple responses allowed when more than 1 staff member):

noninmate with library degree	7 (11.3%)
noninmate without library degree	36 (58.1%)
inmate with library degree	1 (1.6%)
inmate without library degree	33 (53.2%) **(389)**

■ A 1978 survey of law school libraries listed in the 1977 *AALS Directory of Law Teachers* (population: 167; responding: 158 or 95%) *showed that* 134 (85%) respondents reported themselves totally autonomous of any campus unit other than the law school. This compares to 75% so reporting in a 1973 survey and 55% so reporting in a 1937 survey.
(362)

Ibid. . . . *showed that* 124 (78%) respondents reported that the law library book budget was not part of the university library's book budget; 22 (14%)

reported that it was; and 12 (8%) did not reply. Further, 124 (78%) reported that their library's book budget was allocated as part of the law school's budget.   (362)

Organization—Chain of Command

Academic

■ A survey reported in 1964 of the libraries of the colleges of veterinary medicine in the U.S. (sample: 18; responding: 16; usable: 15) *showed that* 13 of the libraries are under the director of libraries, and 2 are under the dean of the veterinary college. 11 of the libraries are headed by professionally trained librarians, and 4 are headed by clerks.   **(169)**

■ A 1972 survey of chief library administrators in public comprehensive community colleges (population: 586; usable responses: 75.9% [no raw number given]) *showed that* 58.7% of the respondents report to the dean of instruction; 13.3% report to the vice-president; 11.5% report to the president; 10% report to other deans; and 6.5% have other reporting arrangments.   **(452)**

■ A 1978 survey of law school libraries listed in the 1977 *AALS Directory of Law Teachers* (population: 167; responding: 158 or 95%) *showed that* 134 (85%) respondents reported themselves totally autonomous of any campus unit other than the law school. This compares to 75% so reporting in a 1973 survey and 55% so reporting in a 1937 survey.   **(362)**

Ibid. . . . *showed that* 124 (78%) respondents reported that the law library book budget was not part of the university library's book budget; 22 (14%) reported that it was; and 12 (8%) did not reply. Further, 124 (78%) reported that their library's book budget was allocated as part of the law school's budget.   **(362)**

Ibid. . . . *showed that*, of the 22 law school libraries whose book budget was part of the university library's budget, the following individuals or groups determined the yearly allocation:

university library director	9 respondents
law librarian and university library director	7 respondents

continued

university library director and higher university officials	3 respondents	
higher university officials	1 respondent	
university library committee	1 respondent	
no reply	1 respondent	**(362)**

Ibid. . . . *showed that* 30 (19%) respondents had to submit an annual report and all other requested data to the university library director; 35 (22%) were not required to submit such material but did so voluntarily or as a courtesy; 43 (27%) were not required to submit such material and did not do so; and 50 (32%) did not reply. **(362)**

Ibid. . . . *showed that* the law school librarian recommended the creation of new positions, reallocation of personnel funds, etc., to the following individuals or groups:

dean of the law school	107	
university library director	16	
both of the above	7	
higher university officials	4	
no reply	24	**(362)**

Ibid. . . . *showed that* 125 (79%) respondents reported that the university library did not hold any veto power over the law library's selection of personnel; 19 (12%) reported that the university library did hold such a veto power; 2 (1.3%) reported that the university library "maybe" held such power; and 12 (8%) did not reply. **(362)**

Ibid. . . . *showed that* if the law librarians were evaluated on a regular basis the evaluations were sent to the following:

law dean	68	
director of university library	17	
law librarian	9	
both law dean and director of university library	6	
personnel	3	
no answer or no evaluation	55	**(362)**

Ibid. . . . *showed that* the source of the head law librarian's salary was as follows:

law school	127
university library	6

continued

both	12	
other	1	
no reply	12	**(362)**

Ibid. . . . *showed that* 151 respondents reported that the head law school librarian attended faculty meetings in the law school, while 32 attended faculty meetings in the library system; 141 voted in law school faculty meetings, while 28 voted in library faculty meetings; and 143 were voting members of faculty committees in the law school, while 29 were voting members of faculty committees in the library.   **(362)**

■ A 1979 survey of libraries in accredited North American veterinary schools (population: 25 libraries; responding: 23 or 92%) *showed that* veterinary libraries were much more integrated into the university library context than their counterparts the medical school libraries. While 28% of the medical school libraries report administratively to the university library, 74% of the veterinary libraries do.   **(740)**

Special

■ A survey reported in 1964 of the libraries of the colleges of veterinary medicine in the U.S. (sample: 18, responding: 16, usable: 15) *showed that* 13 of the libraries are under the director of libraries, and 2 are under the dean of the veterinary college. 11 of the libraries are headed by professionally trained librarians, and 4 are headed by clerks.   **(169)**

■ A survey reported in 1978 of private law firm libraries (sample size: 278; responding: 141 or 51%) concerning budgeting practices *showed that* 87% of the librarians reported to an attorney in charge of the library or a library committee, while 23% were accountable to an office administrator.   **(361)**

■ A 1978 survey of law school libraries listed in the 1977 *AALS Directory of Law Teachers* (population: 167; responding: 158 or 95%) *showed that* 134 (85%) respondents reported themselves totally autonomous of any campus unit other than the law school. This compares to 75% so reporting in a 1973 survey and 55% so reporting in a 1937 survey.   **(362)**

Ibid. . . . *showed that* 124 (78%) respondents reported that the law library book budget was not part of the university library's book budget; 22 (14%) reported that it was; and 12 (8%) did not reply. Further, 124 (78%) reported that their library's book budget was allocated as part of the law school's budget.   **(362)**

Ibid. . . . *showed that* of the 22 law school libraries whose book budget was part of the university library's budget the following individuals or groups determined the yearly allocation:

university library director	9 respondents
law librarian and university library director	7 respondents
university library director and higher university officials	3 respondents
higher university officials	1 respondent
university library committee	1 respondent
no reply	1 respondent **(362)**

Ibid. . . . *showed that* 30 (19%) respondents had to submit an annual report and all other requested data to the university library director; 35 (22%) were not required to submit such material but did so voluntarily or as a courtesy; 43 (27%) were not required to submit such material and did not do so; and 50 (32%) did not reply.   **(362)**

Ibid. . . . *showed that* the law school librarian recommended the creation of new positions, reallocation of personnel funds, etc., to the following individuals or groups:

dean of the law school	107
university library director	16
both of the above	7
higher university officials	4
no reply	24 **(362)**

Ibid. . . . *showed that* 125 (79%) respondents reported that the university library did not hold any veto power over the law library's selection of personnel; 19 (12%) reported that the university library did hold such a veto power; 2 (1.3%) reported that the university library "maybe" held such power; and 12 (8%) did not reply.   **(362)**

Ibid. . . . *showed that*, if the law librarians were evaluated on a regular basis, the evaluations were sent to the following:

law dean	68
director of university library	17
law librarian	9
both law dean and director of university library	6
personnel	3
no answer or no evaluation	55 **(362)**

Ibid. . . . *showed that* the source of the head law librarian's salary was as follows:

law school	127
university library	6
both	12
other	1
no reply	12

(362)

Ibid. . . . *showed that* 151 respondents reported that the head law school librarian attended faculty meetings in the law school, while 32 attended faculty meetings in the library system; 141 voted in law school faculty meetings, while 28 voted in library faculty meetings; and 143 were voting members of faculty committees in the law school, while 29 were voting members of faculty committees in the library.   (362)

■ A 1979 survey of libraries in accredited North American veterinary schools (population: 25 libraries; responding: 23 or 92%) *showed that* veterinary libraries were much more integrated into the university library context than their counterparts, the medical school libraries. While 28% of the medical school libraries report administratively to the university library, 74% of the veterinary libraries do.   (740)

Organization—ILL

Academic

■ A survey reported in 1965 of ILL staffing in college and university libraries (sample: 45; responding: 40; usable: 35) *showed that* ILL was part of reference in 17 libraries, part of circulation in 8, a separate unit in 3, dispersed among divisions in 2, and in miscellaneous arrangements in 5.
(173)

Organization—Library Advisory Committee

Academic

■ A 1967 survey of the 64 ARL library directors (56 responding; 54 with library advisory committees) concerning library advisory committees *showed that* the average number of members on a library advisory committee was 13, with a range from 6 to 66.   (181)

Ibid. . . . *showed that* approximately 2/3 of the respondents reported that the library director was consulted on appointments made to the library advisory committee. The actual appointments were made in 20 cases by the university administration, in 17 cases by the teaching faculty, in 13 cases by the administration and faculty jointly, and by the governing board of the university in 4 cases. **(181)**

Ibid. . . . *showed that* the library director was an ex officio member of 43 library advisory committees, chair of 6, and served in miscellaneous capacities in the remaining 5 instances. Further, in 43 library advisory committees the library director was the only person officially representing the library, while in 11 cases from 1 to 13 staff members other than the director served as members of the committee. **(181)**

Ibid. . . . *showed that* the library advisory committee functions largely in an advisory capacity (45 instances), concerned largely with establishment of policies in the operation of the library (a "major activity" or "active role" in 28 libraries) and involved in the maintenance of liaison with faculty, library, and administration ("active role" 22 libraries), while the committee's role in selecting new key library staff is quite small (none in 44 libraries), as is also its role in book selection (none in 30 libraries). **(181)**

Outreach and Special Programs—General

Academic

■ A survey reported in 1974 of law schools known to have clinical programs (population: 105; responding: 56 or 53.3%) *showed that* 13 (23.2%) reported having separate clinical libraries, and 17 (30.4%) reported an interest in establishing such a library. **(390)**

Ibid. . . . *showed that*, in meeting the teaching needs of the clinical program, 27 (48.2%) of the respondents indicated dissatisfaction with the available printed sources of information, with 25 (44.6%) reporting that they prepared their own clinical teaching materials. **(390)**

■ A 1976 survey of 21 colleges and universities that had or expected to have residence hall libraries *showed that* 12 respondents reported residence hall libraries that were active; 6 reported that their residence hall library system had been discontinued; 2 reported informal collections of materials in residence halls but not libraries as such; and 1 had canceled plans to build a residence hall library.   **(257)**

■ A survey reported in 1978 at the University of Texas Medical Branch, Galveston, of the popularity of various elements of an in-house library publication as rated by UTMB faculty members (survey size: 489 faculty; responding: 295 or 60%) *showed that* the popularity of elements was as follows (in descending order of popularity):

  1. new acquisitions
  2. faculty publications
  3. historical article
  4. news and notes
  5. meet our staff

Further, of the 4 faculty ranks the the faculty rank most interested in the historical article was "full professors."   **(721)**

■ A survey during the 1979-80 academic year of publicly supported, 2-year community colleges in Texas concerning library programs for developmental education students (disadvantaged students) (survey size: 52; responding: 46; usable: 43 or 82.7%) *showed that* 39 (90.7%) of the community colleges had developmental studies programs, 3 (7.0%) did not, and 1 (2.3%) did not reply; while 16 (37.2%) of the learning resource centers reported providing special library instruction to developmental studies students, and 27 (62.8%) reported they did not provide special instruction.   **(517)**

■ A study reported in 1981 at Southern Illinois University, Carbondale, investigating teaching faculty perception of librarians (survey size: 507; responding: 386; usable: 384 or 75.7%) *showed that* 5% of the teaching faculty reported they requested a librarian to talk to one of their classes each semester; 16% reported that they occasionally asked a librarian to speak to one of their classes; and 74% reported that they had never asked a librarian to speak to one of their classes.   **(493)**

■ A survey reported in 1983 of U.S. dental school libraries concerning their service to dental practitioners (population: 60 dental school libraries; responding: 53 or 88%) *showed that* 40 respondents estimated the following monthly use of their library by dental practitioners:

0-10 requests	31 (73.8%) libraries
11-20 requests	7 (16.6%) libraries
21-30 requests	2 (4.8%) libraries
31-40 requests	0 (0.0%) libraries
41-50 requests	2 (4.8%) libraries **(752)**

Ibid. . . . *showed that* 7 (14%) libraries reported participating in continuing education programs to some extent; 2 (3.8%) reported occasionally preparing bibliographies for instructors of continuing education classes but no further involvement; and 44 (83%) libraries reported no participation in continuing education. **(752)**

Ibid. . . . *showed that*, of 51 respondents, 22 (43%) libraries reported using at least 1 method (e.g., articles in local or state association journals, alumni bulletin, information given to graduating students, etc.) to promote library services to dental practitioners, while 29 (57%) reported they do not advertise such services at all. **(752)**

Ibid. . . . *showed that*, of 51 respondents, 36 (70.6%) libraries reported it important to offer library services to dental practitioners; 12 (23.5%) reported that offering such services was important but could not provide such services due to limited resources; and 3 (5.9%) reported that only faculty and students are served by the dental library. **(752)**

Public

■ An informal survey in 1962 of the 50 state library extension agencies (38 responding) to assess trends of library service since 1954 *showed that* the 3 trends least evident were (1) from isolated efforts toward community service to cooperation with other agencies and groups in promoting educational services, (2) from ignoring community problems to assuming increased responsibility in community adult education, (3) from sketchy knowledge of the community to systematic study of the library's relationship to the community. **(063)**

Ibid. . . . *showed that* the 1 trend to which all respondents agreed was a movement away from the traditional emphasis on recreational reading to an increasing recognition of the importance of reference and informational services. The next highest rated trend was movement away from dependence on a limited library staff to provide all programming toward involving more community people in the library's program. The third highest was a trend away from local self-sufficiency toward greater intrastate library cooperation. **(063)**

■ A 1972 survey of 150 public libraries of all sizes throughout the U.S. (126 responding) concerning the state of reader's advisors services *showed that* 23 (18.3%) reported having a "fully designated position, reader's advisor or its equivalent, whose responsibility it is to suggest, guide and develop patron's book reading habits." 16 (12.7%) additional libraries reported formerly having had such a position. **(141)**

Ibid. . . . *showed that* Great Books courses are actively pursued in 30 cities, while 26 libraries reported having either reading skill improvement courses or adult education (usually basic) programs. **(141)**

■ A 1973 study of an experimental SDI service in the Mideastern Michigan Library Cooperative (sample size: 96, responding 42 or 44%) *showed that* 43% of the respondents indicated they found the service "very useful," while an additional 45% reported that they found the service "of some use." 52% indicated that they thought that at least half of the books suggested fit their interests. **(144)**

■ A survey reported in 1976 of current pratices of a diverse group of selected "community aware" public libraries in 25 states (68 responding libraries) *showed that* the kinds of collaborative programs instituted by at least half of the responding libraries were as follows (multiple responses allowed): planning community programs, 58 (85%); joint sponsorship of services, 56 (82%); information and referral services, 49 (72%); conducting community surveys, 40 (59%); and library service placed in multiagency center, 37 (54%). **(215)**

Ibid. . . . *showed that* library staff were solely responsible for initiating 37% of the "most successful" collaborative programs, library administrators for 27%, staff and administrators separately or together for 77%, community groups shared in starting 14%, and library board members were involved in starting 2% of such programs. **(215)**

Ibid. . . . *showed that* library staff were solely responsible for initiating 31% of the "most innovative" programs and library administrators for 28%, staff and administrators separately or together started 65%, community groups were involved in starting 29%, and library board members in 10% of such programs. **(215)**

Ibid. . . . *showed that* a ranking of the most important factors in creating the "most successful" and "most innovative" collaborative programs by responding libraries was essentially the same for both types of programs and was ranked as follows in order of descending importance: good planning, community involvement, project visibility in the community, staff skills, quality of materials, project autonomy. **(215)**

■ A survey reported in 1977 based on a stratified random sample of 300 households (response rate: 251 or 83%) in the Piedmont area of North Carolina *showed that* 122 respondents or 49% of the full sample (67 or 55% of rural respondents; 21 or 36% of small town respondents; and 34 or 49% of urban respondents) reported an interest in bookmobile service; 115 respondents or 46% of the full sample (53 or 43% of rural respondents; 20 or 34% of small town respondents; and 42 or 61% of urban respondents) reported an interest in being able to order library materials over the phone and have them delivered; while 90 respondents or 36% of the full sample (45 or 37% of rural respondents; 14 or 24% of small town respondents; and 31 or 45% of urban respondents) reported an interest in ordering library materials by mail. **(225)**

■ A 1977-78 survey of a random sample of 300 Spanish-surnamed families in the San Bernardino area *showed that* 54% of the sample read the local major daily English newspaper, compared to 17% who reported reading the bilingual weekly. **(237)**

■ A report published in 1979 by the National Library Service for the Blind and Physically Handicapped of the Library of Congress *showed that* the number of circulating Braille materials remained relatively stable between 1969 (500,000) and 1978 (600,000), while the number of circulating recorded books almost tripled between 1969 (5 million) and 1978 (14 million). **(164)**

■ A survey reported in 1982 by the New York Library Association's Film and Video Roundtable of 63 administrators of large and medium-sized public library film collections both in and outside of New York state (38 or 60% responding) *showed that* the following community groups were identified as heavy or moderate film users: nursing homes (100%), senior citizen centers (93%), day care centers (92%), adult clubs and organizations (89%), children's clubs and organizations (86%), hospitals (82%), and social service agencies (79%). **(162)**

School

■ A survey reported in 1967 of teachers and librarians at 2 high schools (sample size 133) *showed that* the greatest areas of disagreement between teachers and school librarians were:

1. Only the librarians should help students select research topics (teacher agreement, 58%; librarian agreement, 88%).

2. The librarian ought to establish separate resource centers equipped with pertinent equipment and supplies for every

academic area (teacher agreement, 75%; librarian agreement, 44%).

3. Librarians should visit classes and give book talks (teacher agreement, 63%; librarian agreement, 88%).

4. Room libraries are more effective than resource centers or a central library (teacher agreement, 25%; librarian agreement, 0%).   **(083)**

Ibid. . . . *showed that* over 90% of the teachers and school librarians agreed with the following 8 statements:

1. Only school librarians should be considered part of the school's instructional staff.

2. High school students should be given instruction in library skills.

3. Librarians should help direct students' leisure reading.

4. Librarians should keep teachers informed of new materials available for their use.

5. Many teachers don't use the library and its facilities effectively.

6. Instruction in effective use of the library should be given as part of a teacher's in-service training.

7. The library staff should include someone to help teachers prepare audiovisual aids.

8. Teachers would use the library more effectively if they knew more about what resources were available and how to locate them.   **(083)**

■ A 1980 survey of 310 public library children's specialists in 74 California library systems (all responding) *showed that* the 3 most frequent kinds of programming reported by libraries were preschool story hours on weekly or monthly basis (63.2% respondents), class visits to library on weekly or monthly basis (52.9% respondents), and film programs on weekly or monthly basis (39.7% respondents).   **(163)**

Special

■ A 1972 survey of physicians who referred patients to the Medical College of Virginia and received short lists of references from the Virginia Medical Information System relevant to the problems of the patients referred (as described in the physicians' letter of referral) (survey size: 123 physicians; responding: 61 or 49.6%) *showed that*, while 6 (10%) physicians did not want to continue receiving the service, 55 (90%) reported that the service was "a good idea and wanted to continue receiving it." 75% of the 55 reported they would be willing to pay for the service in all or some instances.   **(695)**

■ A survey reported in 1974 of law schools known to have clinical programs (population: 105; responding: 56 or 53.3%) *showed that* 13 (23.2%) reported having separate clinical libraries, and 17 (30.4%) reported an interest in establishing such a library.   **(390)**

Ibid. . . . *showed that*, in meeting the teaching needs of the clinical program, 27 (48.2%) of the respondents indicated dissatisfaction with the available printed sources of information, with 25 (44.6%) reporting that they prepared their own clinical teaching materials.   **(390)**

■ A survey reported in 1978 at the University of Texas Medical Branch, Galveston, of the popularity of various elements of an in-house library publication as rated by UTMB faculty members (survey size: 489 faculty; responding: 295 or 60%) *showed that* the popularity of elements was as follows (in descending order of popularity):

    1. new acquisitions
    2. faculty publications
    3. historical article
    4. news and notes
    5. meet our staff

Further, of the 4 faculty ranks the the faculty rank most interested in the historical article was "full professors."   **(721)**

■ A 1979 study and survey of physicians in nonmetropolitan areas of the Pacific Northwest who were offered an opportunity to receive, without charge, table of contents pages from 18 journals relating to cancer research as well as the option to request a photocopy of any article of interest identified through the service (1 day turnaround guaranteed) (study and survey size: 126 physicians, including 63 randomly selected physicians and 63 physicians identified as having a special interest in cancer research and patient care) *showed that* 18 (29%) of the randomly selected physicians chose to participate in the service, while 31 (49%) of the physicians with a special interest in cancer chose to participate.   **(735)**

Ibid. . . . *showed that* a small core of physicians in both groups made very active use of the service. Of the 31 physicians with a special interest in cancer issues who chose to participate in the service, 11 (35%) requested articles; while of the 18 randomly selected physicians who chose to participate in the service, 9 (50%) requested articles. Nevertheless, in a 6-month period 419 articles were requested by those who did request articles.   (735)

Ibid. . . . *showed that*, of the 419 articles requested, the 4 most frequently requested subject areas (out of 6) were as follows:

treatment/survival	230 (54.9%) articles	
disease description/reviews	55 (13.1%) articles	
laboratory/biologic/basic research	52 (12.5%) articles	
epidemiology/occurrence/risk factors/etiology	50 (11.9%) articles	(735)

Ibid. . . . *showed that*, of 56 physicians who had not responded to the original offer of the service but who did respond to a subsequent survey 6 months later, the reasons for not participating were as follows:

access to the journals elsewhere	38% physicians	
did not receive the letter offering the service (conjecture: thrown out by staff before seen by physician)	38% physicians	
too busy	16% physicians	
seldom saw cancer patients	9% physicians	(735)

Ibid. . . . *showed that*, of the 29 physicians who participated in the service but who did not request articles (96% did respond to a subsequent survey 6 months later), the following reasons were given for not requesting articles:

access to the journals elsewhere	11 (40%) physicians	
saw no journals of interest	8 (30%) physicians	
too busy	6 (22%) physicians	
seldom saw cancer patients	2 (7%) physicians	(735)

Ibid. . . . *showed that*, of the 18 physicians who participated in the service and requested articles and responded to a subsequent survey 6 months later, "at least half" read the articles they received in detail and "three-quarters" kept the article for future reference. Further, 17 of the 18 respondents thought that the service should be continued.   (735)

Ibid. . . . *showed that*, including salaries, office supplies, mailing costs, and photocopying costs over the 6-month period, the average cost per person receiving tables of contents was $33.00 for the 6-month period; the average cost per person receiving articles was $80.00 for the 6-month period; and the average cost per article supplied during this time was $3.82. **(735)**

■ A survey reported in 1980 of the largest medical library in each state (sample size: 51 [sic] libraries; responding: 37) *showed that* 26 (91%) reported that they were open to the public; 8 (22%) reported they were partly open to the public; and 3 (8%) reported they were not open to the public. **(236)**

Ibid. . . . *showed that* in terms of providing medical information to non-medical or nonallied health professionals, patients, or laymen, 7 (20%) reported a completely open policy; 24 (65%) reported they were open to the public with limited services; 1 (3%) reported open to some of the public; 1 (3%) reported open to the public through the public library; and 3 (8%) reported not being open to the public at all. **(236)**

Ibid. . . . *showed that* 12 (32%) reported they would like to serve the public extensively; 7 (19%) reported they would perhaps like to serve the public extensively; and 10 (27%) reported they would not like to serve the public extensively. **(236)**

Ibid. . . . *showed that*, in order to provide priority service to the public, 20 (54%) libraries reported the need for additional personnel; 22 (59%) reported the need for additional materials such as patient education books; 7 (19%) reported the need for malpractice insurance; and 17 (46%) reported the need for additional building size, space, and facilities. **(236)**

Ibid. . . . *showed that* 21 (57%) respondents referred questions from the public to public libraries; 8 (22%) referred questions to the local medical association; 10 (27%) referred questions to a physician; and 3 (8%) referred questions to other libraries. **(236)**

■ A study reported in 1981 of citations to a "definitive clinical trial which demonstrated the beneficial effects of photocoagulation in treating diabetic retinopathy," which 18 months after its publication was still not widely known to physicians treating an appreciable number of diabetic patients, *showed that* "a large number of citations in the literature to a clinically significant paper does not of itself ensure that the information reported will readily reach the appropriate practicing physician." Specifically, between 1976 (when the study was published) and 1979, *Science Citation Index* reported 70 citations to the original report. However, "not a single citation which appeared before 1978 came from a general American medical journal, unrestricted in geographic or subject scope." **(738)**

■ A survey reported in 1983 of U.S. dental school libraries concerning their service to dental practitioners (population: 60 dental school libraries; responding: 53 or 88%) *showed that* 40 respondents estimated the following monthly use of their library by dental practitioners:

0-10 requests	31 (73.8%)	libraries
11-20 requests	7 (16.6%)	libraries
21-30 requests	2 (4.8%)	libraries
31-40 requests	0 (0.0%)	libraries
41-50 requests	2 (4.8%)	libraries

(752)

Ibid. . . . *showed that* 7 (14%) libraries reported participating in continuing education programs to some extent; 2 (3.8%) reported occasionally preparing bibliographies for instructors of continuing education classes but no further involvement; and 44 (83%) libraries reported no participation in continuing education. **(752)**

Ibid. . . . *showed that*, of 51 respondents, 22 (43%) libraries reported using at least 1 method (e.g., articles in local or state association journals, alumni bulletin, information given to graduating students, etc.) to promote library services to dental practitioners, while 29 (57%) reported they do not advertise such services at all. **(752)**

Ibid. . . . *showed that*, of 51 respondents, 36 (70.6%) libraries reported it important to offer library services to dental practitioners; 12 (23.5%) reported that offering such services was important but could not provide such services due to limited resources; and 3 (5.9%) reported that only faculty and students are served by the dental library. **(752)**

Outreach and Special Programs—Clinical Medical Librarianship

Academic

■ A 1974 survey by the University of Washington Health Sciences Library concerning the impact of the clinical medical librarianship program (2 reference librarians attended hospital rounds in order to provide physicians, students, nurses, etc., specialized literature on patient-related problems) in 2 hospital areas by surveying all staff who had been present on rounds in those areas (Neonatal Intensive Care Unit: survey size: 36; responding: 30 or 83%; Department of Orthopedics: survey size: 26; responding: 15 or 58%) *showed that* overall response to the program was good, with 100% of the NICU and 93% of the orthopedics "wishing to see the literature service continued." Further, 97% of NICU and 67% of orthopedics reported that the program "was of clinical importance in determining the diagnosis and treatment of patients."   **(710)**

Ibid. . . . *showed that* 100% of the NICU and 93% of the orthopedics reported that the literature service had saved time for the recipients. Further, 53% of the NICU and 60% of the orthopedics reported that they would have looked the materials up on their own if the CML program had not done so.   **(710)**

Ibid. . . . *showed that* 97% of the NICU and 87% of the orthopedics reported that their awareness of the Health Sciences Library and its services and resources had increased as as a result of the CML program. Further, 50% of the NICU and 33% of the orthopedics were interested in more exposure to MEDLINE, while 63% of the NICU and 47% of the orthopedics reported an interest in more information on "specialized bibliographic resources and services."   **(710)**

Ibid. . . . *showed that* 73% of the NICU and 47% of the orthopedics preferred to have the CML present on rounds rather than available full-time within the library.   **(710)**

■ A survey reported in 1978 at the Yale-New Haven Hospital of clinicians concerning their attitudes toward the clinical medical librarian program (4 reference librarians assigned to the departments of pediatrics, psychiatry, internal medicine, and surgery) (survey size: 98 hospital clinicians; responding: 73 or 74%) *showed that* the program was primarily viewed as education-oriented rather than as supporting patient care.
(723)

Ibid. . . . *showed that* respondents reported that the "information pro-vided was exceptionally relevant" (overall average of 3.45 on a scale of 1-4) and that the literature searches were highly accurate (overall average of 3.48 on a scale of 1-4).   **(723)**

Ibid. . . . *showed that* the degree to which respondents reported that the clinical medical librarian had been integrated into their unit was as follows:

not at all   0 (00%) respondents
slightly   7 (10%) respondents
mostly   36 (49%) respondents
fully   30 (41%) respondents   **(723)**

Special

■ A 1974 survey by the University of Washington Health Sciences Library concerning the impact of the clinical medical librarianship program (2 reference librarians attended hospital rounds in order to provide physicians, students, nurses, etc., specialized literature on patient-related problems) in 2 hospital areas by surveying all staff who had been present on rounds in those areas (Neonatal Intensive Care Unit: survey size: 36; responding: 30 or 83%; Department of Orthopedics: survey size: 26; responding: 15 or 58%) *showed that* overall response to the program was good, with 100% of the NICU and 93% of the orthopedics "wishing to see the literature service continued." Further, 97% of NICU and 67% of orthopedics reported that the program "was of clinical importance in determining the diagnosis and treatment of patients."   **(710)**

Ibid. . . . *showed that* 100% of the NICU and 93% of the orthopedics reported that the literature service had saved time for the recipients. Further, 53% of the NICU and 60% of the orthopedics reported that they would have looked the materials up on their own if the CML program had not done so.   **(710)**

Ibid. . . . *showed that* 97% of the NICU and 87% of the orthopedics reported that their awareness of the Health Sciences Library and its services and resources had increased as as a result of the CML program. Further, 50% of the NICU and 33% of the orthopedics were interested in more exposure to MEDLINE, while 63% of the NICU and 47% of the orthopedics reported an interest in more information on "specialized bibliographic resources and services."   **(710)**

Ibid. . . . *showed that* 73% of the NICU and 47% of the orthopedics preferred to have the CML present on rounds rather than available full-time within the library.   **(710)**

■ A survey reported in 1978 at the Yale-New Haven Hospital of clinicians concerning their attitudes toward the clinical medical librarian program (4 reference librarians assigned to the departments of pediatrics, psychiatry, internal medicine, and surgery) (survey size: 98 hospital clinicians; responding: 73 or 74%) *showed that* the program was primarily viewed as education-oriented rather than as supporting patient care.

(723)

Ibid. . . . *showed that* respondents reported that the "information provided was exceptionally relevant" (overall average of 3.45 on a scale of 1-4) and that the literature searches were highly accurate (overall average of 3.48 on a scale of 1-4). **(723)**

Ibid. . . . *showed that* the degree to which respondents reported that the clinical medical librarian had been integrated into their unit was as follows:

not at all	0 (00%)	respondents
slightly	7 (10%)	respondents
mostly	36 (49%)	respondents
fully	30 (41%)	respondents **(723)**

Outreach and Special Programs—Continuing Education

Academic

■ A survey reported in 1977 by the University of Oklahoma Health Sciences Center Library to investigate the relationship between subjects for which physicians had requested literature searches and subjects for which physicians desired continuing education based on a physician population that had requested at least 1 literature search from the Health Sciences Library during 1973-75 (survey size: 396 physicians; responding: 125 or 31.5%) *showed that* "literature searches alone could not be used to determine CME [continuing medical education] topics." Specifically, the 5 most frequently mentioned topics for CME and the 5 topics for which the most literature searches had been requested had only 3 (60%) topics in common. **(717)**

Public

■ A 1974-75 study of the independent learner program (a program jointly sponsored by public libraries and the College Entrance Examination Board and designed to provide information service to adults interested in gaining college credit by examination) provided by the Atlanta Public Library and involving 132 learners *showed that* 43% of the learners were between the ages 26-35, while 71% of the learners were between the ages 18-35.

(147)

Ibid. . . . *showed that* 47% of the learning projects were in humanities-related areas, while 32% were in the science/technology areas. **(147)**

Ibid. . . . *showed that* 63% of the learners reported their goals to be personal development; 28% had job-related goals; and 9% were interested in academic credit. **(147)**

Ibid. . . . *showed that* the length of the learning projects ranged from 1 to 239 days, with an average length of 12.2 days. **(147)**

Special

■ A survey reported in 1977 by the University of Oklahoma Health Sciences Center Library to investigate the relationship between subjects for which physicians had requested literature searches and subjects for which physicians desired continuing education based on a physician population that had requested at least 1 literature search from the Health Sciences Library during 1973-75 (survey size: 396 physicians; responding: 125 or 31.5%) *showed that* "literature searches alone could not be used to determine CME [continuing medical education] topics." Specifically, the 5 most frequently mentioned topics for CME and the 5 topics for which the most literature searches had been requested had only 3 (60%) topics in common. **(717)**

Outreach and Special
Programs—Developmental Education

Academic

■ A survey during the 1979-80 academic year of publicly supported, 2-year community colleges in Texas concerning library programs for developmental education students (disadvantaged students) (survey size: 52; responding: 46; usable: 43 or 82.7%) *showed that* 39 (90.7%) of the community colleges had developmental studies programs, 3 (7.0%) did not, and 1 (2.3%) did not reply; while 16 (37.2%) of the learning resource centers reported providing special library instruction to developmental studies students, and 27 (62.8%) reported they did not provide special instruction. **(517)**

Ibid. . . . *showed that* 5 most frequently reported methods of assisting students in the use of the learning resource center (out of 10) were as follows (multiple responses allowed):

library tour	93.0% respondents	
orientation lecture	83.7% respondents	
course-related instruction	69.8% respondents	
handbooks	62.8% respondents	
point-of-use aids	51.2% respondents	**(517)**

Ibid. . . . *showed that* of 39 respondents at least 1 member of the following ethnic groups was on the staff of the learning resource center:

Anglo	39 (100.0%) LRCs	
black	25 (64.1%) LRCs	
Mexican-American	23 (59.0%) LRCs	
Oriental	5 (12.8%) LRCs	
other	3 (7.7%) LRCs	**(517)**

Outreach and Special Programs—Need

Special

■ A study reported in 1981 of citations to a "definitive clinical trial which demonstrated the beneficial effects of photocoagulation in treating diabetic retinopathy," which 18 months after its publication was still not widely known to physicians treating an appreciable number of diabetic patients, *showed that* "a large number of citations in the literature to a clinically significant paper does not of itself ensure that the information reported will readily reach the appropriate practicing physician." Specifically, between 1976 (when the study was published) and 1979, *Science Citation Index* reported 70 citations to the original report. However, "not a single citation which appeared before 1978 came from a general American medical journal, unrestricted in geographic or subject scope." **(738)**

Outreach and Special Programs—Special Collections

Academic

■ A survey during the 1974-75 academic year at the Queen's University in Kingston (Canada) and Trent University in Peterborough (Canada) of part-time students (survey size: 1,143 students at Trent and 1,408 students at Queen's; responding: 286 or 25.1% students at Trent and 480 or 34.1%

students at Queen's) concerning location of a supplementary library collection off campus *showed that* the 3 locations most frequently chosen by students as their first choice for location of the library collection (or a suitable academic collection) was as follows:

41.7% of the Queen's students and 41.6% of the Trent students selected the university;

24.0% of the Queen's students and 21.3% of the Trent students selected the place of instruction (often not the university);

14.8% of the Queen's students and 21.0% of the Trent students selected the local public library. **(545)**

■ A 1978 survey of academic law libraries concerning the issue of faculty libraries (a separate collection or library set aside for the use of the law faculty) (survey size: 169 libraries; responding: 115 or 68.0%) *showed that* 70 (60.9%) respondents had faculty libraries, while 45 (39.1%) did not. Further, 10 (22.2%) of the 45 respondents without faculty libraries reported that they had previously had such libraries. **(795)**

Ibid. . . . *showed that*, of the 70 faculty libraries, 41 (58.6%) had been established within 7 years of the survey date. However, 14 libraries had been in existence from 20 to 40 years. **(795)**

Ibid. . . . *showed that*, of the 70 respondents with faculty libraries, 35 were located in private institutions, while 35 were located in publicly supported institutions. **(795)**

Ibid. . . . *showed that*, of the 70 respondents with faculty libraries, the collections included "for the most part . . . primary materials related to the individual states in which the libraries [were located] plus Federal materials." Further:

95% of the faculty libraries included periodicals, with an average subscription rate of 75 titles per library;

6 (8.6%) of the faculty libraries included microfilms. **(795)**

Ibid. . . . *showed that* 16 (22.9%) respondents allowed student access to the faculty library, while 54 (77.1%) did not. Further, 41 (58.6%) respondents reported that the faculty library was not set up as a reading room only. "Many of these facilities have kitchens within the faculty library," while 12 (17.1%) respondents reported carrels located in the faculty library. **(795)**

Ibid. . . . *showed that*, of the 70 respondents with faculty libraries, 41 (58.6%) allowed checkout privileges from the main collection to the faculty library. **(795)**

Public

■ A 1976 survey by the Joint Committee on Library Services to Labor Groups, RASD, ALA, of 723 public libraries in communities of more than 10,000 that had a central labor council (385 or 53.2% responding), *showed that* 18 libraries reported that they had special collections of materials for use by labor unions and/or organizations. This compared to 46 libraries reporting such collections (out of 384) in an unpublished 1967 survey. A further 317 libraries (in the 1976 survey) reported labor materials as a part of their regular collections, with size ranging from 4 to 5,250 items and averaging 498 items. **(152)**

Ibid. . . . *showed that* 45 or 11.6% respondents had approached the central labor body or local unions to offer library services to them or secure suggestions for needed library services. This compared to 156 or 41% of the libraries (out of 384) in an unpublished 1967 survey. **(152)**

Ibid. . . . *showed that* 14 or 4% of the responding libraries reported that a staff member was assigned to work with labor organizations and/or labor-related materials. This compares to 22 or 6% of responding libraries (out of 384) in an unpublished 1967 survey. **(152)**

Special

■ A 1978 survey of academic law libraries concerning the issue of faculty libraries (a separate collection or library set aside for the use of the law faculty) (survey size: 169 libraries; responding: 115 or 68.0%) *showed that* 70 (60.9%) respondents had faculty libraries, while 45 (39.1%) did not. Further, 10 (22.2%) of the 45 respondents without faculty libraries reported that they had previously had such libraries. **(795)**

Ibid. . . . *showed that*, of the 70 faculty libraries, 41 (58.6%) had been established within 7 years of the survey date. However, 14 libraries had been in existence from 20 to 40 years. **(795)**

Ibid. . . . *showed that*, of the 70 respondents with faculty libraries, 35 were located in private institutions, while 35 were located in publicly supported institutions. **(795)**

Ibid. . . . *showed that*, of the 70 respondents with faculty libraries, the collections included "for the most part . . . primary materials related to the individual states in which the libraries [were located] plus Federal materials." Further:

95% of the faculty libraries included periodicals, with an average subscription rate of 75 titles per library;

6 (8.6%) of the faculty libraries included microfilms.   **(795)**

Ibid. . . . *showed that* 16 (22.9%) respondents allowed student access to the faculty library, while 54 (77.1%) did not. Further, 41 (58.6%) respondents reported that the faculty library was not set up as a reading room only. "Many of these facilities have kitchens within the faculty library," while 12 (17.1%) respondents reported carrels located in the faculty library.   **(795)**

Ibid. . . . *showed that*, of the 70 respondents with faculty libraries, 41 (58.6%) allowed checkout privileges from the main collection to the faculty library.   **(795)**

Performance Measures

Public

■ An attempt reported in 1982 to establish 4 input measures and 4 output measures for public libraries, based on published statistical reports for 301 New Jersey public libraries over a 6-year period (1974-79) and survey data for 96 public libraries in New Jersey, *showed that* (per capita based on number of residents in the library's service area):

INPUT MEASURES

The proportion of budget spent on materials averaged 19.9%, with a standard deviation of .081 (based on 301 libraries).

The new volumes per capita averaged .181, with a standard deviation of .097 (based on 301 libraries).

The periodical titles per capita averaged .0094, with a standard deviation of .0054 (based on 301 libraries).

The circulation per volume averaged 1.79, with a standard deviation of .77 (based on 301 libraries).

OUTPUT MEASURES

The circulation per capita averaged 5.04, with a standard deviation of 3.07 (based on 301 libraries).

The patron visits per capita averaged 2.82, with a standard deviation of 1.82 (based on 96 libraries).

The reference questions per capita averaged 1.12, with a standard deviation of .79 (based on 96 libraries).

The in-library uses of materials per capita averaged 2.29, with a standard deviation of 2.02 (based on 96 libraries).   **(576)**

Photocopying

Academic

■ A 1970 study of photocopying at the University of Toronto Library (Canada) (photocopies are made by library staff rather than by patrons) during a 2-week period and involving 1,768 items (21,483 pages) *showed that*, of the pages copied, 11% were from Canadian publications, 45% from U.S. publications, 17% from British publications, and 26% from "other" publications.   **(535)**

Ibid. . . . *showed that* 372 (21.0%) of the items photocopied were mono-graphs; 1,334 (75.5%) were serials; 53 (3%) were government publications; 8 (0.5%) were theses; and 1 was "other."   **(535)**

Ibid. . . . *showed that* the numbers of items photocopied per publisher were as follows:

1 item per publisher	909 (51.32%) items
2-5 items per publisher	450 (25.45%) items
6+ items per publisher	409 (23.13%) items

Further, in only 3 cases out of 1,768 was the same article photocopied more than once; in 2 cases the article was copied twice; and in 1 case the article was copied 7 times.   **(535)**

Ibid. . . . *showed that*, of 1,612 items for which the date of publication was known, the distribution was as follows:

published after 1900	96.5% of total
published after 1950	77.0% of total
published after 1960	56.0% of total
published after 1965	37.0% of total
published after 1969	14.3% of total	**(535)**

Ibid. . . . *showed that* photocopies distributed by patron type were as follows:

other libraries	592 (33.48%) of total
graduate students	452 (25.57%) of total
undergraduate students	390 (22.06%) of total
faculty	154 (8.71%) of total
general public	79 (4.47%) of total
library-collection	53 (2.99%) of total
library-staff	48 (2.72%) of total (535)

Ibid. . . . *showed that* 32% of the photocopied items were available at some time through a Canadian agency (i.e., a Canadian publisher or vendor); 12.7% of the photocopied items were Canadian titles; and 0.6% of the photocopied items were Canadian in-print books.   (535)

■ A study reported in 1980 at the Health Sciences Library of the University of California, San Franscisco, over a 21-week period in 1979 to determine the effects of limiting journal circulation *showed that*, when a 5-year backfile of all first-copy journals was made noncirculating, the average weekly circulation dropped 40.8% (from 2,971 items per week to 1,759 items per week), while the average in-house copying increased 135.7% (from 1,938 article equivalents, i.e., total copying divided by 8.5, to 4,567 article equivalents).   (731)

Special

■ A study reported in 1980 at the Health Sciences Library of the University of California, San Franscisco, over a 21-week period in 1979 to determine the effects of limiting journal circulation *showed that*, when a 5-year backfile of all first-copy journals was made noncirculating, the average weekly circulation dropped 40.8% (from 2,971 items per week to 1,759 items per week), while the average in-house copying increased 135.7% (from 1,938 article equivalents, i.e., total copying divided by 8.5, to 4,567 article equivalents).   (731)

Prisons

Special

■ A 1972 survey of prison law libraries (sample size: 90; responding: 68% [no number given, 62 assumed]) *showed that* the type of prison law library staff was as follows (multiple responses allowed when more than 1 staff member):

noninmate with library degree	7 (11.3%)	
noninmate without library degree	36 (58.1%)	
inmate with library degree	1 (1.6%)	
inmate without library degree	33 (53.2%)	**(389)**

Ibid. . . . *showed that* 41 (66.1%) of the prison law libraries had separate law library quarters.   **(389)**

Ibid. . . . *showed that* 7 (11.3%) of the prison law libraries were open 11 to 30 hours per week; 15 (24.2%) were open 31 to 40 hours per week; and 16 (25.8%) were open longer than 40 hours per week.   **(389)**

Ibid. . . . *showed that* 14 (22.6%) of the prison law libraries could comfortably seat 1-5 inmates; 9 (14.5%) could comfortably seat 6-10 inmates; 12 (19.4%) could comfortably seat 11-20 inmates; and 7 (11.3%) could comfortably seat 20+ inmates. No data provided on missing respondents.
(389)

Ibid. . . . *showed that* 19 (30.6%) of the prison law libraries allowed inmates to borrow books; 3 (4.8%) allowed inmates to make photocopies in the library, while 25 (40.3%) allowed inmates to make photocopies outside of the library. 19 (30.6%) of the prison law libraries made no charge for photocopying.   **(389)**

Ibid. . . . *showed that* 26 (41.9%) of the prison law libraries reported 100 linear feet or less of book shelving; 3 (4.8%) reported 101-200 linear feet of book shelving; and 22 (35.5%) reported over 200 linear feet of book shelving. No data provided on missing respondents.   **(389)**

Ibid. . . . *showed that* the 5 types of state legal materials reported most often present in prison law libraries were (multiple responses allowed): compiled statutes (51 or 82.3% respondents), Supreme Court reports (44 or 71.0% respondents), appellate court reports (33 or 53.2% respondents), criminal practice and procedure texts (32 or 51.6% respondents), and digests (31 or 50.0% respondents).   **(389)**

Ibid. . . . *showed that* the 5 types of federal legal materials reported most often present in prison law libraries were (multiple responses allowed) were:

U.S. Code	52 (83.9%) respondents	
Federal Reporter, 2nd	43 (69.4%) respondents	
Supreme Court reports	41 (66.1%) respondents	
Federal Supplement	41 (66.1%) respondents	
Digest (Supreme Court)	29 (46.8%) respondents	**(389)**

Ibid. . . . *showed that* the following 5 types of general legal materials were present, to the degree shown, in prison law libraries:

criminal procedure text	39 (62.9%) respondents	
legal dictionary	37 (59.7%) respondents	
criminal law text	33 (53.2%) respondents	
Criminal Law Reporter	32 (51.6%) respondents	
criminal law forms	27 (43.5%) respondents	**(389)**

Ibid. . . . *showed that* at least 6% of the State prisons (and possibly 34% of the State prisons if nonresponses suggest having no prison law library facilities) had no prison law library facilities, while none of the federal prisons lacked a prison law library facility.   **(389)**

Program Evaluation—General

General

■   A study reported in 1979 of the library performance criteria used in the annual reports of 62 selected libraries (774 total criteria found; average of 12.3 per report) representing all library types *showed that* the following basic categories of criteria were used:

quantifiable measures	462 (59.6%) criteria	
expert opinion	159 (20.5%) criteria	
costs	111 (14.3%) criteria	
comparison to others	15 (01.9%) criteria	
user opinion	9 (01.1%) criteria	
standards/formulas	2 (00.2%) criteria	
other	16 (02.0%) criteria	**(428)**

Academic

■   A study reported in 1977 comparing the performance of a reference unit staffed with nonprofessionals with that of a reference unit staffed with professionals, each in a different library in 2 medium-sized midwestern universities, *showed that*, of 25 questions deliberately containing faulty information, the professional librarians obtained correct information in 13 (52%) cases by themselves and in 15 (67%) cases with the help of referral or consultation. This compares to nonprofessionals, who obtained correct information in 5 (20%) cases by themselves and in 7 (28%) cases with the help of referral or consultation.   **(456)**

Ibid. . . . *showed that*, of 21 deliberately indirect questions, professionals correctly solved 19 (90.5%), while nonprofessionals correctly solved 13 (61.9%).   **(456)**

Public

■ An attempt reported in 1982 to establish 4 input measures and 4 output measures for public libraries, based on published statistical reports for 301 New Jersey public libraries over a 6-year period (1974-79) and survey data for 96 public libraries in New Jersey, *showed that* (per capita based on number of residents in the library's service area):

INPUT MEASURES

The proportion of budget spent on materials averaged 19.9%, with a standard deviation of .081 (based on 301 libraries).

The new volumes per capita averaged .181, with a standard deviation of .097 (based on 301 libraries).

The periodical titles per capita averaged .0094, with a standard deviation of .0054 (based on 301 libraries).

The circulation per volume averaged 1.79, with a standard deviation of .77 (based on 301 libraries).

OUTPUT MEASURES

The circulation per capita averaged 5.04, with a standard deviation of 3.07 (based on 301 libraries).

The patron visits per capita averaged 2.82, with a standard deviation of 1.82 (based on 96 libraries).

The reference questions per capita averaged 1.12, with a standard deviation of .79 (based on 96 libraries).

The in-library uses of materials per capita averaged 2.29, with a standard deviation of 2.02 (based on 96 libraries).   **(576)**

Special

■ A survey reported in 1978 of the 50 state law libraries (40 or 80% responding) *showed that* the 6 (out of 18) most pressing problems they reported facing, listed in descending order of importance based on number of libraries reporting the problem and their rating of its severity were:

increased demands for photocopy service,
not enough shelf space,
not enough study space (tables, desks, etc.),

book budget too low,
nonprofessional staff too small,
and theft of materials.   (358)

Program Evaluation—Reference

Public

■ A 1977-78 study of reference performance in the Suffolk Cooperative
Library System, involving a total of 57 libraries and branches using a
procedure of hidden testing consisting of proxies asking 20 identical
reference questions at each library or branch over a period of 6 months for
a total of 1,110 (sic) queries, *showed that* about 56% of the time an actual
answer was given the proxy, i.e., the proxy was a given a document, fact,
or citation.   (238)

Ibid. . . . *showed that* "about 17%" of the time library respondents
provided neither an answer to a query nor an idea where the proxy could
find it.   (238)

Ibid. . . . *showed that*, of the 56% of the queries to which library respondents gave actual answers, 84% of the time the answer was "correct" or
"mostly correct."   (238)

Ibid. . . . *showed that*, when special queries designed to test library
respondents' willingness to negotiate the proxy's initial inquiry were posed,
67% of the library respondents made no effort to probe for the proxy's
underlying need, while "about 20%" of the respondents did negotiate the
query to its ultimate level.   (238)

■ A study reported in 1978 concerning reference performance in Illinois
public libraries (population: 530 libraries; sample size: 60; response rate 51
or 85%) using one reference librarian from each library to answer 25 test
reference questions *showed that* an average of 59% of the questions were
answered correctly, with a range of 20% to 96%. Upon analysis of each
library's reference collection and considering only those questions for
which the library had appropriate sources, an average of 78% were
answered correctly, with a range of 50% to 100%.   (259)

Ibid. . . . *showed that*, based upon an analysis of each library's reference
collection, the potential range for answering the test questions with local
tools ran from 20% to 100%, with an overall average of 76%.   (259)

Ibid. . . . *showed that,* based upon an analysis of each library's reference collection, at least 275 reference volumes were required before it was potentially possible to answer correctly 50% of the test reference questions, while at least 1,080 volumes would be required before it was potentially possible to answer correctly 70% of the questions. However, given that reference librarians did not work with 100% efficiency, the data suggest that at least 800 reference volumes would be required to answer 50% or more of the test questions correctly, and at least 2,463 reference volumes would be required to answer 70% or more of the questions correctly. **(259)**

Ibid. . . . *showed that* there was a statistically significant positive correlation (.49 at the .05 significance level) between reference collection size and average percentage of correct answers to the test reference questions as well as a statistically significant positive correlation (.52 with no significance level given) between reference collection size and potential percentage of correct answers to the test reference questions. Both relationships, however, were shown to be nonlinearly related; i.e., a point of diminishing returns was reached at about the 3,500-volume point, where increasing the number of reference volumes led to smaller gains in the number of questions correctly answered. **(259)**

Ibid. . . . *showed that* contrary to expectation the reference experience of respondents at their present libraries was not correlated in a statistically significant way with either the percentage of test reference questions answered correctly or the percentage of questions that, given the reference tools available, could have been answered correctly. In fact, the slight direction of the relationship that did occur was negative. **(259)**

Ibid. . . . *showed that* the correlation between the number of reference questions answered per week and the percentage of test reference questions answered correctly by respondent was strong (.52) and statistically significant (significance level not given). There was also a statistically significant relationship between number of reference questions answered per week and the percentage of test questions that, given the reference tools available, could have been answered correctly. (Strength and significance level not given.) **(259)**

Ibid. . . . *showed that* the percentage of test reference questions answered correctly and the percentage of questions that, given the reference tools available, could have been answered correctly did not correlate in a statistically significant way with either age of respondents or total length of reference experience, although the direction of this latter relationship was slightly negative. **(259)**

Ibid. . . . *showed that* perceived adequateness of size of reference collection was related to both percentage of correctly answered questions (.50 with no significance level given) and percentage of those questions that, given the reference tools available, could have been answered correctly (.57 with no significance level given) in a statistically significant manner. **(259)**

■ A 1981 comparison of obtrusive vs. unobtrusive evaluation of reference services in 5 Illinois public libraries serving populations from 10,000 to 100,000, involving 15 obtrusive questions and 9-15 unobtrusive questions in each of the libraries, *showed that* 85% of the obtrusive questions were answered completely and correctly, with a range among the 5 libraries of 67% to 100%; while 70% of the unobtrusive questions were answered completely and correctly, with a range of 33% to 92%. These differences were statistically significant at the .05 level. **(268)**

■ A 1981 comparison of studies of obtrusive vs. unobtrusive evaluation of reference services presented in the literature *showed that* the following percentages of complete and correct answers were given in 7 unobtrusive studies: 54, 55, 40, 40, 50, 47, 70. The percentages of complete and correct answers given in 4 obtrusive studies were as follows: 50, 64, 59, and 85. **(268)**

Staff Evaluation—Professional

Academic

■ A 1967 survey of 4-year state colleges and universities (sample size: 321; responding: 200 or 62.3%; usable: 183 or 57%) showed that the criteria used for promotions of academic librarians were work performance, 137 or 74.9% (32 or 17.5% not responding); advanced degrees, 116 or 63.4% (38 or 20.8% not responding); seniority, 79 or 43.2% (40 or 21.8% not responding); and research, 65 or 35.5% (35 or 19.1% not responding). **(186)**

■ A 1970 survey of Canadian community college libraries concerning academic status, salaries, and fringe benefits (sample size: 108; responding: 49; usable: 43 or 39.8%) *showed that* the criteria for promotion of community college librarians were as follows (multiple responses allowed):

work performance	70.0% of respondents	
seniority	32.5% of respondents	
advanced degree	28.0% of respondents	
research and publication	12.0% of respondents	
teaching	12.0% of respondents	**(537)**

■ A 1971 survey of all university libraries in North America with more than 15 professionals on the staff (population: 185; responding: 138; usable results: 1,230 or 94%) concerning performance appraisal of professionals *showed that* 78 (60%) used some kind of form or set of guidelines to perform the appraisal. Of these 78, a further 38 used the same or a similar form with special modifications for librarians as for the teaching faculty. **(213)**

Ibid. . . . *showed that* 26% of the respondents felt their method of performance appraisal was "very effective"; 64% reported it "somewhat effective"; 8% reported it "ineffective"; and 2% reported it "completely ineffective." **(213)**

■ A survey in 1972 of a stratified random sample of full-time professional librarians in private and public junior colleges, colleges, and universities in the 10 counties of southern California (sample size: 216; responding: 174 or 81%) was analyzed by stepwise regression and showed the following relationships statistically significant at the .05 level or better. While older librarians were more likely than their younger colleagues to advocate faculty titles for librarians and to claim that faculty status would enhance their prestige, they were more likely to oppose the idea of peer appraisal of their work performance. **(092)**

Ibid. . . . *showed that* females were more likely to oppose the idea of peer evaluation than were male librarians. **(092)**

Ibid. . . . *showed that* the more advanced the librarians' educational background, the more likely they were to support the importance of acceptance as equals with faculty members and the less likely they were to agree to the idea of peer appraisal. **(092)**

■ A 1978 survey of law school libraries listed in the 1977 *AALS Directory of Law Teachers* (population: 167; responding: 158 or 95%) *showed that*, if the law librarians were evaulated on a regular basis, the evaluations were sent to the following:

law dean	68	
director of university library	17	
law librarian	9	
both law dean and director of university library	6	
personnel	3	
no answer or no evaluation	55	**(362)**

■ A survey reported in 1983 of the U.S. academic members of the Association of Research Libraries concerning faculty status for professionals (population: 89 libraries; responding: 89 or 100%, including 57 state and 32 private institutions) *showed that* the criteria used for librarian evaluation were as follows:

same as the teaching faculty in 14 (24.6%) of the state and 1 (3.1%) of the private institutions;

modified version of teaching faculty criteria in 17 (29.8%) of the state and 5 (15.6%) of the private institutions;

and a set of professional criteria in 26 (45.6%) of the state and 26 (81.3%) of the private institutions.   **(788)**

Special

■ A 1978 survey of law school libraries listed in the *1977 AALS Directory of Law Teachers* (population: 167; responding: 158 or 95%) *showed that*, if the law librarians were evaluated on a regular basis, the evaluations were sent to the following:

law dean	68	
director of university library	17	
law librarian	9	
both law dean and director of university library	6	
personnel	3	
no answer or no evaluation	55	**(362)**

Staffing Levels

Academic

■ A 1967 survey of medical school libraries concerning reference services (survey size: 93 libraries; responding: 85 or 91.4%) *showed that* the average staffing per library was as follows:

professional	5.2 FTE	
nonprofessional	9.1 FTE	
reference, professional	1.7 FTE	
reference, nonprofessional	0.8 FTE	**(682)**

■ A paper proposed by members of the Library Services Branch of the U.S. Office of Education in 1967 on library manpower *showed that*, during the period 1961-62 through 1964-65, academic libraries had expanded their staffs from 21,099 to 28,080, including a 30% increase in professionals (from 10,300 to 13,030) and a 50% increase in nonprofessionals (from 10,771 to 15,050). The ratio of all library staff to students dropped from 1 for every 186 students in 1961-62 to 1 for every 197 students in 1964-65, including a drop in the library professional/student ratio from 1 to 378 to 1 to 425. **(082)**

■ A 1976 survey of head law librarians in North American schools (sample size: 178; responding: 154 or 86.7%) *showed that* size of professional law school library staff in terms of FTEs was as follows: 116 (75%) reported 0-5 staff, 33 (21%) reported 6-10 staff, 3 (2%) reported 11-15 staff, and 3 (2%) reported 16-20. **(357)**

■ A study of 1977 survey information gathered by the National Center for Educational Statistics (U.S. Office of Education) concerning the degree to which 1,146 college and university libraries (Liberal Arts Colleges I and II; Comprehensive Universities and Colleges I and II) met the 1975 Standards for College Libraries (ACRL) *showed that* the average annual number of student hours worked in the reporting libraries was 10,600 hours, while the median was 6,400 hours. **(486)**

Ibid. . . . *showed that* the overall number of professional librarians per FTE student averaged 1 to 410 with a median of 1 to 350. By type of school the average ran 1 to 440 for private schools with graduate programs, 1 to 310 for private schools with only undergraduate programs, 1 to 570 for publicly supported schools with graduate programs, and 1 to 460 for publicly supported schools with only undergraduate programs. **(486)**

■ A 1977 study of library technician positions (a library technician is a graduate of a 2-year undergraduate program with specialization in library techniques and procedures) in Ontario academic libraries (survey size: 15 libraries; responding: 12 or 80%) *showed that* the number of library technicians employed at the time of the survey in the 12 libraries totaled 27 individuals. Overall, for all 12 libraries, library technicians constituted 5.2% of the total staff and 6.5% of the nonprofessional staff. **(549)**

Ibid. . . . *showed that* 10 (83.3%) of the responding libraries reported that they did not have a position classification designiated specifically for library technicians. **(549)**

■ A 1979 survey of libraries in accredited North American veterinary schools (population: 25 libraries; responding: 23 or 92%) *showed that*, of 18 separately housed veterinary libraries, staff size (based on FTEs) ranged from 1 professional librarian, no paraprofessionals, and 2.5 other staff at Auburn to 2 professionals, 3 paraprofessionals, and 3.5 other staff at Cornell. For all 18 libraries, the staff size averaged 1.2 professionals, 1.1 paraprofessionals, and 2.2 other staff. **(740)**

■ A study reported in 1979 of 30 departmental libraries at the University of Illinois, Urbana, *showed that* 6 variables were very effective in predicting overall staff size of the departmental library. Together, the 6 variables had a multiple correlation of .965, which accounted for 93% of the variance in total staff size. The 6 variables were as follows:

the number of faculty served;
the number of instructional units taught by that faculty;
the average number of hours the library is open per week;
the number of volumes circulated that year;
the total acquisitions budget administered;
and the total number of volumes in the collection. **(563)**

Ibid. . . . *showed that* the formula for predicting total staff size was as follows:

Total staff = A + B1 (circulation) + B2 (volumes) + B3 (hours open per week) + B4 (budget) + B5 (instructional units) + B6 (faculty served)

Where:

A = −2.01
B1 = .039 (per 1,000 circulation)
B2 = .015 (per 1,000 volumes)
B3 = .044 (hours open per week)
B4 = .014 (per $1,000 budgeted)
B5 = .043 (per 1,000 instructional units)
B6 = .004 (faculty served) **(563)**

Ibid. . . . *showed that* the Beta weights for the 6 predictor variables of total staff size were as follows:

circulation	.42
volumes	.32

continued

hours open	.19
total acquisitions budget	.18
instructional units	.16
faculty served	−.15	**(563)**

Ibid. . . . *showed that* 4 variables were important in predicting size of professional staff in the departmental libraries. Together, the 4 variables had a multiple regression coefficient of .89, which explained 80% of the variance in professional staff size. The Beta weights for the 4 variables were as follows (with circulation the most important variable by far):

circulation	.63
monographic budget	.38
faculty served	.08
instructional units	.07	**(563)**

Ibid. . . . *showed that* the formula for predicting professional staff size was as follows:

Professional staff = A + B1 (faculty served) + B2 (instructional units) + B3 (monograph budget) + B4 (circulation)

Where:

A = .344
B1 = −.001 (per faculty served)
B2 = .007 (per 1,000 instructional units)
B3 = .040 (per $1,000 monograph budget)
B4 = .024 (per 1,000 circulation)   **(563)**

Ibid. . . . *showed that* 4 variables were important in predicting size of clerical staff in departmental libraries. Together, the 4 variables had a multiple regression coefficient of .96, which accounted for 93% of the variance in clerical staff size. The Beta weights were as follows (with circulation most important by far):

circulation	.46
number of volumes	.28
student hours supervised	.24
hours open per week	.14	**(563)**

Ibid. . . . *showed that* the formula for predicting clerical staff size in the departmental libraries was as follows:

Clerical staff = A + B1 (circulation) + B2 (volumes) + B3 (student hours) + B4 (hours open)

Where:

A $= -1.4$
B1 $= .04$ (per 1,000 circulation)
B2 $= .01$ (per 1,000 volumes)
B3 $= .0053$ (per student hours)
B4 $= .024$ (per hour open)   **(563)**

■ A survey reported in 1981 of bibliographic instruction in business school libraries (sample size: 120; responding: 65; usable: 61 or 50.8%) *showed that* 48% of the business school libraries have only 1 professional librarian, and 77% have 5 or fewer clerical assistants.   **(436)**

■ A study reported in 1981 of data on 1,146 2-year colleges, as reported in the 1977 Higher Education General Information Surveys and compared to the 1979 Association of College and Research Libraries standards, *showed that* hours of student assistance averaged 3,360 per school annually overall, while the hours of student assistance in 186 private schools averaged 1,860 annually, and in the public schools 3,690 annually. **(500)**

■ A study reported in 1983 of 3 surveys made by the American Medical Association's Division of Library and Archival Services in 1969, 1973, and 1979 concerning the status of health sciences libraries in the U.S.(survey size for each survey ran between 12,000-14,000 health-related organizations, with a response rate for each survey around 95%) *showed that* in 1979 "some 51%" of hospital library personnel were professional library staff; 39% were library technicians/library assistants; and 10% were other library staff. Further, 7% of the professional staff earned $7,000-9,999 per year; 49.5% of the professional staff earned $10,000-14,999 per year; and 43.4% of the professional staff earned $15,000-19,999 per year.   **(747)**

■ A study reported in 1983 of 3 surveys made by the American Medical Association's Division of Library and Archival Services in 1969, 1973 and 1979 concerning the status of health sciences libraries in the U.S.(survey size for each survey ran between 12,000-14,000 health-related organizations, with a response rate for each survey around 95%) *showed that* between 1973 and 1979 the total number of staff decreased from 10,277 FTE staff to 9,302 FTE staff, a decrease of 9%.   **(745)**

Public

■ A paper prepared by members of the Library Services Branch of the U.S. Office of Education in 1967 on library manpower *showed that* during the period 1939-1962 the staff of public libraries increased by 96%. While the U.S. population only grew by 42%, the number of people in library service areas increased by 98%. The number of professional library positions during this period increased only 50%, changing the ratio of 1 public professional librarian for every 6,000 residents to 1 professional for every 7,880 residents. Also, the clerical (nonprofessional) component of public library staffs had increased from 25% in 1939 to 61% in 1962. **(082)**

School

■ A paper prepared by members of the Library Service Branch of the U.S. Office of Education in 1967 on library manpower *showed that* the ratio of school librarians to students increased from 1 to 1,412 students in 1958-59 to 1 to 1,200 students in 1965-66. In 1962, 77% of all school librarians were in secondary schools. **(082)**

■ A 1983 survey of a systematic sample of school library media centers concerning data for fiscal year 1982-83 (survey size: 2,000 centers; responding: 1,297; usable: 1,251 or 62%) *showed that* the number of full-time certified library media specialists per institution was as follows:

1 per school	1,016 (81.2%) respondents
2 per school	141 (11.3%) respondents
3 per school	19 (1.5% [.15% reported]) respondents **(056)**

Ibid. . . . *showed that* staffing assistance for the media specialist was provided as follows:

full-time clerical staff was reported in 63% of the library media centers;

adult volunteers were reported in 34% of the library media centers, ranging from 1 volunteer in 113 centers to 51 volunteers in 1 center;

student volunteers were reported in 71% of the centers, ranging from 1 volunteer in 22 centers to 99 volunteers in 3 centers. **(056)**

Special

■ A 1967 survey of medical school libraries concerning reference services (survey size: 93 libraries; responding: 85 or 91.4%) *showed that* the average staffing per library was as follows:

professional   5.2 FTE
nonprofessional   9.1 FTE
reference, professional   1.7 FTE
reference, nonprofessional   0.8 FTE   (682)

■ A 1973 survey of all county law libraries listed in the 1972 American
Association of Law Libraries *Directory of Law Libraries* (population: 260;
responding: 86 or 33.1%) *showed that*, of 80 respondents, 63 (78.8%)
reported that staff size was adequate, while 65 (81.3%) reported that
staff training and experience was adequate.   (392)

■ A 1974 survey of a random sample of U.S. museum libraries (including
history, art, and science museums) listed in the 1973 Official Museum
Directory (population: 2,556; sample size: 856; responding: 374 or 43.7%)
showed that only 50% of the libraries had a librarian, and only 47% of
them possessed a degree in library science. The largest numbers of
librarians were in libraries with 1,000-5,000 book titles, but full-time
librarians were not reported until library size began to reach 10,000 titles.
                                                                       (412)

Ibid. . . . *showed that* 50% of the libraries reported staffs with total staff
size including paid and volunteer workers averaging 5.8 people (2 FTE)
per library.   (412)

■ A 1976 survey of head law librarians in North American schools
(sample size: 178; responding: 154 or 86.7%) *showed that* size of professional law school library staff in terms of FTEs was as follows: 116 (75%)
reported 0-5 staff; 33 (21%) reported 6-10 staff; 3 (2%) reported 11-15
staff; and 3 (2%) reported 16-20.   (357)

■ A 1979 survey of libraries in accredited North American veterinary
schools (population: 25 libraries; responding: 23 or 92%) *showed that*, of
18 separately housed veterinary libraries, staff size (based on FTEs)
ranged from 1 professional librarian, no paraprofessionals, and 2.5 other
staff at Auburn to 2 professionals, 3 paraprofessionals, and 3.5 other staff
at Cornell. For all 18 libraries, the staff size averaged 1.2 professionals, 1.1
paraprofessionals, and 2.2 other staff.   (740)

■ A 1980 survey of the private law library and corporate law library
membership of the American Association of Law Libraries, excluding

part-time librarians (population: 585; responding: 382; usable: 360 or 61%) *showed that* overall only 26% of the respondents supervise 1 or more professional staff, while 67% supervise 1 or more support staff. **(377)**

■ A study reported in 1983 of 3 surveys made by the American Medical Association's Division of Library and Archival Services in 1969, 1973, and 1979 concerning the status of health sciences libraries in the U.S.(survey size for each survey ran between 12,000-14,000 health-related organizations, with a response rate for each survey around 95%), *showed that* between 1973 and 1979 the total number of staff decreased from 10,277 FTE staff to 9,302 FTE staff, a decrease of 9%. **(745)**

■ A study reported in 1983 of 3 surveys made by the American Medical Association's Division of Library and Archival Services in 1969, 1973, and 1979 concerning the status of health sciences libraries in the U.S.(survey size for each survey ran between 12,000-14,000 health-related organizations, with a response rate for each survey around 95%) *showed that* in 1979 "some 51%" of hospital library personnel were professional library staff; 39% were library technicians/library assistants; and 10% were other library staff. Further, 7% of the professional staff earned $7,000-9,999 per year; 49.5% of the professional staff earned $10,000-14,999 per year; and 43.4% of the professional staff earned $15,000-19,999 per year. **(747)**

Staffing Standards

Academic

■ A study of 1977 survey information gathered by the National Center for Educational Statistics (U.S. Office of Education) concerning the degree to which 1,146 college and university libraries (Liberal Arts Colleges I and II; Comprehensive Universities and Colleges I and II) met the 1975 Standards for College Libraries (ACRL) *showed that* 81% of the libraries fell below the standard in terms of the number of professional librarians needed based on number of students, book collection size, and annual book acquisitions. The average and median number of professional positions needed per library was 2, although 34% of the libraries needed 4 or more professional staff to meet standards. **(486)**

Ibid. . . . *showed that* over half of the libraries had insufficient nonprofessional staff support and fell below the standard in terms of the ratio of professional staff to nonprofessional staff. Standards specify that no more than 25% (ratio of 1 to 3) to 35% (ratio of 1 to 1.9) of the staff should be professional, while the average ratio of professionals to nonprofessionals was 1 to 1.1 and the median was 1 to 1.0. **(486)**

■ A study reported in 1981 of data on 1,146 2-year colleges, as reported in the 1977 Higher Education General Information Surveys and compared to the 1979 Association of College and Research Libraries standards, *showed that* in terms of professional library staff the number of schools meeting minimum standards (by enrollment ranges of FTE students) were as follows:

less than 1,000 students (2 staff minimum)	39% met standards
1,000 to 2,999 students (2.5 staff minimum)	70% met standards
3,000 to 4,999 students (3.5 staff minimum)	65% met standards
5,000 to 6,999 students (6 staff minimum)	32% met standards
7,000 to 8,999 students (7 staff minimum)	46% met standards
9,000 to 10,999 students (8 staff minimum)	73% met standards

Further, in terms of library support staff the number of schools that met minimum standards ranged from 5% of the schools with less than 1,000 FTE students to 33% of the schools with 9,000 to 10,999 FTE students.   **(500)**

Unions—General

Academic

■ A 1968 survey of library staff members of libraries belonging to the Staff Organizations Round Table (SORT) of ALA who did not have collective bargaining contracts (2,185 individuals responding; 1,047 from large public, 614 small public, and 524 from academic libraries; 39% professional, 14% subprofessional, and 46% nonprofessionals) *showed that* 42.7% would probably belong to a union if their library had one; 48.8% would probably not; and 8.3% were undecided. 75% belonged to their staff association.   **(074)**

Ibid. . . . *showed that,* of 23 items related to salaries, fringe benefits and recruitment, the majority response in almost all instances was that collective bargaining would result in little difference. The most likely area collective bargaining was expected to improve was premium pay for night or Sunday work:

professionals expecting such improvement	42%
subprofessionals expecting such improvement	40%
nonprofessionals expecting such improvement	39% **(074)**

Public

■ A 1967 survey of 91 public libraries serving populations of 350,000 or more (80 responding) *showed that*, of 70 administrative responses:

encourage unionization	3%
discourage unionization	20%
neutral	68%
no comment	9%

However, 63% responded that library staff should have recourse to collective bargaining; 64% felt that staff should have the right to affiliate with organized labor; and 11% said library staff should have the right to strike.   **(080)**

Ibid. . . . *showed that* 5 respondents operated under collective bargaining agreements; 56 reported merit employment systems; and 46 had some kind of staff organization "to promote better working conditions."   **(080)**

■ A 1968 survey of library staff members of libraries belonging to the Staff Organization Round Table (SORT) of ALA who did not have collective bargaining contracts (2,185 individuals responding: 1,047 from large public libraries, 614 from small public libraries, and 524 from academic libraries; 39% professionals, 14% subprofessionals, and 46% nonprofessionals) *showed that*, of 23 items related to salaries, fringe benefits, and recruitment, the majority response in almost all instances was that collective bargaining would result in little difference. The most likely area collective bargaining was expected to improve was premium pay for night or Sunday work:

professionals expecting such improvement	42%
subprofessionals expecting such improvement	40%
nonprofessionals expecting such improvement	39% **(074)**

Ibid. . . . *showed that* 42.7% would probably belong to a union if their library had one; 48.8% would probably not; and 8.3% were undecided. 75% belonged to their staff association.   **(074)**

Unions—Nonprofessional

Academic

■ A 1968 survey of library staff members of libraries belonging to the Staff Organization Round Table (SORT) of ALA who did not have collective bargaining contracts (2,185 individuals responding: 1,047 from large public libraries, 614 from small public libraries, and 524 from academic libraries; 39% professionals, 14% subprofessionals, and 46% nonprofessionals) *showed that*, of 23 items related to salaries, fringe benefits, and recruitment, the majority response in almost all instances was that collective bargaining would result in little difference. The most likely area collective bargaining was expected to improve was premium pay for night or Sunday work:

professionals expecting such improvement	42%
subprofessionals expecting such improvement	40%
nonprofessionals expecting such improvement	39% **(074)**

Ibid. . . . *showed that* 42.7% would probably belong to a union if their library had one; 48.8% would probably not; and 8.3% were undecided. 75% belonged to their staff association. **(074)**

■ A survey of 163 classified nonprofessional library employees at the University of Pennsylvania who were union members (99 responding) reported in 1975 *showed that* 70% of the men had a positive attitude toward unions prior to the experience at Penn, as compared to only 33.8% of the women. However, 10 times as many women (33.9%) as men (3.3%) reported never caring one way or the other. Also, only 15% of those employees with some graduate study in librarianship reported a previously favorable attitude toward unions, as compared to 45.3% for the sample as a whole. **(104)**

Public

■ A 1967 survey of 91 public libraries serving populations of 350,000 or more (80 responding) *showed that* 5 operated under collective bargaining agreements; 56 reported merit employment systems; and 46 had some kind of staff organization "to promote better working conditions." **(080)**

Ibid. . . . *showed that* of 70 administrative responses:

encouraged unionization	3%
discouraged unionization	20%
neutral	68%
no comment	9% **(080)**

■ A 1968 survey of library staff members of libraries belonging to the Staff Organization Round Table (SORT) of ALA who did not have collective bargaining contracts (2,185 individuals responding: 1,047 from large public libraries, 614 from small public libraries, and 524 from academic libraries; 39% professionals, 14% subprofessionals, and 46% nonprofessionals) *showed that*, of 23 items related to salaries, fringe benefits, and recruitment, the majority response in almost all instances was that collective bargaining would result in little difference. The most likely area collective bargaining was expected to improve was premium pay for night or Sunday work:

professionals expecting such improvement	42%
subprofessionals expecting such improvement	40%
nonprofessionals expecting such improvement	39% **(074)**

Special

■ A survey reported in 1980 of nondirector, professional law librarians (1 in each school) in U.S. accredited law schools, with the names of individuals being selected randomly from the *Directory of Law Librarians,* 1978 edition (sample size: 145; responding 103 or 71%) *showed that*, of 103 respondents, 20 (19.4%) reported that the law library staff in their libraries was unionized, while 83 (80.6%) reported that it was not unionized. Of the unionized staffs the majority were represented by "private unions." **(371)**

Unions—Professional

Academic

■ A 1968 survey of library staff members of libraries belonging to the Staff Organization Round Table (SORT) of ALA who did not have collective bargaining contracts (2,185 individuals responding: 1,047 from large public libraries, 614 from small public libraries, and 524 from academic libraries; 39% professionals, 14% subprofessionals, and 46% nonprofessionals) *showed that*, of 23 items related to salaries, fringe benefits, and recruitment, the majority response in almost all instances was that collective bargaining would result in little difference. The most likely area collective bargaining was expected to improve was premium pay for night or Sunday work:

professionals expecting such improvement	42%
subprofessionals expecting such improvement	40%
nonprofessionals expecting such improvement	39% **(074)**

■ A survey reported in 1978 of academic libarians at 6 comparable institutions (sample size: 47; responding: 17) comparing academic librarians within bargaining units vs. their counterparts not represented by bargaining units *showed that* there was a statistically significant difference in their perception of some of the criteria for promotion. More non-bargaining unit librarians ranked performance as important, while more bargaining unit librarians ranked both "second masters and/or a doctorate" as important. No statistically significant difference was found between the groups in the responses to research, publication, and professional activities.   **(008)**

Ibid. . . . *showed that* fewer librarians in a bargaining unit were likely to be satisfied with their economic status than librarians without a bargaining unit.   **(008)**

Ibid. . . . *showed that* librarians in a bargaining unit were more likely to have an academic-year contract (67.3% respondents), whereas librarians without a bargaining unit were more likely to have a calendar-year contract (66.7% respondents).   **(008)**

■ A 1979 study of academic librarians in public colleges and universities comparing those in collective bargaining units with those not in such units (sample size: 845 librarians from 38 libraries; responding: 542 librarians) *showed that*, overall, there were no statistically significant differences between professional development activities (e.g., library association membership, library journals read, articles published, etc.) of librarians in bargaining units and librarians not in bargaining units.   **(509)**

Public

■ A 1967 survey of 91 public libraries serving populations of 350,000 or more (80 responding) *showed that* 5 operated under collective bargaining agreements, 56 reported merit employment systems; and 46 had some kind of staff organization "to promote better working conditions."   **(080)**

Ibid. . . . *showed that*, of 70 administrative responses:

encouraged unionization	3%
discouraged unionization	20%
neutral	68%
no comment	9% **(080)**

■ A 1968 survey of library staff members of libraries belonging to the Staff Organization Round Table (SORT) of ALA who did not have collective bargaining contracts (2,185 individuals responding: 1,047 from large public libraries, 614 from small public libraries, and 524 from academic libraries; 39% professionals, 14% subprofessionals and 46% nonprofessionals) *showed that*, of 23 items related to salaries, fringe benefits, and recruitment, the majority response in almost all instances was that collective bargaining would result in little difference. The most likely area collective bargaining was expected to improve was premium pay for night or Sunday work:

professionals expecting such improvement 42%
subprofessionals expecting such improvement 40%
nonprofessionals expecting such improvement 39% **(074)**

Special

■ A 1971 survey of all North American libraries listed in the *Directory* of the American Association of Law Libraries (population: 819 libraries; responding: 437 libraries) *showed that* 412 (94.3%) reported no union activity involving professionals at the time of the survey (although 5 reported that there were plans to unionize the library in the future).

(384)

■ A survey reported in 1980 of nondirector, profesional law librarians (1 in each school) in U.S. accredited law schools with the names of individuals being selected randomly from the *Directory of Law Librarians*, 1978 edition (sample size: 145; responding: 103 or 71%) *showed that*, of 103 respondents, 8 (7.8%) reported that the professional law librarians were unionized, while 95 (92.2%) reported that the professional law librarians were not unionized. The union given "most frequently" by the 8 respondents (though not a majority) was American Association of University Professors. **(371)**

User Fees

Public

■ A 1962 study of nonresident user fees in public libraries in the 6-county Chicago Standard Metropolitan Area (excluding Chicago proper; sample size: 107; return rate: 95), *showed that* the fee was calculated directly to cover the cost of service rendered in 41 cases; was not so calculated in 46 cases; 8 did not respond. Where the fee was not calculated to cover cost of service, it was generally low, $3.00 or under. **(065)**

Ibid. . . . *showed that*, of the 41 libraries who reported establishing a user fee to cover the cost of service, the most common prctice was to set the fee for a family card to reflect the amount an average homeowner paid in library tax. No library reported setting the nonresident user fee at either the per capita library income or establishing it by dividing library income by total number of registered borrowers. **(065)**

Ibid. . . . *showed that* there was a strong positive correlation (r2 = .42) between amount charged for the nonresident user fee and composite municipal socioeconomic rank (median family income, educational level, per capita property valuation, and median value of homes). Rich, well-educated communities tended to charge high nonresident user fees. **(065)**

Ibid. . . . *showed that* only 10 of the 95 responding libraries indicated that the nonresident user fee was set to discourage nonresident use of the library. **(065)**

Ibid. . . . *showed that* 40 were not satisfied with the fee (48 satisfied; 7 undecided). Only 1 library of the 40 felt the fee was too high, the remainder felt the fee failed to accomplish 1 or more of the following: to reflect a fair tax share for service rendered, to keep the number of nonresident borrowers from becoming too much of a burden, or to give some incentive to neighboring areas to start or improve their own libraries. **(065)**

■ A study reported in 1980 of monthly library circulation data for the 12-year period 1965-76 for the Dallas public library system (main library and 14 branches), comparing circulation before and after the institution of the Nonresident Fee Card Program, *showed that* analysis by a series of statistical tests indicated strong evidence for statistically significant circulation declines in 3 libraries, moderate evidence for statistically significant declines in 2 libraries, weak evidence for declines in 4 libraries, and no evidence of statistically significant declines in 6 libraries. (Significance at the .05 level for all tests.) **(266)**

Special

■ A 1974 survey of a random sample of U.S. museum libraries (including history, art, and science museums) listed in the 1973 *Official Museum Directory* (population: 2,556; sample size: 856; responding: 374 or 43.7%) *showed that* 60.4% of the respondents reported either total or partial reliance on private funding, and that 92% of the respondents did not charge user fees. **(412)**

2.

Personnel

Age and Work Experience

Public

■ A survey reported in 1967 of midwestern librarians (37 men, 408 women, total 445) in small public libraries (i.e., serving populations of 10,000 to 35,000) *showed that* the median age was 50.3 years. Years worked in libraries ranged from 1 to 44, with the average being 14.9 years. **(282)**

School

■ A 1983 survey of a systematic sample of school library media centers concerning data for fiscal year 1982-83 (survey size: 2,000 centers; responding: 1,297; usable: 1,251 or 62%) *showed that* the average years of experience and salary for library media specialists by type of library was as follows:

elementary school (587 schools): 10.04 years of experience with a salary of $19,596;

junior high/middle school (308 schools): 11.79 years of experience with a salary of $21,613;

senior high school (304 schools): 12.02 years of experience with a salary of $20,069;

other (49 schools): 9.84 years of experience with a salary of $15,954. **(56)**

Attitudes

General

■ A 1971 study of 2 groups of librarians of all types attending a workshop on motivation (162 responding Americans; 75 responding Canadians) *showed that* they conformed to Herzberg's theoretical framework: The factors that led to job satisfaction/motivation have to do with job content (motivators) and are different from the factors that lead to job dissatisfaction, which have to do with job environment (context or hygiene factors). When asked to identify incidents that caused them to feel "particularly good" or "particularly bad" while at work, 99% of the respondents identified positive factors that were motivators, i.e., related to job content, while 81% of the respondents identified negative factors that were hygiene factors, i.e., factors found in the work environment. **(250)**

Ibid. . . . *showed that* the 3 most frequently reported motivators were achievement (118 or 49.8% respondents), recognition (70 or 29.5%), and work itself (27 or 11.4%). The remaining 3, responsibility, advancement, and professional/personal growth, were reported by only 19 or 8% of the respondents.   **(250)**

Ibid. . . . *showed that* the 3 most frequently reported hygiene factors were institution policy and administration (68 or 28.7% respondents), supervision (56 or 23.6%), and interpersonal relationships (44 or 18.6%). The remaining 4 factors, working conditions, status, salary, and security, were reported by only 24 or 10.1% of the respondents.   **(250)**

Academic

■ A survey reported in 1971 of professional librarians in 2 Canadian university libraries and of graduating library school students in the master's program at one of the schools (survey size: 100 professionals and 126 students; responding: 56 or 56% professionals and 60 or 47.6% students) *showed that* males perceived library work as more creative than female professionals to a statistically significant degree. For example, 43% of the male professionals rated their job as "most creative" compared to 12.5% of the female professionals who so rated their job, while 36.4% of the male students rated "the job" as "most creative" compared to 8.3% of the female students so rating "the job." (Difference was statistically significant at the .02 level.)   **(539)**

Ibid. . . . *showed that* younger students (in their 20s) considered library work more intellectually stimulating than older students (in their 30s and 40s) to a statistically significant degree. (Difference was statistically significant at the .05 level.) Further, professionals who started their careers in their 20s also considered library work more intellectually stimulating than professionals who had started work later in life (in their 30s, 40s, and 50s). (Difference was statistically significant at the .02 level.)   **(539)**

Ibid. . . . *showed that*, of 52 respondents, older librarians tended to see their status as compared to teaching and research faculty as lower than younger librarians to a statistically significant degree. For example, reporting the lowest status compared to teaching and research faculty were:

professionals in their 20s	15 (60%)
professionals in their 30s	12 (75%)
professionals in their 40s	7 (100%)

continued

professionals in their 50s	0 (0%)
professionals in their 60s	1 (50%)

(Statistically significant at the .001 level.) **(539)**

Ibid. . . . *showed that*, of 47 professionals responding, job preference (preferring library work over other kinds of work) varied by library rank to a statistically significant degree, with Librarian II's rating job preference much higher than either Librarian I's or Librarian III's. For example, 6 (33.3%) Librarian I's, 2 (16.7%) Librarian III's, and 12 (70.6%) Librarian II's rated job preference "high" (differences significant at the .05 level). Further, consideration of changing professions also varied by library rank to a statistically significant degree, following the same pattern, with 6 (33.3%) Librarian I's, 1 (10.0%) Librarian III, and 11 (64.7%) Librarian II's reporting never having considered changing their profession (differences significant at the .02 level). **(539)**

Ibid. . . . *showed that*, of 56 professionals responding, the 3 most frequently given reasons for career preference were love for books and people (28 or 50%), profession befitting women (5 or 8.9%), and alternative to teaching (5 or 8.9%). **(539)**

Ibid. . . . *showed that* professionals ranked library departments according to desirability as follows, with the most desirable department ranked first and the least desirable department ranked last (student rankings given in parentheses):

1. reference service (1)
2. serials (8)
3. bibliographic searching (6)
4. acquisitions (2)
5. administration (3)
6. rare books (10)
7. cataloging (7)
8. systems (9)
9. documentation (4)
10. circulation (5) **(539)**

Ibid. . . . *showed that* the impact of automation as viewed by professionals was as follows:

improve both creativity and identity of librarian	19 (33.9%) of total
negative impact	10 (17.9%) of total
improve creativity	8 (14.3%) of total

continued

no change   8 (14.3%) of total
serve as a supportive tool   4 (7.1%) of total
no response   7 (12.5%) of total
                                                    (539)

■ A survey in 1972 of a stratified random sample of full-time professional librarians in private and public junior colleges, colleges, and universities in the 10 counties of southern California (sample size: 216; responding: 174 or 81%) was analyzed by stepwise regression and *showed that* the following relationships were statistically significant at the .05 level or better: While older librarians were more likely than their younger colleagues to advocate faculty titles for librarians and to claim that faculty status would enhance their prestige, they were more likely to oppose the idea of peer appraisal of their work performance.   **(092)**

Ibid. . . . *showed that* females were more likely to oppose the idea of peer evaluation than were male librarians.   **(092)**

Ibid. . . . *showed that* the more advanced the librarians' educational background, the more likely they were to support the importance of acceptance as equals with faculty members and the less likely they were to agree to the idea of peer appraisal.   **(092)**

Ibid. . . . *showed that* public services and administrative librarians were more likely than technical services librarians to feel that faculty status would enhance the librarians' prestige and to agree that librarians function as teachers.   **(092)**

Ibid. . . . *showed that* the longer librarians had held their present jobs the more likely they were to support the view of librarians as teachers.
                                                    (092)

Ibid. . . . *showed that* members of ALA/ACRL were more likely than nonmembers to agree that librarians should have the same ranks and titles as faculty.   **(092)**

■ A survey reported in 1976 of 202 librarians in 23 academic libraries in the greater New York metropolitan area who were given the Need Satisfaction Questionnaire (based on Maslow's Hierarchy of Needs) *showed that*, in terms of need fulfillment (amount of each type of need presently being fulfilled), women reported statistically significantly less fulfillment than men in 2 categories: "esteem" and "autonomy" (significant at the .01 level). In "social" and "security" needs men and women showed similar scores and in "self-actualization" women had lower scores, but not to a statistically significant degree. **(794)**

Ibid. . . . *showed that*, for both men and women, "security" was the need most fulfilled, while "autonomy" was the need least fulfilled for both groups. **(794)**

Ibid. . . . *showed that*, in terms of need deficiency (difference between how much of the need is being met and how much should be met), women perceived statistically significantly higher deficiencies than men in 4 areas: "security," "esteem," "autonomy," and "self-actualization" (significant at the .001 level). Men and women had similar scores in terms of "social" needs. **(794)**

Ibid. . . . *showed that* men perceived "security" to be the least deficient need, while women perceived "social" as the least deficient need. However, both perceived "self-actualization" as the most deficient need. **(794)**

Ibid. . . . *showed that*, in terms of needs importance (how important each of the 5 needs is), women perceived "autonomy" and "self-actualization" as less important than men to a statistically significant degree (significant at the .01 level). "Security," "social," and "esteem" needs were perceived equally important by men and women. Both men and women perceived "self-actualization" as the need of highest importance, while both perceived "esteem" as lowest in importance. **(794)**

■ A 1980 survey of academic librarians in Alabama, Georgia, and Mississippi concerning faculty status (sample size: 416; responding 271; usable: 267 or 64.2%) *showed that* 49.4% of the respondents agreed with the statement "faculty status/rank with its requirement for research and publication for promotion places unrealistic demands on librarians for their advancement." 24.0% disagreed; 21.0% were undecided; and 5.6% gave no response. **(502)**

■ A survey reported in 1983 of circulation professionals in public and academic libraries with more than 50,000 volumes concerning their interest in and use of management data (e.g. loss rates, effectiveness of fines) and the formal methods by which management data was generated (e.g. sampling, statistical tests) (survey size: 200 professionals; responding: 132 or 66%) *showed that* there was more interest in management data itself than in the methods by which it could be generated. Specifically, while 57

(43%) respondents felt "strongly" that use of management data was important for their particular responsibilities, only 41 (31%) felt "strongly" that techniques were likewise important. Further, while 60 (45%) respondents reported they would "definitely" make more use of management data if more were available, only 37 (28%) reported they would "definitely" make more use of techniques to generate management data if information on their use were more easily available. **(804)**

Ibid. . . . *showed that*, both in order to find management information and to acquaint themselves with the techniques for generating such information, respondents most frequently used and found most helpful the published literature. Specifically, the information sources used in the last year (prior to the survey) in descending order of importance were:

1. professional library literature
2. other literature
3. local and regional workshops
4. ALA conferences
5. formal academic classes
6. ALA preconference programs and workshops

The usefulness of each of these sources of information according to the personal experience of the respondents was (in descending order of importance):

1. professional library literature
2. local and regional workshops
3. other literature
4. formal academic classes
5. ALA conferences
6. ALA preconferences and workshops **(804)**

Ibid. . . . *showed that* circulation professionals supported the idea of national standards only in a general way. Specifically, when asked only about national standards, 45% of the respondents reported that they were "very important" or "important." However, when ranked in importance with 11 other specific items, national standards was ranked last in importance. **(804)**

Ibid. . . . *showed that* circulation professionals felt more strongly about the importance of management data and the methods for generating it than they perceived their institutions felt. Specifically, while 57 (43%) respondents felt "strongly" that the use of management data was important for their responsibilities and 41 (31%) felt "strongly" that formal methods for generating such data were important for their responsibilities, only 38 (29%) felt that their institution attached a "great deal" of importance to either the use of management data or to the methods for generating it.

(804)

■ A survey reported in 1983 of reference librarians in 75 U.S. universities with enrollments exceeding 20,000 (survey size: 380; responding: 262 or 69%) *showed that*, based on the Forbes Burnout Survey, reference librarians in academic libraries did not seem to have a burnout problem. Specifically, results of the Burnout Survey showed the following results:

librarians with burnout	none
librarians with mild burnout	1% of total
librarians who were candidates for burnout	12% of total
librarians with burnout under control	87% of total

(789)

Public

■ A survey reported in 1983 of circulation professionals in public and academic libraries with more than 50,000 volumes concerning their interest in and use of management data (e.g. loss rates, effectiveness of fines) and the formal methods by which management data was generated (e.g. sampling, statistical tests) (survey size: 200 professionals; responding: 132 or 66%) *showed that* there was more interest in management data itself than in the methods by which it could be generated. Specifically, while 57 (43%) respondents felt "strongly" that use of management data was important for their particular responsibilities, only 41 (31%) felt "strongly" that techniques were likewise important. Further, while 60 (45%) respondents reported they would "definitely" make more use of management data if more were available, only 37 (28%) reported they would "definitely" make more use of techniques to generate management data if information on their use were more easily available. **(804)**

Ibid. . . . *showed that*, both in order to find management information and to acquaint themselves with the techniques for generating such information, respondents most frequently used and found most helpful the published literature. Specifically, the information sources used in the last year (prior to the survey) in descending order of importance were:

1. professional library literature

  2. other literature
  3. local and regional workshops
  4. ALA conferences
  5. formal academic classes
  6. ALA preconference programs and workshops

The usefulness of each of these sources of information according to the personal experience of the respondents was (in descending order of importance):

  1. professional library literature
  2. local and regional workshops
  3. other literature
  4. formal academic classes
  5. ALA conferences
  6. ALA preconferences and workshops   **(804)**

Ibid. . . . *showed that* circulation professionals supported the idea of national standards only in a general way. Specifically, when asked only about national standards, 45% of the respondents reported that they were "very important" or "important." However, when ranked in importance with 11 other specific items, national standards was ranked last in importance.   **(804)**

Ibid. . . . *showed that* circulation professionals felt more strongly about the importance of management data and the methods for generating it than they perceived their institutions felt. Specifically, while 57 (43%) respondents felt "strongly" that the use of management data was important for their responsibilities and 41 (31%) felt "strongly" that formal methods for generating such data were important for their responsibilities, only 38 (29%) felt that their institution attached a "great deal" of importance to either the use of management data or to the methods for generating it.
                                                                          (804)

Continuing Education—Nonprofessional

Academic

■ A survey reported in 1975 of a stratified random sample of libraries of accredited 4-year colleges and universities to include small, medium, and large institutions based on student enrollment (sample size: 150; usable responses: 141 or 94%) *showed that*, of the responding libraries, more than 80% reported that no formal in-service training was provided for the nonprofessional reference staff. However, 70% of responding libraries indicated that nonprofessionals could take classes during the working day (time had to made up in 1/2 of those cases); 51% of the libraries indicated that tuition waivers are given nonprofessionals taking classes; and 74% of the libraries reported that nonprofessionals could attend professional library meetings during the working day. **(105)**

■ A survey reported in 1976 of the libraries in the largest private and largest public college/university in each state of the continental U.S. (sample size: 100 [sic]; responding: 79 or 79%) *showed that* 39% of the respondents reported availability of in-service training, while only 27 respondents (36%) provided supervisory training for [professional] staff members. **(413)**

Public

■ A survey of current practices of a diverse group of selected "community aware" public libraries in 25 states (68 responding libraries) *showed that* the number of libraries already providing in-service training for paraprofessional staff was as follows: community contacts, 22 (32%); community study, 14 (20%); human relations, 24 (35%); group process, 15 (22%); and community development, 12 (18%). **(215)**

Ibid. . . . *showed that* the number of libraries reporting that further in-service programs were needed for paraprofessionals was as follows: community contacts (29%), community (30%), human relations (43%), group process (38%), and community development (29%). **(215)**

Continuing Education—Professional

Academic

■ A survey reported in 1976 of the libraries in the largest private and largest public college/university in each state of the continental U.S. (sample size: 100 [sic]; responding: 79 or 79%) *showed that* 39% of the respondents reported availability of in-service training, while only 27 respondents (36%) provided supervisory training for [professional] staff members. **(413)**

■ A survey reported in 1983 of circulation professionals in public and academic libraries with more than 50,000 volumes concerning their interest in and use of management data (e.g. loss rates, effectiveness of fines) and the formal methods by which management data was generated (e.g. sampling, statistical tests) (survey size: 200 professionals; responding: 132 or 66%) *showed that* there was more interest in management data itself than in the methods by which it could be generated. Specifically, while 57 (43%) respondents felt "strongly" that use of management data was important for their particular responsibilities, only 41 (31%) felt "strongly" that techniques were likewise important. Further, while 60 (45%) respondents reported they would "definitely" make more use of management data if more were available, only 37 (28%) reported they would "definitely" make more use of techniques to generate management data if information on their use were more easily available.   **(804)**

Ibid. . . . *showed that*, both in order to find management information and to acquaint themselves with the techniques for generating such information, respondents most frequently used and found most helpful the published literature. Specifically, the information sources used in the last year (prior to the survey) in descending order of importance were:

    1. professional library literature
    2. other literature
    3. local and regional workshops
    4. ALA conferences
    5. formal academic classes
    6. ALA preconference programs and workshops

The usefulness of each of these sources of information according to the personal experience of the respondents was (in descending order of importance):

    1. professional library literature
    2. local and regional workshops
    3. other literature
    4. formal academic classes
    5. ALA conferences
    6. ALA preconferences and workshops   **(804)**

Ibid. . . . *showed that* the average monthly time spent by circulation professionals in increasing their awareness of management data or the techniques for generating such data was as follows (including both personal and professional time):

no hours per month	10 (7.6%) respondents
1-5 hours per month	68 (51.5%) respondents
6-10 hours per month	28 (21.2%) respondents
11-30 hours per month	14 (10.6%) respondents
no answer	12 (9.1%) respondents

(804)

Ibid. . . . *showed that* the greatest obstacles to greater use of management data or techniques for generating such data were as follows (in descending order of importance):

1. lack of time
2. lack of appropriate management data
3. lack of training in the formal techniques that could be used to generate management data
4. difficulty in locating appropriate data or sources of skills
5. lack of interest personally **(804)**

Ibid. . . . *showed that* the 5 most highly ranked areas (out of 12) in which more management data was needed were as follows (in descending order of importance):

1. relationship between collection use and collection development
2. collection loss
3. staff training
4. impact of fines and penalties on book return
5. automation costs vs. manual circulation costs **(804)**

Ibid. . . . *showed that* circulation professionals felt more strongly about the importance of management data and the methods for generating it than they perceived their institutions felt. Specifically, while 57 (43%) respondents felt "strongly" that the use of management data was important for their responsibilities and 41 (31%) felt "strongly" that formal methods for generating such data were important for their responsibilities, only 38 (29%) felt that their institution attached a "great deal" of importance to either the use of management data or to the methods for generating it.
(804)

■ A comparison reported in 1983 of 2 surveys of Association of College and Research Libraries members concerning members' educational attainments (1973 survey—survey size: 300 members; responding: 259 or 86.3%; 1978 survey—survey size: 429 members; responding: 357 or 83.2%) *showed that* the proportion of professionals participating in workshops, short courses, and seminars during the 12-month period preceding each of the surveys increased between the 1973 and 1978 surveys. Specifically:

in 1973, 117 (45.2%) respondents reported no participation, while in 1978, only 75 (21.0%) reported no participation;

in 1973, 129 (49.8%) respondents reported participating in 1-3 events, while in 1978, 217 (60.8%) reported participating in 1-3 events;

in 1973, 11 (4.2%) respondents reported participating in 4-6 events, while in 1978, 51 (14.3%) reported participating in 4-6 events;

in 1973, 2 (0.8%) respondents reported participating in 7 or more events, while in 1978, 14 (3.9%) reported participating in 7 or more events.

Overall, the average number of events per participant rose from 1.1 in 1973 to 2.2 in 1978.   **(796)**

Ibid. . . . *showed that* overall a statistically significantly greater proportion of females participated in workshops, short courses, and seminars than males (difference significant at the .05 level).   **(796)**

Ibid. . . . *showed that* overall more librarians had been enrolled in academic course work during the 12 months prior to the 1978 survey (34.4% respondents) than prior to the 1973 survey (22.2% respondents). Based on the 1978 survey, a statistically significantly greater proportion of females had taken such courses than males (difference significant at the .05 level).   **(796)**

Public

■ A survey reported in 1983 of circulation professionals in public and academic libraries with more than 50,000 volumes concerning their interest in and use of management data (e.g. loss rates, effectiveness of fines) and the formal methods by which management data was generated (e.g. sampling, statistical tests) (survey size: 200 professionals; responding: 132 or 66%) *showed that* there was more interest in management data itself than in the methods by which it could be generated. Specifically, while 57 (43%) respondents felt "strongly" that use of management data was important for their particular responsibilities, only 41 (31%) felt "strongly" that techniques were likewise important. Further, while 60 (45%) respondents reported they would "definitely" make more use of management data if more were available, only 37 (28%) reported they would "definitely" make more use of techniques to generate management data if information on their use were more easily available.   **(804)**

Ibid. . . . *showed that*, both in order to find management information and to acquaint themselves with the techniques for generating such information, respondents most frequently used and found most helpful the published literature. Specifically, the information sources used in the last year (prior to the survey) in descending order of importance were:

1. professional library literature
2. other literature
3. local and regional workshops
4. ALA conferences
5. formal academic classes
6. ALA preconference programs and workshops

The usefulness of each of these sources of information according to the personal experience of the respondents was (in descending order of importance):

1. professional library literature
2. local and regional workshops
3. other literature
4. formal academic classes
5. ALA conferences
6. ALA preconferences and workshops   **(804)**

Ibid. . . . *showed that* the average monthly time spent by circulation professionals in increasing their awareness of management data or the techniques for generating such data was as follows (including both personal and professional time):

no hours per month	10 (7.6%) respondents
1-5 hours per month	68 (51.5%) respondents
6-10 hours per month	28 (21.2%) respondents
11-30 hours per month	14 (10.6%) respondents
no answer	12 (9.1%) respondents

(804)

Ibid. . . . *showed that* the greatest obstacles to greater use of management data or techniques for generating such data were as follows (in descending order of importance):

1. lack of time
2. lack of appropriate management data
3. lack of training in the formal techniques that could be used to generate management data
4. difficulty in locating appropriate data or sources of skills
5. lack of interest personally   **(804)**

Ibid. . . . *showed that* the 5 most highly ranked areas (out of 12) in which more management data was needed were as follows (in descending order of importance):

1. relationship between collection use and collection development
2. collection loss

3. staff training
4. impact of fines and penalties on book return
5. automation costs vs. manual circulation costs **(804)**

Ibid. . . . *showed that* circulation professionals felt more strongly about the importance of management data and the methods for generating it than they perceived their institutions felt. Specifically, while 57 (43%) respondents felt "strongly" that the use of management data was important for their responsibilities and 41 (31%) felt "strongly" that formal methods for generating such data were important for their responsibilities, only 38 (29%) felt that their institution attached a "great deal" of importance to either the use of management data or to the methods for generating it.

(804)

Special

■ A 1975 survey of American Association of Law Libraries members concerning interest in continuing education (survey size: 2,100; responding: 742 or 35%) *showed that*:

of 723 respondents, 715 (98.9%) reported that there was a need for continuing education in law librarianship;

of 713 respondents, 697 (97.8%) felt that AALL should sponsor continuing education in law librarianship;

of 714 respondents, 292 (40.9%) felt that AALL should sponsor education programs in basic library skills (e.g. cataloging, acquisitions) for people without library school courses, while 422 (59.1%) felt AALL should not sponsor such courses. **(792)**

Ibid. . . . *showed that* the 8 most frequently mentioned continuing education topics were (multiple responses allowed):

legal bibliography—teaching legal research	279 (37.6%) respondents
public services—new reference tools	272 (36.7%) respondents
administration—budget	253 (34.1%) respondents
microforms—acquisitions and quality control	232 (31.3%) respondents
administration—space utilization	224 (30.2%) respondents
administration—personnel	215 (29.0%) respondents

continued

microforms—microform utilization and reference public services—reference	
	215 (29.0%) respondents
service	212 (28.6%) respondents **(792)**

Demographics

Academic

■ A 1980 survey of academic librarians in Alabama, Georgia, and Mississippi concerning faculty status (sample size: 416; responding 271; usable: 267 or 64.2%) *showed that* 33.7% were male while 66.3% were female. Further, 57.7% were married while 41.5% were single (.8 gave no response). **(502)**

Ibid. . . . *showed that* the library salary was the main income for 68.9% of the respondents, was supplemental for 28.1%, and half and half for 1.9%. 1.1% did not respond. **(502)**

■ A comparison reported in 1983 of 2 surveys of Association of College and Research Libraries members concerning members' educational attainments (1973 survey—survey size: 300 members; responding: 259 or 86.3%; 1978 survey—survey size: 429 members; responding: 357 or 83.2%) *showed that* the proportion of respondents reporting 1 or more specialized work assignments (a foreign language or group of languages, a particular geographic area or a subject speciality) rose 5% between 1973 (32% so reporting) and 1978 (38% so reporting). Further, while 17.4% of the 1973 respondents reported subject speciality assignments, 28.6% of the 1978 respondents reported such assignments. **(796)**

Education—Professional

General

■ A survey in 1970 of all libraries of all types in the 3-county Detroit metropolitan area conducted by the Wayne State University Department of Library Science (116 libraries responding, including 57% of the school libraries, 94% of the academic libraries, 80% of the special libraries, and 92% of the public libraries) *showed that* the employment of librarians (with M.L.S.) and library associates (B.A. only, with or without library science minor) by percentage of the total by library type was as follows:

LIBRARY TYPE	% LIBRARIANS	% ASSOCIATES
academic libraries	16	13
public libraries	46	29

continued

LIBRARY TYPE   % LIBRARIANS   % ASSOCIATES

school libraries	29	53	
special libraries	9	5	(086)

■ A survey reported in 1978 of traceable North American librarians who had earned library doctorates in American Library Association accredited programs between 1930 and 1975 (survey size: 568; responding: 403 or 71%) *showed that* 51.3% reported being in library education; 33.8% reported being in the field of library administration; 11.1% reported library research (as distinct from any other categories); and 3.8% reported being in library operations.   **(463)**

Ibid. . . . *showed that*, based on a scoring system where "3" = essential, "2" = important, "1" = useful and "0" = unimportant, respondents overall rated the library doctorate 2.4 in obtaining their present posts and 1.99 in performing the duties of their present post. Specifically:

library educators rated the library doctorate 2.81 in obtaining their present posts and 2.33 in performing their duties;

library administrators ranked the library doctorate 2.06 in obtaining their present position and 1.73 in performing their duties;

library researchers ranked the library doctorate 1.86 in obtaining their present position and 1.51 in performing their duties;

individuals in library operations ranked the library doctorate 1.20 in obtaining their present position and 1.07 in performing their duties.   **(463)**

■ A study of academic job advertisements at 5-year intervals (1959, 1964, 1969, 1974, and 1979) over a 20-year period, taken from 3 library journals (*Library Journal, ALA Bulletin/American Libraries*, and *College and Research Libraries/College and Research Libraries News*) and excluding jobs that were primarily administrative or technical in nature for a total of 1,254 jobs, *showed that* in 1959, 48 (26.0%) of the jobs advertised required an M.L.S., of which only 9 (4.9%) of the jobs required an ALA-accredited M.L.S.; while by 1979, 244 (97.6%) of the jobs required an M.L.S., of which 193 (77.2%) required an ALA-accredited M.L.S.   **(515)**

Ibid. . . . *showed that* in 1959, 1 (.5%) job required a subject master's degree and no particular subject was specificied, while by 1979 69 (27.6%)

of the jobs required a subject master's degree of which 40 (16.0%) required a specific subject area. **(515)**

Ibid. . . . *showed that* generally the number of qualifications for professional jobs had increased during the 20-year period. Specifically, the number of jobs requiring:

a foreign language increased from 38 (20.5%) of the jobs in 1959 to 88 (35.2%) of the jobs in 1979;

computer expertise increased from 0 in 1959 to 103 (41.2%) of the jobs in 1979;

subject background increased from 20 (10.8%) of the jobs in 1959 to 81 (32.4%) of the jobs in 1979;

AV knowledge increased from 1 (.5%) of the jobs in 1959 to 18 (7.2%) of the jobs in 1979;

teaching experience increased from 2 (1.1%) of the jobs in 1959 to 11 (4.4%) of the jobs in 1979;

specific library expertise increased from 10 (5.4%) of the jobs in 1959 to 52 (20.8%) of the jobs in 1979;

communicative ability increased from 2 (1.1%) of the jobs in 1959 to 34 (13.6%) of the jobs in 1979;

administrative ability increased from 1 (.5%) job in 1959 to 28 (11.2%) of the jobs in 1979. **(515)**

Ibid. . . . *showed that* generally prior experience was associated with higher salaries, while subject master's degrees were associated with higher salaries only recently. Specifically, advertised salaries of positions requiring experience were statistically significantly higher than salaries of positions not requiring experience in 4 of the 5 years studied (significance level at .001 or better), while advertised salaries of positions requiring subject master's degrees were statistically significantly higher only in the 1974 and 1979 periods studied (significance level at .05 or better). **(515)**

Academic

■ A 1968 survey of academic library salaries in a 7-state area (North and South Dakota, Minnesota, Iowa, Nebraska, Wyoming, and Montana) (sample size: 96; responding: 68 or 70.8%) *showed that* approximately 12% of all academic librarians in the sample did not have a master's degree (fifth-year B.A. in library science was counted as a master's degree). Such individuals are employed in 29 of the 66 responding libraries. **(198)**

Ibid. . . . *showed that* nearly 15% of librarians in responding institutions had at least 2 master's degrees. Such individuals are employed in 31 of the 66 responding libraries. However, only 16 institutions (24.2%) automatically paid extra for such additional academic preparation.   **(198)**

■ A 1970 survey of Canadian community college libraries concerning academic status, salaries, and fringe benefits (sample size: 108; responding: 49; usable: 43 or 39.8%) *showed that* educational attainment of community college librarians was as follows:

bachelor's degree in library science	58% of total
master's degree in library science	26% of total
second master's degree	4% of total
work beyond master's degree	5% of total
foreign qualification	7% of total

                                                                       (537)

■ A 1974-75 study of university libraries including all Association of Research Libraries libraries (sample size: 92; responding: 72 or 78%) and all library schools with ALA-accredited programs (sample size: not given; responding: 44 or 80%) *showed that* the 72 libraries reported employing as of February 1, 1975, 207 Ph.D's of which 173 (84.3%) were subject Ph.D.'s (i.e. in a subject field rather than in library science). The number of subject Ph.D.'s with M.L.S.'s was 106 (60.6%).   **(445)**

Ibid. . . . *showed that* responding libraries reported [some individuals apparently worked in more than 1 area] that 52 (30.1%) subject Ph.D.'s were employed in archives/special collections, 44 (25.4%) in subject bibliography, 39 (22.5%) in administration, 34 (19.7%) in reference or technical services, and 6 (3.5%) as branch librarians.   **(445)**

■ A 1978 survey of law school libraries listed in the 1977 *AALS Directory of Law Teachers* (population: 167; responding: 158 or 95%) *showed that* the degrees held by the head law librarian were as follows:

undergraduate degree only	1 (0.6%) respondent
undergraduate and library science degrees	12 (07.6%) respondents
undergraduate and law degrees	20 (12.7%) respondents
all three degrees	121 (76.6%) respondents
no degree	1 (0.6%) respondent
no response	3 (1.9%) respondents

                                                                       (362)

■ A study of academic job advertisements at 5-year intervals (1959, 1964, 1969, 1974, and 1979) over a 20-year period taken from 3 library journals (*Library Journal, ALA Bulletin/American Libraries*, and *College and Research Libraries/College and Research Libraries News*) and excluding jobs that were primarily administrative or technical in nature for a total of 1,254 jobs, *showed that* generally the number of qualifications for professional jobs had increased during the 20-year period. Specifically, the number of jobs requiring:

a foreign language increased from 38 (20.5%) of the jobs in 1959 to 88 (35.2%) of the jobs in 1979;

computer expertise increased from 0 in 1959 to 103 (41.2%) of the jobs in 1979;

subject background increased from 20 (10.8%) of the jobs in 1959 to 81 (32.4%) of the jobs in 1979;

AV knowledge increased from 1 (.5%) of the jobs in 1959 to 18 (7.2%) of the jobs in 1979;

teaching experience increased from 2 (1.1%) of the jobs in 1959 to 11 (4.4%) of the jobs in 1979;

specific library expertise increased from 10 (5.4%) of the jobs in 1959 to 52 (20.8%) of the jobs in 1979;

communicative ability increased from 2 (1.1%) of the jobs in 1959 to 34 (13.6%) of the jobs in 1979;

administrative ability increased from 1 (.5%) job in 1959 to 28 (11.2%) of the jobs in 1979. **(515)**

Ibid. . . . *showed that* generally prior experience was associated with higher salaries, while subject master's degrees were associated with higher salaries only recently. Specifically, advertised salaries of positions requiring experience were statistically significantly higher than salaries of positions not requiring experience in 4 of the 5 years studied (significance level at .001 or better), while advertised salaries of positions requiring subject master's degrees were statistically significantly higher only in the 1974 and 1979 periods studied (significance level at .05 or better). **(515)**

■ A 1980 survey of academic librarians in Alabama, Georgia, and Mississippi concerning faculty status (sample size: 416; responding 271; usable: 267 or 64.2%) *showed that* 87.3% of the respondents reported having the M.L.S. degree. Other degrees were reported as follows:

none/no answer	64.0%
M.S.	17.0%

continued

Ph.D.	9.8%	
M.A.	6.9%	
sixth-year	2.3%	**(502)**

■ A study reported in 1981 of job listings for college and university libraries reported in *Library Journal* and *College and Research Libraries News* during 1970-79 (5,269 job listings) *showed that* educational requirements for nondirector positions generally increased from 1970 through 1976, with a peak in the 1974-76 period and decline in educational requirements subsequently. The only exception to this pattern was college director positions, whose educational requirements increased throughout the survey period. **(494)**

Ibid. . . . *showed that,* overall for the survey period for nondirector university positions, 1.9% required a Ph.D., 27.0% required a second master's, while 71% required no additional educational certification. Overall for nondirector college positions, 2.8% required a Ph.D., 21.4% required a second master's, while 75.8% required no additional educational certification. **(494)**

Ibid. . . . *showed that* both director and nondirector positions in the university environment listed statistically significantly higher educational requirements than director and nondirector positions in the college environment. Significant at the .05 level or less. **(494)**

■ A comparison reported in 1983 of 2 surveys of Association of College and Research Libraries members concerning members' educational attainments (1973 survey—survey size: 300 members; responding: 259 or 86.3%; 1978 survey—survey size: 429 members; responding: 357 or 83.2%) *showed that* overall the educational level of members had increased. Specifically:

bachelor's degrees: 100% of both surveys had bachelor's degrees;

second bachelor's degrees: 54 (20.9%) of the 1973 sample compared to 42 (11.8%) of the 1978 sample had or were pursuing second bachelor's degrees;

master's degrees: 236 (91.1%) of the 1973 sample compared to 334 (93.5%) of the 1978 sample had or were pursuing master's degrees;

second master's degrees: 50 (19.3%) of the 1973 sample compared to 134 (37.6%) of the 1978 sample had or were pursuing second master's degrees;

sixth-year certificate: 11 (4.3%) of the 1973 sample compared to 20 (5.6%) of the 1978 sample had or were pursuing sixth-year certificates;

doctorates: 18 (6.9%) of the 1973 sample compared to 58 (16.2%) of the 1978 sample had or were pursuing doctoral degrees. **(796)**

Ibid. . . . *showed that*, of 343 respondents to the 1978 survey, the highest degree held was as follows:

bachelor's degree	5 (1.5%)	respondents
second bachelor's degree	11 (3.2%)	respondents
master's degree	169 (49.3%)	respondents
second master's degree	94 (27.4%)	respondents
sixth-year certificate	11 (3.2%)	respondents
doctorate	53 (15.5%)	respondents

(796)

Ibid. . . . *showed that*, based on the 1978 sample, younger professionals tended to be more highly educated than older professionals to a statistically significant degree. For example, the number of professionals in each of 3 age groups who held second master's degrees was as follows:

23-36 years of age	46 (35.9%)	respondents
37-47 years of age	25 (25.3%)	respondents
48-69 years of age	23 (19.8%)	respondents

Also, the number of professionals in each of 3 age groups who held doctorates was as follows:

23-36 years of age	19 (14.8%)	respondents
37-47 years of age	23 (23.2%)	respondents
48-69 years of age	11 (9.5%)	respondents

(Differences significant at the .05 level.) **(796)**

Ibid. . . . *showed that*, based on the 1978 sample, the highest degree being held or pursued by gender was as follows (153 males responding; 192 females responding):

bachelor's degree: no males compared to 5 (2.6%) females;

second bachelor's degree: 2 (1.3%) males compared to 9 (4.7%) females;

master's degree: 62 (40.5%) males compared to 109 (56.8%) females;

second master's degree: 48 (31.4%) males compared to 46 (24.0%) females;

sixth year certificate: 6 (3.9%) males compared to 5 (2.6%) females;

doctorate: 35 (22.9%) males compared to 18 (9.4%) females. **(796)**

Ibid. . . . *showed that*, based on the 1978 sample, males had a statistically significantly higher level of education than females. For example, males were more likely to hold degrees above the first master's degree, while females were more likely to hold degrees at or below the level of the first master's degree. Specifically, 41.8% of the males had their highest degrees at or below the level of the first master's degree, while 64.1% of the females had such degrees (difference significant at the .05 level). **(796)**

Ibid. . . . *showed that* overall more librarians had been enrolled in academic course work during the 12 months prior to the 1978 survey (34.4% respondents) than prior to the 1973 survey (22.2% respondents). Based on the 1978 survey a statistically significantly greater proportion of females had taken such courses than males (difference significant at the .05 level). **(796)**

Public

■ A survey reported in 1967 of midwestern librarians (37 men, 408 women, total 445) in small public libraries (i.e., serving populations of 10,000 to 35,000) *showed that*, of those librarians under 30 years of age, 91.6% had completed 4 years of college; of librarians in their 30s, 85.0% had completed college; of librarians in their 40s, 65.3% had completed college; of librarians in their 50s, 52.0% had completed college; of librarians in their 60s, 53.1% had completed college; and of those librarians 70+, 50.0% had completed college. **(282)**

Ibid. . . . *showed that*, of the respondents as a group, 36.0% had no college degree; 26.4% had no more than a college degree; 13.3% had no more than a fifth-year bachelor's degree; and 24.1% had no more than a master's degree. **(282)**

Ibid. . . . *showed that* 54.3% of the librarians with professional degrees worked in communities with median incomes of less than $7,000, while

72.2% of the librarians with less training worked in such communities; 19.4% of the librarians with professional degrees worked in communities with median incomes 10,000+, while only 6.5% of the librarians with less training worked in such communities. A positive correlation (correlation coefficient = .20) between professional training and community income was determined (no significance level given). **(282)**

Ibid. . . . *showed a* slight statistical relationship (correlation coefficient = .14) between size of community and professional education of the librarian. 29.4% of the librarians with professional degrees and 40.3% of the librarians with less education worked in libraries serving communities of 10,000 to 14,999, while 16.5% of the librarians with professional degrees and 10.9% of the librarians with less education worked in libraries serving communities of 30,000 to 34,999 (no significance level given). **(282)**

Special

■ A preliminary analysis reported in 1976 of a survey of American Association of Law Library members (survey size: "approximately 2,000" individuals; responding: "approximately 1,400" or 70%, of which responses from 888 respondents were analyzed at the time of the report) *showed that* education of respondents was as follows:

graduate degrees in library science	50% respondents
degree in law	26% respondents
both of the above	17% respondents
working on 1 of the above	9% respondents

Since an earlier survey of AALL members in 1970, the number of members with law degrees had increased from 40% to 43%; the members holding both degrees decreased from 23% to 17%; and the members holding neither degree decreased from 25% to 16%. Further, AALL members who had completed a formal course in law librarianship or legal bibliography had increased to 54% compared to the 1970 survey. **(793)**

■ A 1978 survey of law school libraries listed in the 1977 *AALS Directory of Law Teachers* (population: 167; responding: 158 or 95%) *showed that* the degrees held by the head law librarian were as follows:

undergraduate degree only	1 (0.6%) respondent
undergraduate and library science degrees	12 (07.6%) respondents
undergraduate and law degrees	20 (12.7%) respondents

continued

all three degrees   121 (76.6%) respondents
no degree   1 (0.6%) respondent
no response   3 (1.9%) respondents
                                                (362)

Job Satisfaction—Nonprofessional

Academic

■ A 1971-72 survey of full-time employees (both professional and
nonprofessional) in 3 U.S. university libraries in selected departments
(book selection, acquisitions, cataloging, circulation, and reference) concerning job satisfaction as measured by the Hage/Aiken satisfaction scale
(survey size: 521 employees; responding: 384 or 73%) *showed that* there
was no statistically significant relationship between job satisfaction and
gender.   **(806)**

Ibid. . . . *showed that* there was a statistically significant relationship
between job satisfaction and age. Specifically, the least satisfied group
were those under 25 years of age, and their job satisfaction was statistically
significantly lower than all other groups except for those 25-29 years old
and those 55-59 years old (significant at the .001 level).   **(806)**

Ibid. . . . *showed that* employees with more years of experience tended to
report higher levels of job satisfaction than employees with fewer years of
experience, while employees who had worked in a particular library longer
tended to report higher job satisfaction than employees who had worked in
a particular library a shorter length of time. Specifically, in terms of total
library experience, the 3-4 year group reported the lowest job satisfaction
and differed to a statistically significant degree in job satisfaction from
those in the 5-6, 9-10, 11-14, and 15-24 year groups (significant at the .05
level). Further, among those working in a particular library, employees
with 1-2 or 3-4 years of experience in that library reported statistically
significantly lower job satisfaction than those who had worked 11-14 or
15-24 years in that library (significant at the .05 level).   **(806)**

Ibid. . . . *showed that* job satisfaction increased as administrative level
rose. Specifically, the average job satisfaction scores were as follows (the
higher the score the less job satisfaction):

no supervisory responsibility   15.64 average score
first-level supervisor   14.10 average score
unit manager   12.73 average score
department head   11.11 average score

Further, employees with no supervisory responsibility reported statistically significantly lower job satisfaction scores than unit or department heads (significant at the .001 level). **(806)**

Ibid. . . . *showed that* job satisfaction varied by department as follows (the higher the score the less job satisfaction):

reference	12.21	average	score
acquisitions	14.03	average	score
cataloging	14.45	average	score
serials	15.89	average	score
circulation	16.25	average	score
searching	17.45	average	score

Further, reference librarians reported statistically significantly higher job satisfaction scores than any other department except for acquisitions (significant at the .01 level). **(806)**

Ibid. . . . *showed that* professional librarians reported statistically significantly higher job satisfaction scores than nonprofessional employees (significant at the .001 level). **(806)**

Ibid. . . . *showed that*, of 137 professionals, 24 (17%) reported they intended to leave the full-time work force or go into another type of work within 5 years (12 of the 24 respondents were over the age of 55, which suggested that retirement was the reason for leaving). On the other hand, 54 (40%) of the professionals and 67 (27%) of the nonprofessionals reported that they expected to be working in the same library in 5 years' time. **(806)**

■ A survey of 163 classified nonprofessional library employees at the University of Pennsylvania who were union members (99 responding), reported in 1975, *showed that* job satisfaction increased with age. 24.3% of the 20-25 year olds, 28.1% of the 26-30 year olds, and 51.6% of those 31 or older rated their job interesting. **(105)**

Job Satisfaction—Professional

Academic

■ A 1971-72 survey of full-time employees (both professional and nonprofessional) in 3 U.S. university libraries in selected departments (book selection, acquisitions, cataloging, circulation, and reference) concerning job satisfaction as measured by the Hage/Aiken satisfaction scale (survey size: 521 employees; responding: 384 or 73%) *showed that* there was no statistically significant relationship between job satisfaction and gender. **(806)**

Ibid. . . . *showed that* there was a statistically significant relationship between job satisfaction and age. Specifically, the least satisfied group were those under 25 years of age, and their job satisfaction was statistically significantly lower than all other groups except for those 25-29 years old and those 55-59 years old (significant at the .001 level). **(806)**

Ibid. . . . *showed that* employees with more years of experience tended to report higher levels of job satisfaction than employees with fewer years of experience, while employees who had worked in a particular library longer tended to report higher job satisfaction than employees who had worked in a particular library a shorter length of time. Specifically, in terms of total library experience, the 3-4 year group reported the lowest job satisfaction and differed to a statistically significant degree in job satisfaction from those in the 5-6, 9-10, 11-14, and 15-24 year groups (significant at the .05 level). Further, among those working in a particular library, employees with 1-2 or 3-4 years of experience in that library reported statistically significantly lower job satisfaction than those who had worked 11-14 or 15-24 years in that library (significant at the .05 level). **(806)**

Ibid. . . . *showed that* job satisfaction increased as administrative level rose. Specifically, the average job satisfaction scores were as follows (the higher the score the less job satisfaction):

no supervisory responsibility	15.64 average score
first-level supervisor	14.10 average score
unit manager	12.73 average score
department head	11.11 average score

Further, employees with no supervisory responsibility reported statistically significantly lower job satisfaction scores than unit or department heads (significant at the .001 level). **(806)**

Ibid. . . . *showed that* job satisfaction varied by department as follows (the higher the score the less job satisfaction):

reference	12.21 average score
acquisitions	14.03 average score
cataloging	14.45 average score
serials	15.89 average score
circulation	16.25 average score
searching	17.45 average score

Further, reference librarians reported statistically significantly higher job satisfaction scores than any other department except for acquisitions (significant at the .01 level). **(806)**

Ibid. . . . *showed that* professional librarians reported statistically significantly higher job satisfaction scores than nonprofessional employees (significant at the .001 level). **(806)**

Ibid. . . . *showed that,* of 137 professionals, 24 (17%) reported they intended to leave the full-time work force or go into another type of work within 5 years (12 of the 24 respondents were over the age of 55, which suggested that retirement was the reason for leaving). On the other hand, 54 (40%) of the professionals and 67 (27%) of the nonprofessionals reported that they expected to be working in the same library in 5 years' time. **(806)**

■ A survey reported in 1983 of reference librarians in 75 U.S. universities with enrollments exceeding 20,000 (survey size: 380; responding: 262 or 69%) *showed that,* based on the Forbes Burnout Survey, reference librarians in academic libraries did not seem to have a burnout problem. Specifically, results of the Burnout Survey showed the following results)

librarians with burnout	none
librarians with mild burnout	1% of total
librarians who were candidates for burnout	12% of total
librarians with burnout under control	87% of total **(789)**

Special

■ A 1975 survey of participants at a management development program for a southwestern chapter of the Special Libraries Association (survey size: 72 librarians; usable: 64 or 88.9%) investigating the relationships between age and tenure and job satisfaction (the last measured by the Job Descriptive Index developed by Smith, et al.) *showed that* there was no statistically significant difference in job satisfaction between special librarians under 30 years of age and special librarians over 30 years of age; and no statistically significant difference in job satisfaction between special librarians who had 3 or fewer years of full-time library experience and those with greater full-time library experience. Further, although the results were somewhat ambiguous there was also no statistically significant difference found between individual job satisfaction and age or between individual job satisfaction and length of full-time work in libraries. **(783)**

Level of Work—Nonprofessional

General

■ A survey in 1974 of the 47 charter members of the OCLC network, including site visits and interviews (148) with all levels of library personnel in member libraries *showed that* 74% of the interviewees stated that the nonprofessional work had been made more demanding, while only 3 interviewees reported that professional cataloging had been made more demanding.   **(112)**

Level of Work—Professional

General

■ A survey reported in 1965 of 163 professional librarians in academic and public libraries in Michigan who indicated which of 50 professional and 50 nonprofessional tasks (from the ALA *Descriptive List of Professional and Non-Professional Duties in Libraries*) they did *showed that* of the total sample 64.97% of all tasks reported were professional. 72.04% of the tasks reported by academic librarians were professional compared to 62.93% of nonacademic librarians' tasks; 64.28% of the public service librarians' tasks were reported as professional compared to 70.14% of nonpublic service librarians'; and 58.89% of the junior librarians' tasks were professional compared to 65.98% of the senior librarians' tasks.   **(174)**

■ A survey in 1974 of the 47 charter members of the OCLC network, including site visits and interviews (148) with all levels of library personnel in member libraries *showed that* 74% of the interviewees stated that the nonprofessional work had been made more demanding, while only 3 interviewees reported that professional cataloging had been made more demanding.   **(112)**

Library Technicians

General

■ A study reported in 1971 of library technician graduates during the period 1967-1969 (sample size: 200; responding: 154 or 77%) *showed that* the average full-time salary after training was $5,357 per year compared to $4,089 (adjusted for inflation and cost of living increases) before training. This is an average difference of $1,262, a statistically significant difference at the .001 significance level.   **(398)**

Ibid. . . . *showed that* 147 (95%) respondents reported they were happy that they took the library technician program (requiring 2 years' work past high school), while 7 (5%) reported they were not happy to have taken the program. Of those unhappy, 4 reported they were not displeased with the courses but displeased because they could not find a job after graduation.
(398)

Ibid. . . . *showed that,* of 91 respondents, 70 (77%) felt their course work had done a "good" or "excellent" job of preparing them for their present position; 16 (18%) felt that it had done a "fair" job; and 5 (5%) felt that it had done a "poor" or "unsatisfactory" job of preparation.   **(398)**

Ibid. . . . *showed that,* of 91 respondents, 64 (70.3%) felt they were accepted as part of the library staff; 13 (14.3%) felt they were moderately accepted by the library staff; 12 (13.2%) felt they were considered another clerical assistant; and 2 (2.2%) felt they were not accepted by the professional librarian.   **(398)**

Ibid. . . . *showed that* before entering the library technician program 61 (40%) respondents had worked in a high school library; 7 (4%) in a college or university library; 7 (4%) in a public library; and 8 (5%) worked as volunteers in an elementary school library.   **(398)**

Ibid. . . . *showed that* 5 (3%) of the library technician graduates were male, while 149 (97%) were female.   **(398)**

Academic

■ A 1977 study of library technician positions (a library technician is a graduate of a 2-year undergraduate program with specialization in library techniques and procedures) in Ontario academic libraries (survey size: 15 libraries; responding: 12 or 80% libraries) *showed that* the number of library technicians employed at the time of the survey in the 12 libraries totaled 27 individuals. Overall for all 12 libraries, library technicians constituted 5.2% of the total staff and 6.5% of the nonprofessional staff.
(549)

Ibid. . . . *showed that* 10 (83.3%) of the responding libraries reported that they did not have a position classification designated specifically for library technicians.   **(549)**

Ibid. . . . *showed that*, of 5 respondents ranking the importance of courses taken by library technicians, the courses were (in descending order of importance):

1. library techniques
2. library-related courses
3. communications
4. business
5. human relations and social sciences
6. humanities
7. sciences **(549)**

Ibid. . . . *showed that*, of 5 respondents ranking the advantages of library technicians using a weighted scale, the top 3 advantages (out of 6) were (in descending order of importance):

1. relieve librarians of routine library tasks
2. save professional time and money necessary for on-the-job training
3. upgrade librarians by making it necessary to have a clear distinction between professional and nonprofessional tasks **(549)**

Ibid. . . . *showed that*, of 6 respondents ranking the disadvantags of library technicians using a weighted scale, the 2 greatest disadvantages were (in descending order of importance):

1. not possessing the necessary personnel category, salary, and advancement possibilities necessary to attract library technicians
2. not considering the training of library technicians adequate so that on-the-job training was still necessary **(549)**

Ibid. . . . *showed that*, of 27 presently employed library technicians plus 6 individuals formerly in library technician positions, 21 (63.6%) were located in technical services, while 11 (33.3%) were employed in public services operations. **(549)**

Minorities

Academic

■ A 1969 survey by the Library Administration Division (LAD) of ALA of the largest public and academic libraries, the state library agencies, and 1 public library system in most states (65% libraries responding) *showed that* the average percentage of minority staff representation was as follows:

RESPONDENTS	TOTAL %	% PROFESSIONAL	% OTHER
state agencies	9+	4+	11+
public libraries	16+	8+	23+
systems	8+	8+	8+
academic	4+	4+	5+

(075)

Ibid. . . . *showed that* 84% of responding libraries had minority employees (either full- or part-time) in the following breakdown:

American Indians	1%	
Spanish-Americans	15+%	
Negroes	73+%	
Oriental-Americans	11+%	**(075)**

Ibid. . . . *showed that*, while 27+% of all employees were in professional positions, 14+% of minority group employees were in professional positions. **(075)**

Public

■ A 1969 survey by the Library Administration Division (LAD) of ALA of the largest public and academic libraries, the state library agencies, and 1 public library system in most states (65% libraries responding) *showed that* the average percentage of minority staff representation was as follows:

RESPONDENTS	TOTAL %	% PROFESSIONAL	% OTHER
state agencies	9+	4+	11+
public libraries	16+	8+	23+
systems	8+	8+	8+
academic	4+	4+	5+

(075)

Ibid. . . . *showed that* 84% of responding libraries had minority employees (either full- or part-time) in the following breakdown:

American Indians	1%	
Spanish-Americans	15+%	
Negroes	73+%	
Oriental-Americans	11+%	**(075)**

Ibid. . . . *showed that*, while 27+% of all employees were in professional positions, 14+% of minority group employees were in professional positions. **(075)**

Special

■ A survey reported in 1972 of black employment in law school libraries (sample size: 136; responding: 95 or 70%) *showed that* responding libraries reported a total of 12 black law librarians out of 346 professional law librarians (3.4% of the professional law librarians). This included 7 black women out of 204 women professionals (2%) and 5 black men out of 123 male professionals (1.4%). **(386)**

Ibid. . . . *showed that* responding libraries reported 69 black sub-professionals out of a total of 552 subprofessionals (12.5% of the sub-professionals). This included 44 black women out of 342 female subprofessionals (12.9%) and 25 black men out of 210 male subprofessionals (11.9%). **(386)**

Personality Traits—Professional

General

■ A survey reported in 1979 of job satisfaction among beginning librarians (6 to 18 months on the job) using the Minnesota Importance Questionnaire (MIQ), the Minnesota Job Description Questionnaire (MJDQ), and the Minnesota Satisfaction Questionnaire (MSQ) sent to 314 graduates of 6 library schools (response rate: MJDQ and MSQ, 228 or 73%; MIQ, 193 or 61%) *showed that* there was no statistically significant difference in vocational needs (MIQ) among groups divided by age or previous work experience (significance level .01). **(632)**

Ibid. . . . *showed that* analysis of the 22 MSQ scales revealed that the mean creativity scale score of the school librarians was significantly higher than the mean creativity scale scores of the technical services librarians in academic libraries and public services librarians in public libraries; that the mean independence scale score of the technical services librarians in academic libraries was significantly higher than the mean independence scale scores of the public services librarians in public libraries and school libraries; and that the mean social service scale score of technical services librarians in academic libraries was significantly lower than the mean social service scale scores of public services librarians in both academic and public libraries and school librarians (significance level .01). **(632)**

Ibid. . . . *showed that* the 5 most highly ranked items on the MSQ for the whole group were moral values (mean 3.90), social service (mean 3.79), security (mean 3.71), co-workers (mean 3.56), and autonomy (mean 3.52).

(632)

Ibid. . . . *showed that* correlation of the MIQ scale scores and the MJDQ scale scores with the MIQ scale scores revealed that the need profiles of satisfied and dissatisfied librarian were quite similar, while the job environments in which satisfied and dissatisfied librarians worked were perceived to be quite dissimilar. Stepwise multiple regression of the MJDQ scale scores with the general satisfaction scale scores *showed that* the 2 most important elements in this environment were the supervision-human relations scale (measuring respondent's assessment of the human relations skills of his immediate supervisor) and the ability-utilization scale (measuring the respondent's assessment of the degree to which his job allows him to make full use of his abilities), which accounted for 38% of the variance of the general satisfaction scale scores. **(632)**

■ A survey reported in 1981 that requested a systemic sample of special librarians to take the Rokeach Value Survey (sample size: 200; responding: 101), which was then compared to Value Survey results from librarians in public libraries, library school faculty, and library school students, *showed that* special librarians differed most from these other groups in the importance they assigned to sense of accomplishment. Public librarians and library school faculty ranked it higher (both ranked it 1 of 18) while library school students ranked it lower (9 of 18). Special librarians ranked it 6 of 18. These differences were statistically significant at the .05 level.

(434)

Academic

■ A study reported in 1963 of 676 academic librarians from across the U.S. who had been given the Ghiselli "Self Description Inventory" (an instrument that required each subject to choose the adjectives he felt best described him in a forced choice context) plus a supplementary questionnaire *showed that* the average librarian scored in the 76th percentile of the adult working population in intelligence, in the 70th percentile in terms of occupational level, and in the 41st percentile in terms of initiative. **(131)**

Ibid. . . . *showed that* only 13% indicated any regret at having chosen librarianship as a profession. This was a much smaller proportion than for most other occupational groups. **(131)**

Ibid. . . . *showed that* the average librarian scored in the 52nd percentile of the adult working population in supervisory qualities. Furthermore, only 2% of the respondents gave supervision or personnel work as a major source of satisfaction in their work, and 20% found supervision the least attractive aspect of librarianship.   (131)

■ A survey reported in 1975 to determine levels of job satisfaction, using a Maslow needs hierarchy of 202 men and women library professionals from 23 college and university libraries in the greater New York metropolitan area, *showed that* in terms of needs fulfillment (degree to which job met needs) men and women showed similar levels of fulfillment in lower order needs, i.e., "social" and "security" needs, but that women expressed statistically significantly lower levels of fulfillment than men in meeting "esteem" and "autonomy" needs.   (103)

Ibid. . . . *showed that* in terms of needs deficiency (size of gap between actual and desired degree to which job fills needs) women have statistically significantly higher deficiencies than men in "security," "autonomy," "esteem," and "self-actualization." There was no statistically significant difference between men and women in the area of social needs.   (103)

Ibid. . . . showed in terms of importance of needs (degree to which respondents considered the need important) both men and women ranked autonomy and self-actualization needs as most important. The judged importance of security, social, and esteem needs were similar for both men and women, while women considered autonomy and self-actualization as having less importance than men.   (103)

■ A survey reported in 1976 of 202 librarians in 23 academic libraries in the greater New York metropolitan area who were given the Need Satisfaction Questionnaire (based on Maslow's Hierarchy of Needs) *showed that*, in terms of need fulfillment (amount of each type of need presently being fulfilled), women reported statistically significantly less fulfillment than men in 2 categories: "esteem" and "autonomy" (significant at the .01 level). In "social" and "security" needs men and women showed similar scores, and in "self-actualization" women had lower scores but not to a statistically significant degree.   (794)

Ibid. . . . *showed that* for both men and women, "security" was the need most fulfilled, while "autonomy" was the need least fulfilled for both groups.   (794)

Ibid. . . . *showed that*, in terms of need deficiency (difference between how much of the need is being met and how much should be met), women perceived statistically significantly higher deficiencies than men in 4 areas: "security," "esteem," "autonomy," and "self-actualization" (significant at the .001 level). Men and women had similar scores in terms of "social" needs. **(794)**

Ibid. . . . *showed that* men perceived "security" to be the least deficient need, while women perceived "social" as the least deficient need. However, both perceived "self-actualization" as the most deficient need. **(794)**

Ibid. . . . *showed that*, in terms of needs importance (how important each of the 5 needs is), women perceived "autonomy" and "self-actualization" as less important than men to a statistically significant degree (significant at the .01 level). "Security," "social," and "esteem" needs were perceived as equally important by men and women. Both men and women perceived "self-actualization" as the need of highest importance, while both perceived "esteem" as lowest in importance. **(794)**

■ A 1977 study in a library school at a major university in the western United States, involving 16 males and 26 females taking the Bem Sex-Role Inventory, *showed that* there were no statistically significant differences between library school males and the normative male group on masculinity, femininity, or androgyny scores. **(485)**

Ibid. . . . *showed that* there were no statistically significant differences between library school females and the normative female group on masculinity or androgyny scores. There were statistically significant differences between the two groups on femininity scores, with the library school females scoring higher (significant at the .05 level). **(485)**

Ibid. . . . *showed that* a comparison of scores for library school males and library school females showed a statistically significant difference on masculinity, femininity, and androgyny scores, with males scoring higher on the masculinity scales and females scoring higher on the female and androgynous scales (significant at the .01 level). **(485)**

Special

■ A survey reported in 1981 that requested a systemic sample of special librarians to take the Rokeach Value Survey (sample size: 200; responding: 101), which was then compared to Value Survey results from librarians in public libraries, library school faculty, and library school students *showed that* the 3 top-ranked values (out of 18) for special librarians were (1) self-respect (i.e., self-esteem), (2) freedom (i.e., independence, free choice), and (3) inner harmony (freedom from inner conflict).   **(434)**

Ibid. . . . *showed that* there were no statistically significant differences in values held by special librarians by gender; however, 3 values did show increases in importance by age of special librarians (sense of accomplish-
. ment; equality, i.e.,brotherhood, equal opportunity for all; and wisdom), and 2 values showed decreases in importance by age of special librarians (happiness and pleasure).   **(434)**

Ibid. . . . *showed that* the 3 least important values (out of 18) for special librarians were (16) social recognition; (17) national security; and (18) salvation, i.e., saved, eternal life.   **(434)**

Productivity

Academic

■ A 1977 study at the University of North Carolina at Chapel Hill, based on the time logs of 67 searchers in the Bibliographic Searching Section over a 4-month period and involving just under 14,000 items *showed that* during the 4-month period the 6 searchers actually worked only 77.4% of the salaried hours (due to sick leave, vacations, etc.), and of the time actually worked only 71% of the time was actually spent searching (due to breaks, meetings, etc.). Consequently, only 55% of the salaried hours were spent actually searching.   **(305)**

Professional-Support Staff Ratio

Academic

■ A 1966 survey of Catholic college and university libraries in institutions with at least 1,000 full-time students (sample size: 70; responding: 56 or 80%) *showed that* the median ratio of professionals to nonprofessionals was 5:19. (Similar libraries in the population at least had a median ratio of 5:6.5.)   **(187)**

■ A 1967 survey of medical school libraries concerning reference services (survey size: 93 libraries; responding: 85 or 91.4%) *showed that* the average staffing per library was as follows:

professional	5.2 FTE
nonprofessional	9.1 FTE
reference, professional	1.7 FTE
reference, nonprofessional	0.8 FTE

(682)

■ A study of 1977 survey information gathered by the National Center for Educational Statistics (U.S. Office of Education) concerning the degree to which 1,146 college and university libraries (Liberal Arts Colleges I and II; Comprehensive Universities and Colleges I and II) met the 1975 Standards for College Libraries (ACRL) *showed that* over half of the libraries had insufficient nonprofessional staff support and fell below the standard in terms of the ratio of professional staff to nonprofessional staff. Standards specify that no more than 25% (ratio of 1 to 3) to 35% (ratio of 1 to 1.9) of the staff should be professional, while the average ratio of professionals to nonprofessionals was 1 to 1.1 and the median was 1 to 1.0.

(486)

■ A study reported in 1981 of data on 1,146 2-year colleges, as reported in the 1977 Higher Education General Information Surveys and compared to the 1979 Association of College and Research Libraries standards, *showed that* the ratio of professional to support staff averaged 1 professional to 1.30 nonprofessional overall, with a ratio among the 214 private schools of 1 to .64 and among the 897 public schools of 1 to 1.46. **(500)**

■ A study reported in 1983 of 3 surveys made by the American Medical Association's Division of Library and Archival Services in 1969, 1973, and 1979 concerning the status of health sciences libraries in the U.S. (survey size for each survey ran between 12,000-14,000 health-related organizations, with a response rate for each survey around 95%) *showed that* in 1979 "some 51%" of hospital library personnel were professional library staff; 39% were library technicians/library assistants; and 10% were other library staff. Further, 7% of the professional staff earned $7,000-9,999 per year; 49.5% of the professional staff earned $10,000-14,999 per year; and 43.4% of the professional staff earned $15,000-19,999 per year. **(747)**

Special

■ A 1967 survey of medical school libraries concerning reference services (survey size: 93 libraries; responding: 85 or 91.4%) *showed that* the average staffing per library was as follows:

professional	5.2 FTE
nonprofessional	9.1 FTE

continued

reference, professional   1.7 FTE

reference, nonprofessional   0.8 FTE

(682)

■ A study reported in 1983 of 3 surveys made by the American Medical
Association's Division of Library and Archival Services in 1969, 1973, and
1979 concerning the status of health sciences libraries in the U.S. (survey
size for each survey ran between 12,000-14,000 health-related organizations, with a response rate for each survey around 95%) *showed that* in
1979 "some 51%" of hospital library personnel were professional library
staff; 39% were library technicians/library assistants; and 10% were other
library staff. Further, 7% of the professional staff earned $7,000-9,999 per
year; 49.5% of the professional staff earned $10,000-14,999 per year; and
43.4% of the professional staff earned $15,000-19,999 per year.   **(747)**

Staffing Patterns

School

■ A 1983 survey of a systematic sample of school library media centers
concerning data for fiscal year 1982-83 (survey size: 2,000 centers; responding: 1,297; usable: 1,251 or 62%) *showed that* the number of full-time
certified library media specialists per institution was as follows:

1 per school   1,016 (81.2%) respondents
2 per school   141 (11.3%) respondents
3 per school   19 (.15% sic [1.5%]) respondents   **(56)**

Ibid. . . . *showed that* a comparison of schools with (666 schools) and
without (597 schools) district-level library media coordinators revealed
that schools without district coordinators spent more money per student on
resources and had more books per student than schools with district
coordinators. However, schools with district coordinators paid media
specialists higher salaries, had more AV items per student, had more
clerical assistance, and used more adult volunteers than schools without
district coordinators. Specifically:

total materials expenditure per student in schools with
coordinators averaged $8.80, and in schools without
coordinators averaged $10.92;

average books per student in schools with coordinators
averaged 18, and in schools without coordinators averaged 20;

number of AV items per student in schools with coordinators

averaged 3.45, and in schools without coordinators averaged 3.03;

media specialist salary in schools with coordinators averaged $20,699, and in schools without coordinators averaged $19,354;

the number of clerical assistants and adult volunteers in schools with coordinators averaged .83 and 2.46, respectively, and in schools without coordinators averaged .77 and 1.85, respectively. **(56)**

Staffing Standards

Academic

■ A study of 1977 survey information gathered by the National Center for Educational Statistics (U.S. Office of Education) concerning the degree to which 1,146 college and university libraries (Liberal Arts Colleges I and II; Comprehensive Universities and Colleges I and II) met the 1975 Standards for College Libraries (ACRL) *showed that* 81% of the libraries fell below the standard in terms of the number of professional librarians needed based on number of students, book collection size, and annual book acquisitions. The average and median number of professional positions needed per library was 2, although 34% of the libraries needed 4 or more professional staff to meet standards. **(486)**

Ibid. . . . *showed that* over half of the libraries had insufficient nonprofessional staff support and fell below the standard in terms of the ratio of professional staff to nonprofessional staff. Standards specify that no more than 25% (ratio of 1 to 3) to 35% (ratio of 1 to 1.9) of the staff should be professional, while the average ratio of professionals to nonprofessionals was 1 to 1.1 and the median was 1 to 1.0. **(486)**

■ A study reported in 1981 of data on 1,146 2-year colleges, as reported in the 1977 Higher Education General Information Surveys and compared to the 1979 Association of College and Research Libraries standards, *showed that* in terms of professional library staff the numbers of schools meeting minimum standards (by enrollment ranges of FTE students) were as follows:

less than 1,000 students
 (2 staff minimum) 39% met standards
1,000 to 2,999 students
 (2.5 staff minimum) 70% met standards

continued

3,000 to 4,999 students
    (3.5 staff minimum)   65% met standards
5,000 to 6,999 students
    (6 staff minimum)   32% met standards
7,000 to 8,999 students
    (7 staff minimum)   46% met standards
9,000 to 10,999 students
    (8 staff minimum)   73% met standards

Further, in terms of library support staff, the number of schools that met minimum standards ranged from 5% of the schools with less than 1,000 FTE students to 33% of the schools with 9,000 to 10,999 FTE students.
(500)

Student Workers

Academic

■ A survey of the time spent by student workers on various library tasks undertaken at Bowling Green State University in academic 1975-76 *showed that* the most time-consuming tasks library-wide were:

shelving	17.2%
monitoring (e.g., security)	13.4%
checking out materials	8.0%
checking in materials	5.8% **(033)**

■ A study of 1977 survey information gathered by the National Center for Educational Statistics (U.S. Office of Education) concerning the degree to which 1,146 college and university libraries (Liberal Arts Colleges I and II; Comprehensive Universities and Colleges I and II) met the 1975 Standards for College Libraries (ACRL) *showed that* the average annual number of student hours worked in the reporting libraries was 10,600 hours, while the median was 6,400 hours. **(486)**

■ A survey of circulation staff (including supervisors, clerks, and students) activity at the University of Illinois, Urbana, in 1978, based on 4,304 random checks of activity during 44 randomly selected days, *showed that* the activity that accounted for the largest percentage of time for circulation student staff was absenteeism, which involved 26.4% of student staff time.
(119)

■ A study reported in 1981 of data on 1,146 2-year colleges, as reported in the 1977 Higher Education General Information Surveys and compared to the 1979 Association of College and Research Libraries standards, *showed that* hours of student assistance averaged 3,360 per school annually overall, while the hours of student assistance in 186 private schools averaged 1,860 annually and in the public schools 3,690 annually. **(500)**

Turnover—Nonprofessional Staff

Academic

■ A 1971-72 survey of full-time employees (both professional and nonprofessional) in 3 U.S. university libraries in selected departments (book selection, acquisitions, cataloging, circulation, and reference) concerning job satisfaction as measured by the Hage/Aiken satisfaction scale (survey size: 521 librarians; responding: 384 or 73%) *showed that*, of 137 professionals, 24 (17%) reported they intended to leave the full-time work force or go into another type of work within 5 years (12 of the 24 respondents were over the age of 55, which suggested that retirement was the reason for leaving). On the other hand, 54 (40%) of the professionals and 67 (27%) of the nonprofessionals reported that they expected to be working in the same library in 5 years' time. **(806)**

Turnover—Professional Staff

General

■ A survey in 1970 of all libraries of all types in the 3-county Detroit metropolitan area conducted by the Wayne State University Department of Library Science (116 libraries responding, including 57% of the school libraries, 94% of the academic libraries, 80% of the special libraries, and 92% of the public libraries) *showed that* a total of 559 librarians resigned during the 5 years previous to the survey, constituting the following percentages of the total professional workforce of the following types of libraries:

LIBRARY TYPE	% PROFESSIONAL WORKFORCE	
school libraries	28	
academic libraries	39	
special libraries	64	
public libraries	85	**(086)**

Ibid. . . . *showed that*, of 559 librarians who resigned during the five years previous to the survey, the following estimated percentages of the total professional workforce by library type left the profession:

LIBRARY TYPE	% PROFESSIONAL WORKFORCE	
school libraries	30	
academic libraries	16	
special libraries	29	
public libraries	34	(086)

Ibid. . . . *showed that* 75% of all libraries of all types reported no preference for any particular age level, while 25% indicated their greatest need was for librarians under 35 years of age; the need for black librarians was reported only by the large public and school library systems; and 4 school districts and 10 public libraries reported their greatest need was for male librarians.   (086)

Academic

■ A 1971-72 survey of full-time employees (both professional and nonprofessional) in 3 U.S. university libraries in selected departments (book selection, acquisitions, cataloging, circulation, and reference) concerning job satisfaction as measured by the Hage/Aiken satisfaction scale (survey size: 521 librarians; responding: 384 or 73%) *showed that*, of 137 professionals, 24 (17%) reported they intended to leave the full-time work force or go into another type of work within 5 years (12 of the 24 respondents were over the age of 55, which suggested that retirement was the reason for leaving). On the other hand, 54 (40%) of the professionals and 67 (27%) of the nonprofessionals reported that they expected to be working in the same library in 5 years' time.   (806)

Workload—Professional Staff

General

■ A 1968 survey of library staff members belonging to the Staff Organization Round Table (SORT) of ALA who did not have collective bargaining contracts (2,185 individuals responding, including 1,047 from large public libraries, 614 from small public libraries, and 524 from academic libraries; 39% professionals, 14% subprofessionals, and 46% nonprofessionals) *showed that* the following ratios obtained between librarians and populations/enrollments:

public elementary & secondary schools: .57 librarians/1,000 enrollees
college & university libraries: 2.7 librarians/1,000 enrollees

public libraries: .11 librarians/1,000 population
special libraries: .054 librarians/1,000 population **(074)**

Academic

■ A study published in 1980 of how 17 public service librarians spent their work time, based on a minute-by-minute account of 5 days selected over a 6-week period, *showed that* their priorities as a group by time spent were as follows:

reference	13.5 hours
professional development	9.0 hours
meetings	6.4 hours
acquisitions (i.e., selection)	5.7 hours
processing	3.6 hours
miscellaneous	1.8 hours **(030)**

3.

Buildings and Equipment

Audiovisual

General

■ A 1980-81 survey of 198 U.S. libraries with cable facilities (86 or 43% response rate including 63 public libraries, 18 academic, 4 school, and 1 special library) *showed that* 33 (39%) respondents reported the ability to both transmit and receive video; 29 (34%) reported ability to receive only—regular CATV subscriber; 14 (16%) reported no CATV connection; 9 (10%) reported no CATV in their area; and 1 (1%) did not answer.
(341)

Ibid. . . . *showed that* 43 respondents were categorized as technically able to immediately participate in a national video-teleconferencing network in that they were currently connected with an operational cable system with a satellite receiving station that had excess capacity. The remaining libraries reported lacking one of the above technical features or (in the case of 5 respondents) indicated no interest in joining such a network.   **(341)**

Academic

■ A 1972 survey of chief library administrators in public comprehensive community colleges (population: 586; usable responses: 75.9% [no raw number given]) *showed that* types of holdings were as follows:

slides, records, filmstrips, audiotapes and microforms	90.0% respondents
transparencies	83.2% respondents
films	74.2% respondents
videotape	69.5% respondents
self-instructional carrels with media outlets	64.6% respondents **(452)**

■ A study reported in 1975 of the degree to which 2-year college libraries (sample size: 26; responding: 23) in the state of Ohio conformed to the "Guidelines for Two-Year College Learning Resources Programs" established by the ACRL Board of Directors in 1972 *showed that* half of the learning resource centers provided autotutorial carrels of some sort, a third had learning laboratory services and telecommunication production, but almost none provided computer services, campus duplicating (other than library photocopying), printing services, or dial access services.   **(127)**

Ibid. . . . *showed that* more than a third did not have control over or records for the location of learning equipment; however, most did control and keep catalogs of all learning materials.   **(127)**

■ A survey reported in 1983 of Medical Library Association institutional members concerning their use of audiovisual materials (survey size: 300; responding: 201; usable: 198 or 66%) *showed that* 65 (33%) respondents reported providing no AV services of any kind, while 143 (77%) respondents did provide some sort of AV service.   **(750)**

Ibid. . . . *showed that*, of 143 respondents (91 hospital, 29 medical school, and 13 "other" libraries) that did provide AV services, the numbers of libraries collecting the various types of AV materials were as follows:

audiocassettes: collected by 91% of the hospital, 79% of the medical school, and 77% of the other libraries;

videocassettes: collected by 88% of the hospital, 90% of the medical school, and 77% of the other libraries;

filmstrips/cassettes: collected by 82% of the hospital, 76% of the medical school, and 77% of the other libraries;

slide/cassettes: collected by 80% of the hospital, 86% of the medical school, and 85% of the other libraries;

films (both 16 mm and super 8): collected by 62% of the hospital, 76% of the medical school, and 85% of the other libraries;

color microfiche: collected by 52% of the hospital, 62% of the medical school, and 70% of the other libraries.   **(750)**

Ibid. . . . *showed that* of 143 respondents (91 hospital, 29 medical school, and 13 "other" libraries) that did provide AV services, the 2 most frequently consulted sources for the acquisition of AV hardware were colleagues and reviews in AV journals. For example, (multiple responses allowed):

recommendation by colleagues was reported as a source of information on AV hardware by 79% of the hospital, 71% of the medical school, and 70% of the other libraries;

reviews in AV journals were reported as a source of information on AV hardware by 44% of the hospital, 43% of the medical school, and 40% of the other libraries.   **(750)**

Special

■ A 1972 study of audiovisual use in U.S. law schools undertaken by the American Association of Law Libraries Audio-Visual Committee (population: 149 law schools taken from the 1970 edition of the *Directory of Law Libraries*; responding: 142 or 95.3%) *showed that* the five types of AV equipment most frequently reported as permanently located in the law school were:

microcard reader	(52.82% respondents)	
microfilm reader	(51.41% respondents)	
microfiche reader	(48.59% respondents)	
cassette tape recorder	(48.59% respondents)	
standard tape recorder	(32.39% respondents)	**(387)**

Ibid. . . . *showed that* the 4 types of AV media most commonly reported as heavily used (i.e. more than several times a year) were: standard TV receiver (20.59% respondents), television camera (16.28% respondents), videotape recorder (14.00% respondents), and a cassette tape recorder (12.93% respondents). **(387)**

■ A survey reported in 1983 of Medical Library Association institutional members concerning their use of audiovisual materials (survey size: 300; responding: 201; usable: 198 or 66%) *showed that* 65 (33%) respondents reported providing no AV services of any kind, while 143 (77%) respondents did provide some sort of AV service. **(750)**

Ibid. . . . *showed that* of 143 respondents (91 hospital, 29 medical school, and 13 "other" libraries) that did provide AV services, the numbers of libraries collecting the various types of AV materials were as follows:

audiocassettes: collected by 91% of the hospital, 79% of the medical school, and 77% of the other libraries;

videocassettes: collected by 88% of the hospital, 90% of the medical school, and 77% of the other libraries;

filmstrips/cassettes: collected by 82% of the hospital, 76% of the medical school, and 77% of the other libraries;

slide/cassettes: collected by 80% of the hospital, 86% of the medical school, and 85% of the other libraries;

films (both 16 mm and super 8): collected by 62% of the hospital, 76% of the medical school, and 85% of the other libraries;

color microfiche: collected by 52% of the hospital, 62% of the medical school, and 70% of the other libraries. **(750)**

Ibid. . . . *showed that* of 143 respondents (91 hospital, 29 medical school, and 13 "other" libraries) that did provide AV services, the 2 most frequently consulted sources for the acquisition of AV hardware were colleagues and reviews in AV journals. For example, (multiple responses allowed):

> recommendation by colleagues was reported as a source of information on AV hardware by 79% of the hospital, 71% of the medical school, and 70% of the other libraries;

> reviews in AV journals were reported as a source of information on AV hardware by 44% of the hospital, 43% of the medical school, and 40% of the other libraries.   **(750)**

Automation

General

■ A review of data provided by 3 "leading educational research firms" (Quality Education Data, TALMIS, and Market Data Retrieval) concerning use of microcomputers in U.S. schools *showed that*, as of Fall 1982, the number of schools with microcomputers by type of school was as follows:

> elementary schools: 21% had microcomputers with 67% of them keeping the computer in the resource or media center;

> junior high schools: 30% had microcomputers with 71% of them keeping the computer in the resource center;

> high schools: 60% had microcomputers with 42% of them keeping the computer in the resource center.   **(309)**

Academic

■ A 1974 comparison of a semiautomated (Mohawk punched card) system vs. manual circulation system at Colorado State University *showed that* the unit costs of the manual system were $0.365 vs. $0.474 for the automated system, an increase of 29.9%.   **(331)**

■ A study reported in 1977 at the University of Minnesota Twin Cities campus concerning attitudes held by heads of academic units toward departmental libraries independent of the university library system (sample size: 167; responding: 108 or 64.7% including 67 respondents with independent departmental libraries and 41 respondents without such libraries) *showed that*, while 88% of both groups indicated that an online terminal for interface with the official library system would be "helpful" or "essential," 31% of the respondents with independent department libraries and 20% of the respondents without independent departmental libraries rated the terminals as "essential."   **(451)**

■ A 1979 survey of academic libraries listed in the 1979 edition of *OCLC Participating Libraries Arranged by Network and Institution* (survey size: 200 libraries; responding: 166 or 83%) *showed that* of 163 respondents the number of OCLC terminals used for cataloging per library was as follows:

1 terminal	104 (63.8%)	libraries
2 terminals	36 (22.1%)	libraries
3 terminals	8 (4.9%)	libraries
4 terminals	9 (5.5%)	libraries
5-17 terminals	6 (3.7%)	libraries **(764)**

■ A 1981 survey of U.S. depository libraries, both academic and public (sample size: 221; responding: 171 or 77%), concerning their use of online data bases (DIALOG, ORBIT, and BRS), particularly with regard to government documents *showed that* 35% of the academic libraries and 65% of the public libraries did not have online terminals in the library. **(317)**

Ibid. . . . *showed that* the 2 main reasons academic depository librarians reported for not doing online searching were that other librarians do online data base searching (53%), and that no terminals were available (35%); while the 2 main reasons public depository librarians reported for not doing online searching were no terminals (60%) and no money available (38%). **(317)**

Public

■ A 1981 survey of U.S. depository libraries, both academic and public (sample size: 221; responding: 171 or 77%), concerning their use of online data bases (DIALOG, ORBIT, and BRS), particularly with regard to government documents *showed that* 35% of the academic libraries and 65% of the public libraries did not have online terminals in the library. **(317)**

Ibid. . . . *showed that* the 2 main reasons academic depository librarians reported for not doing online searching were that other librarians do online data base searching (53%), and that no terminals were available (35%);

while the 2 main reasons public depository librarians reported for not doing online searching were no terminals (60%) and no money available (38%). **(317)**

School

■ A 1983 survey of a systematic sample of school library media centers concerning data for fiscal year 1982-83 (survey size: 2,000 centers; responding: 1,297; usable: 1,251 or 62%) *showed that* the use of microcomputers by type of library was as follows [total respondents for each type of library not given]:

> elementary schools: 186 centers reported an average of 2.46 microcomputers located in the library media center, while 84 centers reported an average of 3.69 microcomputers located outside of the media center but managed by the media specialists;

> junior high/middle schools: 70 centers reported an average of 2.0 microcomputers located in the library media center, while 22 centers reported an average of 4.09 microcomputers located outside of the media center but managed by the media specialists;

> senior high school: 96 centers reported an average of 2.52 microcomputers located in the library media center, while 32 reported an average of 5.75 microcomputers located outside of the media center but managed by the media specialists;

> combination of the above schools: 9 centers reported an average of 2.0 microcomputers located in the library media center, while 6 centers reported an average of 7.33 microcomputers located outside of the media center but managed by the media specialists. **(056)**

Ibid. . . . *showed that* [in 1982-83] the average expenditure for microcomputer software reported by 81 elementary centers was $595; for 37 junior high/middle school centers was $322; for 46 senior high centers was $381; and for 5 combinations of the above schools was $523. **(056)**

Special

■ A study reported in 1978 of LEXIS subscribers in 4 different cities (Cleveland, Chicago, New York City, and Washington, D.C.) (sample size: 62; responding: 39; usable: 38 or 61.3%) involving 35 law firms, 2 law schools, and 1 government agency *showed that* 31 (81.6%) of the respondents had 1 LEXIS terminal, 6 (15.8%) had 2 LEXIS terminals, and 1 (2.6%) had more than 2 LEXIS terminals. **(359)**

Ibid. . . . *showed that* 15 (39.5%) respondents had had a LEXIS terminal for more than 2 years, 11 (28.9%) had had such a terminal for 1-2 years, 8 (21.1%) had had one for 1/2 to 1 year, and 4 (10.5%) had had one for less than 1/2 year. **(359)**

Ibid. . . . *showed that* of 41 terminals, 32 (78.1%) were located in the library or adjacent office, 1 (2.4%) was located in the librarian's office, 6 (14.6%) were located in an assigned office, and 2 (4.9%) were located in branch offices. **(359)**

Carrels

Academic

■ A 1964-67 study of northern California university, 4-year college, and 2-year college libraries (including 1 Oregon library) *showed that* the 3 aspects of the physical library environment that 1,112 students at 16 institutions most often rated as needing improvement were snack facilities (53%), number of carrels (44%), and quietness (44%). **(244)**

■ A survey reported in 1968 of 32 urban universities (32 responding; 24 usable responses) concerning faculty studies ("a small enclosed area of individual study; not an open study station") in the library *showed that* 65% of the libraries had faculty studies. **(180)**

Ibid. . . . *showed that* the ratio of faculty to faculty studies in institutions where the number of faculty studies was reported as inadequate (82% of respondents) ranged from 4.0:1 (126 studies) to 337.0:1 (8 studies), while the ratio of faculty to faculty studies in institutions where the number of faculty studies was reported as adequate (18% of respondents) ranged from 1.6:1 (238 studies) to 31.0:1 (48 studies). **(180)**

Ibid. . . . *showed that* 66% of responding libraries did not use a separate circulation policy for faculty studies. **(180)**

Ibid. . . . *showed that* smoking was permitted in faculty studies by 71% of responding libraries, while none of the libraries permitted eating or drinking in faculty studies. However, 80% of respondents reported housekeeping problems along these lines. **(180)**

■ A 1979 survey of libraries in accredited North American veterinary schools (population: 25 libraries; responding: 23 or 92%) *showed that*, of the 18 veterinary libraries housed separately, the physical size of the library ranged from 2,163 square feet at Tuskegee to 15,437 square feet at Kansas State University, with the average veterinary library occupying 5,785 square feet of space. The number of reader stations available ranged from 33 at Washington State University to 225 at Iowa State University, with the average veterinary library providing 120 reader stations.   **(740)**

Special

■ A 1979 survey of libraries in accredited North American veterinary schools (population: 25 libraries; responding: 23 or 92%) *showed that* of the 18 veterinary libraries housed separately, the physical size of the library ranged from 2,163 square feet at Tuskegee to 15,437 square feet at Kansas State University, with the average veterinary library occupying 5,785 square feet of space. The number of reader stations available ranged from 33 at Washington State University to 225 at Iowa State University, with the average veterinary library providing 120 reader stations.   **(740)**

Comfort

Special

■ A 1973 survey of all county law libraries listed in the 1972 American Association of Law Libraries' *Directory of Law Libraries* (population: 260; responding: 86 or 33.1%) *showed that*, of 85 respondents reporting on comfort in their libraries, 21 (24.7%) reported "excellent," 32 (37.6%) reported "good," 23 (27.1%) reported "fair," and 9 (10.6%) reported "poor."   **(392)**

General Equipment

Academic

■ A 1964-67 study of northern California university, 4-year college, and 2-year college libraries (including 1 Oregon library) *showed that* the 3 aspects of the physical library environment that 1,112 students at 16 institutions most often rated as needing improvement were snack facilities (53%), number of carrels (44%), and quietness (44%).   **(244)**

■ A 1967 survey by the Institute of Higher Education at Teachers College, Columbia University, of innovative programs in libraries in academic institutions with liberal arts programs (sample size: 1,193;

responding 781 or 65%) *showed that* 578 (74%) of responding libraries had copying machines, of which 476 (61%) libraries reported having them only since 1961. 32 libraries (4%) were planning to make copying machines available at the time of the study. 330 (42%) libraries reported the presence of reader-printers, and an additional 134 (17%) reported plans to install reader-printers at the time of the study. **(190)**

■ A 1978 survey of academic law libraries concerning the issue of faculty libraries (a separate collection or library set aside for the use of the law faculty) (survey size: 169 libraries; responding: 115 or 68.0%) *showed that* 16 (22.9%) respondents allowed student access to the faculty library, while 54 (77.1%) did not. Further, 41 (58.6%) respondents reported that the faculty library was not set up as a reading room only. "Many of these facilities have kitchens within the faculty library," while 12 (17.1%) respondents reported carrels located in the faculty library. **(795)**

■ A 1979 survey of libraries in accredited North American veterinary schools (population: 25 libraries; responding: 23 or 92%) *showed that* all respondents reported that online search services were available. 10 (43.5%) libraries reported they had their own terminals, 22 (95.7%) reported direct or indirect access to the National Library of Medicine data bases and 19 (82.6%) reported access to Lockheed or Systems Development Corporation data bases. **(740)**

■ A 1981 survey of U.S. depository libraries, both academic and public (sample size: 221; responding: 171 or 77%) concerning their use of online data bases (DIALOG, ORBIT and BRS) particularly with regard to government documents *showed that* 35% of the academic libraries and 65% of the public libraries did not have online terminals in the library. **(317)**

Ibid. . . . *showed that* the two main reasons academic depository librarians reported for not doing online searching were that other librarians do online data base searching (53%), and that no terminals were available (35%); while the two main reasons public depository librarians reported for not doing online searching were no terminals (60%) and no money available (38%). **(317)**

Ibid. . . . *showed that* the top 3 reasons given by respondents for not ordering government documents microfiche as the result of an online search were: library does not have computer terminals (academic depositories, 33%; public depositories, 59%), didn't know that microfiche government documents could be ordered online (academic depositories, 24%; public depositories, 25%) and prefer hard copy to microfiche copy (academic depositories, 27%; public depositories, 20%).   **(317)**

Public

■ A 1981 survey of U.S. depository libraries, both academic and public (sample size: 221; responding: 171 or 77%), concerning their use of online data bases (DIALOG, ORBIT, and BRS), particularly with regard to government documents *showed that* 35% of the academic libraries and 65% of the public libraries did not have online terminals in the library.
(317)

Ibid. . . . *showed that* the 2 main reasons academic depository librarians reported for not doing online searching were that other librarians do online data base searching (53%), and that no terminals were available (35%); while the two main reasons public depository librarians reported for not doing online searching were no terminals (60%) and no money available (38%).   **(317)**

Ibid. . . . *showed that* the top 3 reasons given by respondents for not ordering government documents microfiche as the result of an online search were: library does not have computer terminals (academic depositories, 33%; public depositories, 59%), didn't know that microfiche government documents could be ordered online (academic depositories, 24%; public depositories, 25%) and prefer hard copy to microfiche copy (academic depositories, 27%; public depositories, 20%).   **(317)**

Special

■ A 1978 survey of academic law libraries concerning the issue of faculty libraries (a separate collection or library set aside for the use of the law faculty) (survey size: 169 libraries; responding: 115 or 68.0%) *showed that* 16 (22.9%) respondents allowed student access to the faculty library, while 54 (77.1%) did not. Further, 41 (58.6%) respondents reported that the faculty library was not set up as a reading room only. "Many of these facilities have kitchens within the faculty library," while 12 (17.1%) respondents reported carrels located in the faculty library.   **(795)**

■ A study reported in 1978 of LEXIS subscribers in 4 different cities (Cleveland, Chicago, New York City and Washington, D.C.) (sample size: 62; responding: 39; usable: 38 or 61.3%) involving 35 law firms, 2 law schools and 1 government agency *showed that* 31 (81.6%) of the respondents had 1 LEXIS terminal, 6 (15.8%) had 2 LEXIS terminals, and 1 (2.6%) had more than 2 LEXIS terminals.   **(359)**

Ibid. . . . *showed that* 15 (39.5%) respondents had had a LEXIS terminal for more than 2 years, 11 (28.9%) had had such a terminal for 1-2 years, 8 (21.1%) had had one for 1/2 to 1 year, and 4 (10.5%) had had one for less than 1/2 year.   **(359)**

Ibid. . . . *showed that* of 41 terminals, 32 (78.1%) were located in the library or adjacent office, 1 (2.4%) was located in the librarian's office, 6 (14.6%) were located in an assigned office and 2 (4.9%) were located in branch offices.   **(359)**

■ A 1979 survey of libraries in accredited North American veterinary schools (population: 25 libraries; responding: 23 or 92%) *showed that* all respondents reported that online search services were available. 10 (43.5%) libraries reported they had their own terminals, 22 (95.7%) reported direct or indirect access to the National Library of Medicine data bases and 19 (82.6%) reported access to Lockheed or Systems Development Corporation data bases.   **(740)**

Handicapped Needs

Academic

■ A 1976 study at Ohio State University of visually impaired students (population 38; surveyed, i.e., who could be reached: 26 including 6 blind students and 20 partially sighted students) concerning their special equipment needs *showed that* 4 of the blind students reported a need for a braille writer; 1 blind student reported a need for an Optacon; 4 of the partially sighted students reported a need for a television-type magnifier; and 16 of both blind and partially sighted groups reported a need for a tape recorder. 7 of the partially sighted students reported no need for any of the equipment.   **(462)**

Ibid. . . . *showed that* 9 (45.0%) of the partially sighted students and 1 (16.7%) of the blind students reported using none of the available library equipment for the visually impaired.   **(462)**

Public

■ A 1971 survey of Canadian public libraries serving communities with populations of more than 8,000 people conducted by the Adult Services Section of the Canadian Library Association concerning service to the physically handicapped (survey size: 222; responding: 111 or 50%) *showed that* the number of libraries providing various special materials was as follows:

large print books	90	(81.1%) libraries
films	64	(57.7%) libraries
cassettes	23	(20.7%) libraries
cassette players	16	(14.4%) libraries
opaque projectors	9	(8.1%) libraries
overhead projectors	7	(6.3%) libraries
talking books	4	(3.6%) libraries
talking book machines	3	(2.7%) libraries (540)

Ibid. . . . *showed that* the following number of libraries provided the following types of services or facilities for handicapped patrons:

home delivery service	46	(41.4%) libraries
wheel chair ramps, elevators	31	(27.9%) libraries
books or other material by mail	24	(21.6%) libraries
programs for the handicapped	13	(11.7%) libraries
television/radio programs	3	(2.7%) libraries
deposit collections:		
senior citizen homes	60	(54.1%) libraries
nursing homes	32	(28.8%) libraries
hospitals	28	(25.2%) libraries
senior citizen centers	22	(19.8%) libraries
drop-in centers	4	(3.6%) libraries
other	14	(12.6%) libraries (540)

Microforms

Academic

■ An investigation reported in 1960 into the comparative differences between microfilm and bound periodical volumes at Colby Junior College (New London, New Hampshire) and Abraham Baldwin College (Tifton, Georgia) *showed that* storing bound volumes of journals on traditional stack shelving required approximately 7.5 times as many cubic feet and 4.6 times as many square feet of storage space as storing the same number of volumes of microfilm. This is based on a 9-drawer microfilm cabinet requiring 167.2 cubic feet of space and holding 540 reels of microfilm or an estimated 725 periodicals volumes. (107)

■ A 1967 survey by the Institute of Higher Education at Teachers College, Columbia University, of innovative programs in libraries in academic institutions with liberal arts programs (sample size: 1193; responding 781 or 65%) *showed that* 578 (74%) of responding libraries had copying machines, of which 476 (61%) libraries reported having them only since 1961. 32 libraries (4%) were planning to make copying machines available at the time of the study. 330 (42%) libraries reported presence of reader-printers, and an additional 134 (17%) reported plans to install reader-printers at the time of the study.   **(190)**

■ A study reported in 1981 at San Jose State University Library comparing graduate library school students' lookup speeds of 16 entries (3 author, 8 title/added entries, and 5 subject entries) in fiche vs. microfilm forms of a dictionary public library catalog with 436,791 entries (using a Micro-Desing 4020 fiche reader and an Information Design ROM 3 film reader) *showed that* the average speed of the film users was 16.7 minutes compared to 25.3 minutes for the fiche users. (This was a statistically significant difference at the .01 level.)   **(340)**

■ A 1982 survey of economics and political science faculty members in 9 colleges and universities serving as academic depository institutions in Massachusetts for the Government Printing Office (sample size: 216 faculty members, including 105 economists and 111 political scientists; responding: 155 or 71.8%, including 86 economists and 69 political scientists) *showed that* 120 (6%) of the 125 respondents who reported using federal government documents reported that they did not have ready access to microform readers in their office, department, or home. Only 5 reported immediate access to viewing equipment outside the central library.   **(316)**

Parking

Public

■ A 1966 survey of 21,385 adult (12 years old or older) public library users in the Baltimore-Washington metropolitan region of Maryland who entered the library during a 6-week period (79.1% of patrons approached filled out the survey instrument) *showed that* 67.9% of the respondents traveled to the library by car, 24.6% walked, and 4.9% traveled by bus. According to self-report, 39.7% of the respondents traveled less than 1 mile, 44.4% between 1 and 5 miles, 9.1% between 5 and 10 miles, 3.5% between 10 and 15 miles, 1.8% over 15 miles, and 1.5% did not respond.   **(301)**

Ibid. . . . *showed that* the top 3 difficulties given by 5,029 respondents in trying to use the library were getting parking space (9.2%), library too noisy (5.4%), and difficult to figure out the library arrangement (4.7%).   **(301)**

■ A survey reported in 1978 of all libraries reporting in *Library Journal* that they had completed main and branch buildings with on-site parking in FY 1972, 1973, and 1974 (population: 150; responding 108 or 72%, including 72 main buildings and 36 branches) *showed that*, of the 38 respondents willing to state an opinion for a standard, the "prevailing opinion" was that 1 square foot of parking should be allowed for each square foot of public library building.   **(228)**

Ibid. . . . *showed that* the average number of parking spaces per square foot of library building was .0025 for main library buildings and .0034 spaces per square foot for branch library buildings.   **(228)**

■ A questionnaire survey of 3,500 public library cardholders in 5 medium-sized Pennsylvania cities in conjunction with interviews of a randomly selected sample of householders in 1 city by the Institute of Public Administration (at Pennsylvania State University) under contract to the Pennsylvania State Library in 1965 *showed that* the most consistent criticism of the library was the absence of adequate patron parking space. Criticism of the building, the collection, and the reference materials all took second place to parking. The importance of parking was also shown in that improved parking accommodations were given more often as the most important change patrons recommended for improving library service in 4 out of 5 cities.   **(084)**

Physical Layout

Academic

■ A 1978 study at the State University of New York College at Cortland concerning seating arrangements and noise levels as measured by accoustical equipment and survey questionnaires *showed that* replacing tables and upholstered chairs in the central area with individual study carrels and distributing the tables and upholstered chairs thoughout the floor did not reduce the frequency of bursts of noise over 50 decibels. However subjective ratings of noise levels by students using the library decreased from an average of 4.38 (scale of 10 with 1 = quiet, 10 = noisy; 438 students sampled) to 3.90 (347 students sampled), while annoyance ratings decreased from an average of 4.13 to 3.61 . Both changes were statistically significant at the .005 level.   **(501)**

Ibid. . . . *showed that* after the furniture had been rearranged [no sample size or raw numbers given] 64% of the students reported that the affected floors were "very much" or "somewhat" quieter, 24% reported "no difference," 4% reported that the floors were "noisier," and 8% did not respond.   **(501)**

Ibid. . . . *showed that* after the furniture had been rearranged [no sample size or raw numbers given] 47% of the students reported that they liked the change, 25% were indifferent, and 28% disliked the change. Further, 44% reported being able to accomplish more work, 52% reported no difference in work accomplished, and 4% reported being able to do less work. (Both of these distributions were significantly statistically different from chance at the .001 level.) **(501)**

■ A 1979 survey of libraries in accredited North American veterinary schools (population: 25 libraries; responding: 23 or 92%) *showed that,* of the 18 veterinary libraries housed separately, the physical size of the library ranged from 2,163 square feet at Tuskegee to 15,437 square feet at Kansas State University, with the average veterinary library occupying 5,785 square feet of space. The number of reader stations available ranged from 33 at Washington State University to 225 at Iowa State University, with the average veterinary library providing 120 reader stations. **(740)**

■ A survey reported in 1981 of bibliographic instruction in business school libraries (sample size: 120 libraries; responding: 65; usable: 61 or 50.8%) *showed that* 28 (45.9%) of the business school libraries were located in the same building as the business school while 33 (54.1%) were located in the main library building. Of these 33, 14% had separate collections while 86% had their collections in the general stacks. **(436)**

Special

■ A 1979 survey of libraries in accredited North American veterinary schools (population: 25 libraries; responding: 23 or 92%) *showed that,* of the 18 veterinary libraries housed separately, the physical size of the library ranged from 2,163 square feet at Tuskegee to 15,437 square feet at Kansas State University, with the average veterinary library occupying 5,785 square feet of space. The number of reader stations available ranged from 33 at Washington State University to 225 at Iowa State University, with the average veterinary library providing 120 reader stations. **(740)**

Space Needs

Special

■ A 1972 survey of prison law libraries (sample size: 90; responding: 68% [no number given, 62 assumed]) *showed that* 41 (66.1%) of the prison law libraries had separate law library quarters. **(389)**

Ibid. . . . *showed that* 14 (22.6%) of the prison law libraries could comfortably seat 1-5 inmates; 9 (14.5%) could comfortably seat 6-10 inmates; 12 (19.4%) could comfortably seat 11-20 inmates; and 7 (11.3%) could comfortably seat 20+ inmates. No data provided on missing respondents.
(389)

■ A 1973 survey of all county law libraries listed in the 1972 American Association of Law Libraries *Directory of Law Libraries* (population: 260; responding: 86 or 33.1%) *showed that*, of 84 respondents, 18 (21%) reported their quarters as "excellent" in terms of size, 25 (30%) reported it as "good" in terms of size, 15 (18%) reported it as "fair" in terms of size, and 26 (31%) reported it as "poor" in terms of size.   **(392)**

■ A survey reported in 1978 of the 50 state law libraries (40 or 80% responding) *showed that* the 6 (out of 18) most pressing problems they reported facing, listed in descending order of importance based on number of libraries reporting the problem and their rating of its severity were:

> increased demands for photocopy service
> not enough shelf space
> not enough study space (tables, desks,etc.)
> book budget too low
> nonprofessional staff too small
> theft of materials   **(358)**

Stacks

General

■ A review of shelving arrangements by Keys Metcalf *showed that* with ordinary shelving (ranges 55 inches on center), 2/3 of the building space consists of aisles; with very narrow aisles (ranges 40 inches on centers with 24-inch aisles) the space devoted to shelving rises to 40%. With hinged or drawer-type shelving the space devoted to shelving could be increased to approximately 66%; with roller-type compact shelving approximately 80% of the space could be shelving.   **(114)**

Academic

■ An investigation reported in 1960 into the comparative differences between microfilm and bound periodical volumes at Colby Junior College (New London, New Hampshire) and Abraham Baldwin College (Tifton,

Georgia) *showed that* storing bound volumes of journals on traditional stack shelving required approximately 7.5 times as many cubic feet and 4.6 times as many square feet of storage space as storing the same number of volumes of microfilm. This was based on a 9-drawer microfilm cabinet requiring 167.2 cubic feet of space and holding 540 reels of microfilm or an estimated 725 periodicals volumes.   (107)

■ A study of the effect of meeting standards for the handicapped in New York State *showed that* increasing aisle width from 3 feet to 4 feet to accommodate wheelchair patrons would reduce stack capacity by 23%.
(052)

■ A 1981 study in the science section of the University of Guelph Library (Canada) of the amount of shelf space an average item required, based on sampling "several thousand items in the monograph and serials collection" *showed that* an average size of 1.13 linear inches per monograph volume and 2.18 linear inches per periodical volume was required.   (531)

Special

■ A 1972 survey of prison law libraries (sample size: 90; responding: 68% [no number given, 62 assumed]) *showed that* 26 (41.9%) of the prison law libraries reported 100 linear feet or less of book shelving; 3 (4.8%) reported 101-200 linear feet of book shelving; and 22 (35.5%) reported over 200 linear feet of book shelving. No data provided on missing respondents.   (389)

Storage Costs

Academic

■ An investigation reported in 1960 into the comparative differences between microfilm and bound periodical volumes at Colby Junior College (New London, New Hampshire) and Abraham Baldwin College (Tifton, Georgia) *showed that* the comparative costs of microform storage and use were less than those for bound journals even when initial costs of storage cabinets and readers were factored in. The cost of storing 725 bound volumes was computed at 40.5 square feet at $11.00 per square foot building costs plus $175 for 9 feet of standard shelving ($620.50), compared to building costs for 8.87 square feet plus $500.00 for a storage cabinet and reader for microfilm ($597.57).   (107)

Terminals

Academic

■ A 1979 survey of libraries in accredited North American veterinary schools (population: 25 libraries; responding: 23 or 92%) *showed that* all respondents reported that online search services were available. 10 (43.5%) libraries reported they had their own terminals, 22 (95.7%) reported direct or indirect access to the National Library of Medicine data bases, and 19 (82.6%) reported access to Lockheed or Systems Development Corporation data bases.   **(740)**

BIBLIOGRAPHY OF ARTICLES

Note: This Bibliography cites all articles summarized in the six-volume set of *Handbooks*. Entries in the Bibliography are sequentially arranged by the citation reference numbers that correspond to the numbers appearing at the end of each research summary throughout the six volumes. The numbers in boldface located at the end of some citations refer only to those research summaries contained in this volume. Alphabetic access to the Bibliography is provided through the Author Index.

1 Pamela Kobelski and Jean Trumbore. "Student Use of On-line Bibliographic Services," *Journal of Academic Librarianship* 4:1 (March 1978), 14-18.

2 John V. Richardson, Jr. "Readability and Readership of Journals in Library Science," *Journal of Academic Librarianship* 3:1 (March 1977), 20-22.

3 Elizabeth Gates Kesler. "A Campaign against Mutilation," *Journal of Academic Librarianship* 3:1 (March 1977), 29-30.

4 Bruce Miller and Marilyn Sorum. "A Two Stage Sampling Procedure for Estimating the Proportion of Lost Books in a Library," *Journal of Academic Librarianship* 3:2 (May 1977), 74-80.

5 Jeffrey St. Clair and Rao Aluri. "Staffing the Reference Desk: Professionals or Nonprofessionals," *Journal of Academic Librarianship* 3:3 (July 1977), 149-153.

6 Valentine DeBruin. "Sometimes Dirty Things Are Seen on the Screen," *Journal of Academic Librarianship* 3:5 (November 1977), 256-266.

7 Herbert S. White. "The View from the Library School," *Journal of Academic Librarianship* 3:6 (January 1970), 321.

8 Stella Bentley. "Collective Bargaining and Faculty Status," *Journal of Academic Librarianship* 4:2 (May 1978), 75-81. **(27, 170)**

9 Steven Seokho Chwe. "A Comparative Study of Job Satisfaction: Catalogers and Reference Librarians in University Libraries," *Journal of Academic Librarianship* 4:3 (July 1978), 139-143.

10 Jo Bell Whitlatch and Karen Kieffer. "Service at San Jose State University: Survey of Document Availability," *Journal of Academic Librarianship* 4:4 (September 1978), 196-199.

11 Joan Grant and Susan Perelmuter. "Vendor Performance Evaluation," *Journal of Academic Librarianship* 4:5 (November 1978), 366-367.

12 Robert Goehlert. "Book Availability and Delivery Service," *Journal of Academic Librarianship* 4:5 (November 1978), 368-371.

13 Linda L. Phillips and Ann E. Raup. "Comparing Methods for Teaching Use of Periodical Indexes," *Journal of Academic Librarianship* 4:6 (January 1979), 420-423.

14 Margaret Johnson Bennett, David T. Buxton and Ella Capriotti. "Shelf Reading in a Large, Open Stack Library," *Journal of Academic Librarianship* 5:1 (March 1979), 4-8.

15 Sarah D. Knapp and C. James Schmidt. "Budgeting To Provide Computer-Based Reference Services: A Case Study," *Journal of Academic Librarianship* 5:1 (March 1979), 9-13.

16 Herbert S. White. "Library Materials Prices and Academic Library Practices: Between Scylla and Charybdis," *Journal of Academic Librarianship* 5:1 (March 1979), 20-23. **(19, 20, 21)**

17 Dorothy P. Wells. "Coping with Schedules for Extended Hours: A Survey of Attitudes and Practices," *Journal of Academic Librarianship* 5:1 (March 1979), 24-27.

18 Johanna E. Tallman. "One Year's Experience with CONTU Guidelines for Interlibrary Loan Photocopies," *Journal of Academic Librarianship* 5:2 (May 1979), 71-74.

19 Robert Goehlert. "The Effect of Loan Policies on Circulation Recalls," *Journal of Academic Librarianship* 5:2 (May 1979), 79-82.

20 James R. Dwyer. "Public Response to an Academic Library Microcatalog," *Journal of Academic Librarianship* 5:3 (July 1979), 132-141.

21 Paul Metz. "The Role of the Academic Library Director," *Journal of Academic Librarianship* 5:3 (July 1979), 148-152. **(62)**

22 Anne B. Piternick. "Problems of Resource Sharing with the Community: A Case Study," *Journal of Academic Librarianship* 5:3 (July 1979), 153-158.

23 Shelley Phipps and Ruth Dickstein. "The Library Skills Program at the University of Arizona: Testing, Evaluation and Critique," *Journal of Academic Librarianship* 5:4 (September 1979), 205-214.

24 Michael Stuart Freeman. "Published Study Guides: What They Say about Libraries," *Journal of Academic Librarianship* 5:5 (November 1979), 252-255.

25 James H. Richards, Jr. "Missing Inaction," *Journal of Academic Librarianship* 5:5 (November 1979), 266-269.

26 Philip H. Kitchens. "Engineers Meet the Library," *Journal of Academic Librarianship* 5:5 (November 1979), 277-282.

27 Michael Rouchton. "OCLC Serials Records: Errors, Omissions, and Dependability," *Journal of Academic Librarianship* 5:6 (January 1980), 316-321.

28 Charles R. McClure. "Academic Librarians, Information Sources, and Shared Decision Making," *Journal of Academic Librarianship* 6:1 (March 1980), 9-15. **(24, 25, 62, 63)**

29 Marjorie E. Murfin. "The Myth of Accessibility: Frustration and Failure in Retrieving Periodicals," *Journal of Academic Librarianship* 6:1 (March 1980), 16-19.

30 Anthony W. Ferguson and John R. Taylor. "What Are You Doing? An Analysis of Activities of Public Service Librarians at a Medium-sized Research Library," *Journal of Academic Librarianship* 6:1 (March 1980), 24-29. **(217)**

31 Regina Shelton. "Adaption: A One-Year Survey of Reserve Photocopying," *Journal of Academic Librarianship* 6:2 (May 1980), 74-76.

32 Dorothea M. Thompson. "The Correct Uses of Library Data Bases Can Improve Interlibrary Loan Efficiency," *Journal of Academic Librarianship* 6:2 (May 1980), 83-86.

33 Joan Repp and Julia A. Woods. "Student Appraisal Study and Allocation Formula: Priorities and Equitable Funding in a University Setting," *Journal of Academic Librarianship* 6:2 (May 1980), 87-90. **(214)**

34 Elaine S. Friedman. "Patron Access to Online Cataloging Systems: OCLC in the Public Service Environment," *Journal of Academic Librarianship* 6:3 (July 1980), 132-139.

35 Edward C. Jestes. "Manual vs. Automated Circulation: A Comparison of Operating Costs in a University Library," *Journal of Academic Librarianship* 6:3 (July 1980), 144-150.

36 Kathleen A. Johnson and Barbara S. Plake. "Evaluation of PLATO Library Instructional Lessons: Another View," *Journal of Academic Librarianship* 6:3 (July 1980), 154-158.

37 Priscilla C. Yu. "International Gift and Exchange: The Asian Experience," *Journal of Academic Librarianship* 6:6 (January 1981), 333-338.

38 George W. Black, Jr. "Estimating Collection Size Using the Shelf List in a Science Library," *Journal of Academic Librarianship* (January 1981), 339-341.

39 Beth Macleod. *"Library Journal* and *Choice*: A Review of Reviews," *Journal of Academic Librarianship* 7:1 (March 1981), 23-28.

40 Frank Wm. Goudy. "HEA, Title II-C Grant Awards: A Financial Overview from FY 1978-79 through FY 1981-82," *Journal of Academic Librarianship* 8:5 (November 1982), 264-269. **(77)**

41 Larry Hardesty and John Wright. "Student Library Skills and Attitudes and Their Change: Relationships to Other Selected Variables," *Journal of Academic Librarianship* 8:4 (September 1982), 216-220.

42 Penelope Pearson and Virginia Teufel. "Evaluating Undergraduate Library Instruction at the Ohio State University," *Journal of Academic Librarianship* 7:6 (January 1982), 351-357.

43 David S. Ferrioro. "ARL Directors as Proteges and Mentors," *Journal of Academic Librarianship* 7:6 (January 1982), 358-365. **(64, 65)**

44 Albert F. Maag. "So You Want to be a Director...," *Journal of Academic Librarianship* 7:4 (September 1981), 213-217. **(43, 44)**

45 Mary Noel Gouke and Sue Pease. "Title Searches in an Online Catalog and a Card Catalog: A Comparative Study of Patron Success in Two Libraries," *Journal of Academic Librarianship* 8:3 (July 1982), 137-143.

46 John K. Mayeski and Marilyn T. Sharrow. "Recruitment of Academic Library Managers: A Survey," *Journal of Academic Librarianship* 8:3 (July 1982), 151-154. **(93)**

47 Linda K. Rambler. "Syllabus Study: Key to a Responsive Academic Library," *Journal of Academic Librarianship* 8:3 (July 1982), 155-159.

48 Marion T. Reid. "Effectiveness of the OCLC Data Base for Acquisitions Verification," *Journal of Academic Librarianship* 2:6 (January 1977), 303-326.

49 James D. Culley, Denis F. Healy and Kermit G. Cudd. "Business Students and the University Library: An Overlooked Element in the Business Curriculum," *Journal of Academic Librarianship* 2:6 (January 1977), 293-296.

50 Edward Kazlauskas. "An Exploratory Study: A Kenesic Analysis of Academic Library Service Points," *Journal of Academic Librarianship* 2:3 (July 1976), 130-134.

51 Helen Gothberg. "Immediacy: A Study of Communication Effect on the Reference Process," *Journal of Academic Librarianship* 2:3 (July 1976), 126-129.

52 John Vasi. "Building Libraries for the Handicapped: A Second Look," *Journal of Academic Librarianship* 2:2 (May 1976), 82-83. **(237)**

53 Elliot S. Palais. "The Significance of Subject Dispersion for the Indexing of Political Science Journals," *Journal of Academic Librarianship* 2:2 (May 1976), 72-76.

54 Ruth Carol Cushman. "Lease Plans—A New Lease on Life for Libraries," *Journal of Academic Librarianship* 2:1 (March 1976), 15-19.

55 Charles R. McClure. "Subject and Added Entries as Access to Information," *Journal of Academic Librarianship* 2:1 (March 1976), 9-14.

56 Marilyn L. Miller and Barbara B. Moran. "Expenditures for Resources in School Library Media Centers FY '82-'83," *School Library Journal* 30:2 (October 1983), 105-114. **(82, 86, 163, 226)**

57 Karen Lee Shelley. "The Future of Conservation in Research Libraries," *Journal of Academic Librarianship* 1:6 (January 1976), 15-18.

58 Maryan E. Reynolds. "Challenges of Modern Network Development," *Journal of Academic Librarianship* 1:2 (May 1975), 19-22.

59 Marjorie E. Martin and Clyde Hendrick. "Ripoffs Tell Their Story: Interviews with Mutilators in a University Library," *Journal of Academic Librarianship* 1:2 (May 1975), 8-12.

60 Audrey Tobias. "The Yule Curve Describing Periodical Citations by Freshmen: Essential Tool or Abstract Frill?" *Journal of Academic Librarianship* 1:1 (March 1975), 14-16.

61 Allan J. Dyson. "Organizing Undergraduate Library Instruction," *Journal of Academic Librarianship* 1:1 (March 1975), 9-13.

62 David F. Kohl. "High Efficiency Inventorying through Predictive Data," *Journal of Academic Librarianship* 8:2 (May 1982), 82-84.

63 Eleanor Phinney. "Trends in Public Library Adult Services," *ALA Bulletin* 57:3 (March 1963), 262-266. **(97, 133)**

64 Zelia J. French. "Library-Community Self-studies in Kansas," *ALA Bulletin* 56:1 (January 1962), 37-41.

65 Guy Garrison. "Nonresident Library Fees in Suburban Chicago," *ALA Bulletin* 55:6 (June 1961), 1013-1017. **(171, 172)**

66 James E. Bryan. "The Christmas Holiday Jam," *ALA Bulletin* 55:6 (June 1961), 526-530.

67 Joint Libraries Committee on Fair Use in Photocopying, American Library Association. "Fair Use in Photocopying: Report on Single Copies," *ALA Bulletin* 55:6 (June 1961), 571-573.

68 Henry J. Dubester. "Stack Use of a Research Library," *ALA Bulletin* 55:10 (November 1961), 891-893.

69 Mary Virginia Gaver. "Teacher Education and School Libraries," *ALA Bulletin* 60:1 (January 1966), 63-72.

70 Richard Waters. "Free Space: Can Public Libraries Receive It?" *ALA Bulletin* 58:3 (March 1964), 232-234. **(12)**

71 Frank L. Schick. "Professional Library Manpower," *ALA Bulletin* 58:4 (April 1964), 315-317.

72 Milbrey Jones. "Socio-Economic Factors in Library Service to Students," *ALA Bulletin* 58:11 (December 1964), 1003-1006.

73 Elizabeth W. Stone. "Administrators Fiddle while Employees Burn or Flee," *ALA Bulletin* 63:2 (February 1969), 181-187.

74 Staff Organizations Round Table, American Library Association. "Opinions on Collective Bargaining," *ALA Bulletin* 63:6 (June 1969), 803-808. **(166, 167, 168, 169, 171, 217)**

75 Library Administration Division, American Library Association. "Library Employment of Minority Group Personnel," *ALA Bulletin* 63:7 (July-August 1969), 985-987. **(118, 205)**

76 Eli M. Oboler. "The Case for ALA Regional Annual Conferences," *ALA Bulletin* 63:8 (September 1969), 1099-1101.

77 Edward N. Howard. "Breaking the Fine Barrier," *ALA Bulletin* 63:11 (December 1969), 1541-1545.

78 Elin B. Christianson. "Variation of Editorial Material in Periodicals Indexed in *Reader's Guide*," *ALA Bulletin* 62:2 (February 1968), 173-182.

79 Insurance for Libraries Committee, American Library Association. "The Makings of a Nationwide Scandal," *ALA Bulletin* 62:4 (April 1968), 384-386. **(89)**

80 George L. Gardiner. "Collective Bargaining: Some Questions Asked," *ALA Bulletin* 62:8 (September 1968), 973-976. **(167, 168, 170)**

81 Barbara M. Conant. "Trials and Tribulations of Textbook Price Indexing," *ALA Bulletin* 61:2 (February 1967), 197-199.

82 Henry T. Drennan and Sarah R. Reed. "Library Manpower," *ALA Bulletin* 61:8 (September 1967), 957-965. **(159, 163)**

83 Jerry L. Walker. "Changing Attitudes toward the Library and the Librarian," *ALA Bulletin* 61:8 (September 1967), 977-981. **(136)**

84 William R. Monat. "The Community Library: Its Search for a Vital Purpose," *ALA Bulletin* 61:11 (December 1967), 1301-1310. **(234)**

85 Irene A. Braden. "Pilot Inventory of Library Holdings," *ALA Bulletin* 62:9 (October 1968), 1129-1131.

86 Genevieve Casey. "Library Manpower in the Detroit Metropolitan Region," *American Libraries* 1:8 (September 1970), 787-789. **(190, 215, 216)**

87 Nora Cambier, Barton Clark, Robert Daugherty and Mike Gabriel. "Books in Print 1969: An Analysis of Errors," *American Libraries* 1:9 (October 1970), 901-902.

88 Tom Childers and Beth Krevitt. "Municipal Funding of Library Services," *American Libraries* 3:1 (January 1972), 53-57. **(15)**

89 Albert H. Rubenstein, David J. Werner, Gustave Rath, John A. Kernaghan, and Robert D. O'Keefe. "Search versus Experiment—the Role of the Research Librarian," *College and Research Libraries* 34:4 (July 1973), 280-286.

90 Frank F. Kuo. "A Comparison of Six Versions of Science Library Instruction," *College and Research Libraries* 34:4 (July 1973), 287-290.

91 Laurence Miller. "The role of Circulation Services in the Major University Library," *College and Research Libraries* 34:6 (November 1973), 463-471.

92 Ruth Hyman and Gail Schlachter. "Academic Status: Who Wants It?" *College and Research Libraries* 34:6 (November 1973), 472-478. **(157, 178)**

93 Larry E. Harrelson. "Large Libraries and Information Desks," *College and Research Libraries* 35:1 (January 1974), 21-27.

94 Robert B. Downs. "Library Resources in the United States," *College and Research Libraries* 35:2 (March 1974), 97-108.

95 Richard J. Beeler. "Late-Study Areas: A Means of Extending Library Hours," *College and Research Libraries* 35:3 (May 1974), 200-203. **(78, 79)**

96 Rolland E. Stevens. "A Study of Interlibrary Loan," *College and Research Libraries* 35:5 (September 1974), 336-343.

97 Jay B. Clark. "An Approach to Collection Inventory," *College and Research Libraries* 35:5 (September 1974), 354-359.

98 Jan Baaske, Don Tolliver and Judy Westerberg. "Overdue Policies: A Comparison of Alternatives," *College and Research Libraries* 35:5 (September 1974), 354-359.

99 Clyde Hendrick and Marjorie E. Murfin. "Project Library Ripoff: A Study of Periodical Mutilation in a University Library," *College and Research Libraries* 35:6 (November 1974), 402-411.

100 Peter Marshall. "How Much, How Often?" *College and Research Libraries* 35:6 (November 1974), 453-456.

101 Robert Balay and Christine Andres. "Use of the Reference Service in a Large Academic Library," *College and Research Libraries* 36:1 (January 1975), 9-26.

102 Guy Walker. "Preservation Efforts in Larger U.S. Academic Libraries," *College and Research Libraries* 36:1 (January 1975), 39-44.

103 Susanne Patterson Wahba. "Job Satisfaction of Librarians: A Comparison between Men and Women," *College and Research Libraries* 36:1 (January 1975), 45-51. **(208)**

104 Grant T. Skelley. "Characteristics of Collections Added to American Research Libraries 1940-1970: A Preliminary Investigation," *College and Reseach Libraries* 36:1 (January 1975), 52-60. **(168)**

105 Laura M. Boyer and William C. Theimer, Jr. "The Use and Training of Nonprofessional Personnel at Reference Desks in Selected College and University Libraries," *College and Research Libraries* 36:3 (May 1975), 193-200. **(183, 199)**

106 Robert J. Greene. "LENDS: An Approach to the Centralization/Decentralization Dilemma," *College and Research Libraries* 36:3 (May 1975), 201-207.

107 Frances L. Meals and Walter T. Johnson. "We Chose Microfilm," *College and Research Libraries* 21:3 (May 1960), 223-228. **(232, 237)**

108 George Caldwell. "University Libraries and Government Publications: A Survey," *College and Research Libraries* 22:1 (January 1961), 30-34.

109 Allen Story. "Leo in Libraryland," *American Libraries* 7:9 (October 1976), 569-571. **(90, 91)**

110 Leslie R. Morris. "The Rise and Fall of the Library Job Market," *American Libraries* 12:9 (October 1981), 557-558. **(92)**

111 Richard De Gennaro. "Escalating Journal Prices: Time To Fight Back," *American Libraries* 8:1 (January 1977), 69-74.

112 Joe A. Hewitt. "The Impact of OCLC," *American Libaries* 7:5 (May 1976), 268-275. **(202)**

113 Fritz Veit. "Book Order Procedures in the Publicly Controlled Colleges and Universities of the Midwest," *College and Research Libraries* 23:1 (January 1962), 33-40.

114 Keyes D. Metcalf. "Compact Shelving," *College and Research Libraries* 23:2 (March 1962), 103-111. **(236)**

115 Natalie N. Nicholson and Eleanor Bartlett. "Who Uses University Libraries," *College and Research Libraries* 23:3 (May 1962), 217-259.

116 H. William Axford. "Rider Revisited," *College and Research Libraries* 23:4 (July 1962), 345-347.

117 E.J. Josey. "The Role of the College Library Staff in Instruction in the Use of the Library," *College and Research Libraries* 23:6 (November 1962), 492-498.

118 Edwin E. Williams. "Magnitude of the Paper-Deterioration Problems as Measured by a National Union Catalog Sample," *College and Research Libraries* 23:6 (November 1962), 499.

119 Stella Frank Mosborg. "Measuring Circulation Desk Activities Using a Random Alarm Mechanism," *College and Research Libraries* 41:5 (September 1980), 437-444. **(214)**

120 Jean E. Koch and Judith M. Pask. "Working Papers in Academic Business Libraries," *College and Research Libraries* 41:6 (November 1980), 517-523.

121 Paul Metz. "Administrative Succession in the Academic Library," *College and Research Libraries* 39:5 (September 1978), 358-364. **(33, 42, 55, 56, 59)**

122 Libby Trudell and James Wolper. "Interlibrary Loan in New England," *College and Research Libraries* 39:5 (September 1978), 365-371.

123 Richard M. Dougherty. "The Evaluation of Campus Library Document Delivery Service," *College and Research Libraries* 34:1 (January 1973), 29-39.

124 Ung Chon Kim. "A Comparison of Two Out-of-Print Book Buying Methods," *College and Research Libraries* 34:5 (September 1973), 258-264.

125 Ann Gwyn, Anne McArthur and Karen Furlow. "Friends of the Library," *College and Research Libraries* 36:4 (July 1975), 272-282. **(107, 108)**

126 John J. Knightly. "Library Collections and Academic Curricula: Quantitative Relationships," *College and Research Libraries* 36:4 (July 1975), 295-301.

127 Alice S. Clark and Rita Hirschman. "Using the 'Guidelines': A Study of the State-Supported Two-Year College Libraries in Ohio," *College and Research Libraries* 36:5 (September 1975), 364-370. **(49, 83, 221)**

128 Virginia E. Yagello and Gerry Gutherie. "The Effect of Reduced Loan Periods on High Use Items," *College and Research Libraries* 36:5 (September 1975), 411-414.

129 George Piternick. "Library Growth and Academic Quality," *College and Research Libraries* 24:3 (May 1963), 223-229.

130 Robert N. Broadus. "An Analysis of Faculty Circulation in a University Library," *College and Research Libraries* 24:4 (July 1963), 323-325.

131 Perry D. Morrison. "The Personality of the Academic Librarian," *College and Research Libraries* 24:5 (September 1963), 365-368. **(207, 208)**

132 W.J. Bonk. "What is Basic Reference?" *College and Research Libraries* 25:3 (May 1964), 5-8.

133 Jean Legg "The Periodical Scene," *RQ* 7:3 (Spring 1968), 129-132.

134 Richard H. Perrine. "Catalog Use Difficulties," *RQ* 7:4 (Summer 1968), 169-174.

135 Thelma E. Larson. "A Survey of User Orientation Methods," *RQ* 8:3 (Spring 1969), 182-187.

136 Phil Hoehn and Jean Hudson. "Academic Library Staffing Patterns," *RQ* 8:4 (Summer 1969), 242-244.

137 T.H. Milby. "Two Approaches to Biology," *RQ* 11:3 (Spring 1972), 231-235.

138 James B. Way. "Loose Leaf Business Services," *RQ* 9:2 (Winter 1969), 128-133.

139 Mary Jane Swope and Jeffrey Katzer. "Why Don't They Ask Questions?" *RQ* 12:2 (Winter 1972), 161-165.

140 Robert M. Simmons. "Finding That Government Document," *RQ* 12:2 (Winter 1972), 167-171.

141 Lee Regan. "Status of Reader's Advisory Service," *RQ* 12:3 (Spring 1973), 227-233. **(134)**

142 Bruce Cossar. "Interlibrary Loan Costs," *RQ* 12:3 (Spring 1973), 243-246.

143 Mary R. Turtle and William C. Robinson. "The Relationship between Time Lag and Place of Publication in *Library and Information Science Abstracts* and *Library Literature*," *RQ* 14:1 (Fall 1974), 28-31.

144 Rosemary Magrill and Charles H. Davis. "Public Library SDI; A Pilot Study," *RQ* 14:2 (Winter 1974), 131-137. **(134)**

145 Steve Parker and Kathy Essary. "A Manual SDI System for Academic Libraries," *RQ* 15:1 (Fall 1975), 47-54.

146 Carl F. Orgren and Barbara J. Olson. "Statewide Teletype Reference Service," *RQ* 15:3 (Spring 1976), 203-209.

147 Anne S. Mavor, Jose Orlando Toro and Ernest R. Deprospo. "An Overview of the National Adult Independent Learning Project," *RQ* 15:4 (Summer 1976), 293-308. **(144)**

148 Danuta A. Nitecki. "Attitudes toward Automated Information Retrieval Services among RASD Members," *RQ* 16:2 (Winter 1976), 133-141. **(4)**

149 Rhoda Garoogian. "Library Use of the New York Times Information Bank: A Preliminary Survey," *RQ* 16:1 (Fall 1976), 59-64.

150 Marcella Ciucki. "Recording of Reference/Information Service Activities: A Study of Forms Currently Used," *RQ* 16:4 (Summer 1977), 273-283.

151 Mollie Sandock. "A Study of University Students' Awareness of Reference Services," *RQ* 16:4 (Summer 1977), 284-296.

152 Kathleen Imhoff and Larry Brandwein. "Labor Collections and Services in Public Libraries throughout the United States, 1976," *RQ* 17:2 (Winter 1977), 149-158. **(147)**

153 Cynthia Swenk and Wendy Robinson. "A Comparison of the Guides to Abstracting and Indexing Services Provided by Katz, Chicorel and Ulrich," *RQ* (Summer 1978), 317-319.

154 John P. Wilkinson and William Miller. "The Step Approach to Reference Service," *RQ* (Summer 1978), 293-299.

155 Gerald Johoda, Alan Bayer and William L. Needham. "A Comparison of On-Line Bibliographic Searches in One Academic and One Industrial Organization," *RQ* 18:1 (Fall 1978), 42-49.

156 Stephen P. Harter and Mary Alice S. Fields. "Circulation, Reference and the Evaluation of Public Library Service," *RQ* 18:2 (Winter 1978), 147-152.

157 Daniel Ream. "An Evaluation of Four Book Review Journals," *RQ* 19:2 (Winter 1979), 149-153.

158 Joseph W. Palmer. "Review Citations for Best-Selling Books," *RQ* 19:2 (Winter 1979), 154-158.

159 "An Evaluation of References to Indexes and Abstracts in Ulrich's 17th Edition," *RQ* 20:2 (Winter 1980), 155-159.

160 Victoria T. Kok and Anton R. Pierce. "The Reference Desk Survey: A Management Tool in an Academic Research Library," *RQ* 22:2 (Winter 1982), 181-187.

161 Sheila S. Intner. "Equality of Cataloging in the Age of AACR2," *American Libraries* 14:2 (February 1983), 102-103.

162 Joseph W. Palmer. "The Future of Public Library Film Service," *American Libraries* 13:2 (February 1982), 140-142. **(135)**

163 Robert Grover and Mary Kevin Moore. "Print Dominates Library Service to Children," *American Libraries* 13:4 (April 1982), 268-269. **(136)**

164 Richard H. Evensen and Mary Berghaus Levering. "Services Are 500% Better," *American Libraries* 10:6 (June 1979), 373. **(135)**

165 Judith Schick. "Job Mobility of Men and Women Librarians and How It Affects Career Advancement," *American Libraries* 10:11 (December 1979), 643-647.

166　Elizabeth Rountree. "Users and Nonusers Disclose Their Needs," *American Libraries* 10:8 (September 1979), 486-487.

167　George Bobinski. "A Survey of Faculty Loan Policies," *College and Research Libraries* 24:6 (November 1963), 483-486. add

168　L. Miles Raisig and Frederick G. Kilgour. "The Use of Medical Theses as Demonstrated by Journal Citations, 1850-1960," *College and Research Libraries* 25:2 (March 1964), 93-102.

169　George H. Fadenrecht. "Library Facilities and Practices in Colleges of Veterinary Medicine," *College and Research Libraries* 25:4 (July 1964), 308-335. **(126, 128)**

170　Donald Thompson. "Working Conditions in Selected Private College Libraries," *College and Research Libraries* 25:4 (July 1964), 261-294. **(6)**

171　Benedict Brooks and Frederick G. Kilgour. "Catalog Subject Searches in the Yale Medical Library," *College and Research Libraries* 25:6 (November 1964), 483-487.

172　Patrick Barkey. "Patterns of Student Use of a College Library," *College and Research Libraries* 26:2 (March 1965), 115-118.

173　Genevieve Porterfield. "Staffing of Interlibrary Loan Service," *College and Research Libraries* 26:4 (July 1965), 318-320. **(130)**

174　Harold Mathis. "Professional or Clerical: A Cross-Validation Study," *College and Research Libraries* 26:6 (November 1965), 525-531. **(94, 95, 202)**

175　David H. Doerrer. 'Overtime' and the Academic Librarian," *College and Research Libraries* 27:3 (May 1966), 194-239. **(29)**

176　Lois L. Luesing. "Church Historical Collections in Liberal Arts Colleges," *College and Research Libraries* 27:5 (July 1966), 291-317.

177　W.C. Blankenship. "Head Librarians: How Many Men? How Many Women?" *College and Research Libraries* 28:1 (January 1967), 41-48. **(38, 41, 58)**

178　Morrison C. Haviland. "Loans to Faculty Members in University Libraries," *College and Research Libraries* 28:3 (May 1967), 171-174.

179　R. Vernon Ritter. "An Investigation of Classroom-Library Relationships on a College Campus as Seen in Recorded Circulation and GPA's," *College and Research Libraries* 29:1 (January 1968), 3-4.

180　Peter Spyers-Duran. "Faculty Studies: A Survey of Their Use in Selected Libraries," *College and Research Libraries* 29:1 (January 1968), 55-61.

181　Raymond Kilpela. "The University Library Committee," *College and Research Libraries* 29:2 (March 1968), 141-143. **(60, 130, 131, 227)**

182 W. Porter Kellam and Dale L. Barker. "Activities and Opportunities of University Librarians for Full Participation in the Educational Enterprise," *College and Research Libraries* 29:5 (May 1968), 195-199. **(7, 8, 61)**

183 Lloyd A. Kramer and Martha B. Kramer. "The College Library and the Drop-Out," *College and Research Libraries* 29:4 (July 1968), 310-312.

184 Carl Hintz. "Criteria for Appointment to and Promotion in Academic Rank," *College and Research Libraries* 29:5 (September 1968), 341-346.

185 Desmond Taylor. "Classification Trends in Junior College Libraries," *College and Research Libraries* 29:6 (September 1968), 351-356.

186 Raj Madan, Eliese Hetler and Marilyn Strong. "The Status of Librarians in Four-Year State Colleges and Universities," *College and Research Libraries* 29:5 (September 1968), 381-386. **(7, 27, 156)**

187 Victor Novak. "The Librarian in Catholic Institutions," *College and Research Libraries* 29:5 (September 1968), 403-410. **(32, 210)**

188 Barbara H. Phipps. "Library Instruction for the Undergraduate," *College and Research Libraries* 29:5 (September 1968), 411-423.

189 Ashby J. Fristoe. "Paperbound Books: Many Problems, No Solutions," *College and Research Libraries* 29:5 (September 1968), 437-442.

190 Sidney Forman. "Innovative Practices in College Libraries," *College and Research Libraries* 29:6 (November 1968), 486-492. **(229, 233)**

191 Richard W. Trueswell. "Some Circulation Data from a Research Library," *College and Research Libraries* 29:6 (November 1968), 493-495.

192 Jane P. Kleiner. "The Information Desk: The Library's Gateway to Service," *College and Research Libraries* 29:6 (November 1968), 496-501.

193 J.E.G. Craig, Jr. "Characteristics of Use of Geology Literature," *College and Research Libraries* 3:3 (May 1969), 230-236.

194 Ronald A. Hoppe and Edward C. Simmel. "Book Tearing: The Bystander in the University Library," *College and Research Libraries* 3:3 (May 1969), 247-251.

195 Stephen L. Peterson. "Patterns of Use of Periodical Literature," *College and Research Libraries* 30:5 (September 1969), 422-430.

196 Mary B. Cassata. "Teach-in: The Academic Librarian's Key to Status," *College and Research Libraries* 31:1 (January 1970), 22-27.

197 E.J. Josey. "Community Use of Junior College Libraries—A Symposium," *College and Research Libraries* 31:3 (May 1970), 185-198.

198 Virgil F. Massman. "Academic Library Salaries in a Seven-State Area," *College and Research Libraries* 3:6 (November 1969), 477-482. **(191, 192)**

199 James Krikelas. "Subject Searches Using Two Catalogs: A Comparative Evaluation," *College and Research Libraries* 30:6 (November 1969), 506-517.

200 James Wright. "Fringe Benefits for Academic Library Personnel," *College and Research Libraries* 31:1 (January 1970), 18-21. **(6, 8, 9, 25, 26, 29, 30)**

201 Howard Clayton. "Femininity and Job Satisfaction among Male Library Students at One Midwestern University," *College and Research Libraries* 31:6 (November 1970), 388-398.

202 Philip V. Rzasa and John H. Moriarty. "The Types and Needs of Academic Library Users: A Case Study of 6,568 Responses," *College and Research Libraries* 31:6 (November 1970),403-409.

203 Bob Carmack and Trudi Loeber. "The Library Reserve System—Another Look," *College and Research Libraries* 32:2 (March 1971), 105-109.

204 C. James Schmidt and Kay Shaffer. "A Cooperative Interlibrary Loan Service for the State-Assisted University Libraries in Ohio," *College and Research Libraries* 32:3 (May 1971), 197-204.

205 Edward S. Warner. "A Tentative Analytical Approach to the Determination of Interlibrary Loan Network Effectiveness," *College and Research Libraries* 32:3 (May 1971), 217-221.

206 Irving Zelkind and Joseph Sprug. "Increased Control through Decreased Controls: A Motivational Approach to a Library Circulation Problem," *College and Research Libraries* 32:3 (May 1971), 222-226.

207 William E. McGrath. "Correlating the Subjects of Books Taken Out Of and Books Used Within an Open-Stack Library," *College and Research Libraries* 32:4 (July 1971), 280-285.

208 Thomas Kirk. "A Comparison of Two Methods of Library Instruction for Students in Introductory Biology," *College and Research Libraries* 32:6 (November 1971), 465-474.

209 Dawn McCaghy and Gary Purcell. "Faculty Use of Government Publications," *College and Research Libraries* 33:1 (January 1972), 7-12.

210 Joe A. Hewitt. "Sample Audit of Cards from a University Library Catalog," *College and Research Libraries* 33:1 (January 1972), 24-27.

211 William E. McGrath. "The Significance of Books Used According to a Classified Profile of Academic Departments," *College and Research Libraries* 33:3 (May 1972), 212-219.

212 Carlos A. Cuadra and Ruth J. Patrick. "Survey of Academic Library Consortia in the U.S.," *College and Research Libraries* 33:4 (July 1972), 271-283. **(96)**

213 Marjorie Johnson. "Performance Appraisal of Librarians—A Survey," *College and Research Libraries* 33:5 (September 1972), 359-367. **(157)**

214 Marvin E. Wiggins. "The Development of Library Use Instruction Programs," *College and Research Libraries* 33:6 (November 1972), 473-479.

215 Margaret E. Monroe. "Community Development as a Mode of Community Analysis," *Library Trends* 24:3 (January 1976), 497-514. **(134, 183)**

216 Janet K. Rudd and Larry G. Carver. "Topographic Map Acquisition in U.S. Academic Libraries," *Library Trends* 29:3 Winter 1981), 375-390.

217 John Belland. "Factors Influencing Selection of Materials," *School Media Quarterly* 6:2 (Winter 1978), 112-119.

218 Virginia Witucke. "A Comparative Analysis of Juvenile Book Review Media," *School Media Quarterly* 8:3 (Spring 1980), 153-160.

219 M. Carl Drott and Jacqueline C. Mancall. "Magazines as Information Sources: Patterns of Student Use," *School Media Quarterly* 8:4 (Summer 1980), 240-250.

220 Jerry J. Watson and Bill C. Snider. "Book Selection Pressure on School Library Media Specialists and Teachers," *School Media Quarterly* 9:2 (Winter 1981), 95-101.

221 Jerry J. Watson and Bill C. Snider. "Educating the Potential Self-Censor," *School Media Quarterly* 9:4 (Summer 1981), 272-276.

222 Lucy Anne Wozny. "Online Bibliographic Searching and Student Use of Information: An Innovative Teaching Approach," *School Library Media Quarterly* 11:1 (Fall 1982), 35-42.

223 Carol A. Doll. "School and Public Library Collection Overlap and the Implications for Networking," *School Library Media Quarterly* 11:3 (Spring 1983), 193-199.

224 Arthur Tannenbaum and Eva Sidhom. "User Environment and Attitudes in an Academic Microform Center," *Library Journal* 101:18 (October 15, 1976), 2139-2143.

225 Timothy Hays, Kenneth D. Shearer and Concepcion Wilson. "The Patron Is Not the Public," *Library Journal* 102:16 (September 15, 1977), 1813-1818. **(135)**

226 Wilma Lee Woolard. "The Combined School and Public Library: Can It Work?" *Library Journal* 103:4 (February 15, 1978), 435-438. **(97, 98, 99, 100, 105, 106, 124, 125)**

227 David C. Genaway. "Bar Coding and the Librarian Supermarket: An Analysis of Advertised Library Vacancies," *Library Journal* 103:3 (February 1, 1978), 322-325. **(3, 92, 117, 118)**

228 Hoyt Galvin. "Public Library Parking Needs," *Library Journal* 103:2 (November 15, 1978), 2310-2313. **(234)**

229 Harold J. Ettelt. "Book Use at a Small (Very) Community College Library," *Library Journal* 103:2 (November 15, 1978), 2314-2315.

230 Frederick G. Kilgour. "Interlibrary Loans On-Line," *Library Journal* 104:4 (February 15, 1979), 460-463.

231 Paul Little. "The Effectiveness of Paperbacks," *Library Journal* 104:2 (November 15, 1979), 2411-2416.

232 Ken Kister. "Encyclopedias and the Public Library: A National Survey," *Library Journal* 104:8 (April 15, 1979), 890-893.

233 Arlene T. Dowell. "Discrepancies in CIP: How Serious Is the Problem," *Library Journal* 104:19 (November 1, 1979), 2281-2287.

234 Gary D. Byrd, Mary Kay Smith and Norene McDonald. "MINET in K.C.," *Library Journal* 104:17 (October 1, 1979), 2044-2047.

235 Ray L. Carpenter. "The Public Library Patron," *Library Journal* 104:3 (February 1, 1979), 347-351.

236 Cathy Schell. "Preventive Medicine: The Library Prescription," *Library Journal* 105:8 (April 15, 1980), 929-931. **(87, 99, 139)**

237 Michael Gonzalez, Bill Greeley and Stephen Whitney. "Assessing the Library Needs of the Spanish-speaking," *Library Journal* 105:7 (April 1, 1980), 786-789. **(135)**

238 Thomas Childers. "The Test of Reference," *Library Journal* 105:8 (April 15, 1980), 924-928. **(154)**

239 Mary Noel Gouke and Marjorie Murfin. "Periodical Mutilization: The Insidious Disease," *Library Journal* 105:16 (September 15, 1980), 1795-1797.

240 Sheila Creth and Faith Harders. "Requirements for the Entry Level Librarian," *Library Journal* 105:18 (October 15, 1980), 2168-2169.

241 Kathleen M. Heim and Leigh S. Estabrook. "Career Patterns of Librarians," *Drexel Library Quarterly* 17:3 (Summer 1981), 35-51. **(40, 66, 67)**

242 Margaret Peil. "Library Use by Low-Income Chicago Families," *Library Quarterly* 33:4 (October 1963), 329-333.

243 Herbert Goldhor and John McCrossan. "An Exploratory Study of the Effect of a Public Library Summer Reading Club on Reading Skills," *Library Quarterly* 36:1 (June 1966), 14-24.

244 Robert Sommer. "Reading Areas in College Libraries," *Library Quarterly* 38:3 (July 1968), 249-260. **(121, 227, 228)**

245 Isaac T. Littleton. "The Literature of Agricultural Economics: Its Bibliographic Organization and Use," *Library Quarterly* 39:2 (April 1969), 140-152.

246 G. Edward Evans. "Book Selection and Book Collection Usage in Academic Libraries," *Library Quarterly* 40:3 (July 1970), 297-308.

247 Marilyn Werstein Greenberg. "A Study of Reading Motivation of Twenty-Three Seventh-Grade Students," *Library Quarterly* 40:3 (July 1970), 309-317.

248 Ben-Ami Lipetz. "Catalog Use in a Large Research Library," *Library Quarterly* 42:1 (January 1972), 129-130.

249 John Aubry. "A Timing Study of the Manual Searching of Catalogs," *Library Quarterly* 42:4 (October 1972), 399-415.

250 Kenneth H. Plate and Elizabeth W. Stone. "Factors Affecting Librarians' Job Satisfaction: A Report of Two Studies," *Library Quarterly* 44:2 (April 1974), 97-109. (**175, 176**)

251 Elizabeth Warner McElroy. "Subject Variety in Adult Reading: I. Factors Related to Variety in Reading," *Library Quarterly* 38:1 (April 1968), 154-167.

252 James C. Baughman. "A Structural Analysis of the Literature of Sociology," *Library Quarterly* 44:4 (October 1974), 293-308.

253 Edd E. Wheeler. "The Bottom Lines: Fifty Years of Legal Footnoting in Review," *Law Library Journal* 72:2 (Spring 1979), 245-259.

254 Daniel O'Connor and Phyllis Van Orden. "Getting into Print," *College and Research Libraries* 39:5 (September 1978), 389-396.

255 Howard Fosdick. "Library Education in Information Science: Present Trends," *Special Libraries* 69:3 (March 1978), 100-108.

256 Paula de Simone Watson. "Publication Activity among Academic Librarians," *College and Research Libraries* 38:5 (September 1977), 375-384.

257 Susan Andriette Ariew. "The Failure of the Open Access Residence Hall Library," *College and Research Libraries* 39:5 (September 1978), 372-380. (**132**)

258 Mary Ellen Soper. "Characteristics and Use of Personal Collections," *Library Quarterly* (October 1976), 397-415.

259 Ronald R. Powell. "An Investigation of the Relationships Between Quantifiable Reference Service Variables and Reference Performance in Public Libraries," *Library Quarterly* 48:1 (January 1978), 1-19. (**154, 155, 156**)

260 Mary Jo Lynch. "Reference Interviews in Public Libraries," *Library Quarterly* 48:2 (April 1978), 119-142.

261 William A. Satariano. "Journal Use in Sociology: Citation Analysis versus Readership Patterns," *Library Quarterly* 48:3 (July 1978), 293-300.

262 Paul Metz. "The Use of the General Collection in the Library of Congress," *Library Quarterly* 49:4 (October 1979), 415-434.

263 Michael Halperin and Maureen Strazdon. "Measuring Students' Preferences for Reference Service: A Conjoint Analysis," *Library Quarterly* 50:2 (April 1980), 208-224.

264 Herbert S. White. "Factors in the Decisions by Individuals and Libraries To Place or Cancel Subscriptions to Scholarly and Research Journals," *Library Quarterly* 50:3 (July 1980), 287-309. **(96)**

265 George D'Elia. "The Development and Testing of a Conceptual Model of Public Library User Behavior," *Library Quarterly* 50:4 (October 1980), 410-430.

266 Donald A. Hicks. "Diversifying Fiscal Support by Pricing Public Library Services: A Policy Impact Analysis," *Library Quarterly* 50:4 (October 1980), 453-474. **(172)**

267 Theodora Hodges and Uri Block. "Fiche or Film for COM Catalogs: Two Use Tests," *Library Quarterly* 52:2 (April 1982), 131-144.

268 Terry L. Weech and Herbert Goldhor. "Obtrusive versus Unobtrusive Evaluation of Reference Service in Five Illinois Public Libraries: A Pilot Study," *Library Quarterly* 52:4 (October 1982), 305-324. **(156)**

269 Stephen E. Wiberley, Jr. "Journal Rankings From Citation Studies: A Comparison of National and Local Data From Social Work," *Library Quarterly* 52:4 (October 1982), 348-359.

270 George D'Elia and Sandra Walsh. "User Satisfaction with Library Service— A Measure of Public Library Performance?" *Library Quarterly* 53:2 (April 1983), 109-133.

271 Edward A. Dyl. "A Note on Price Discrimination by Academic Journals," *Library Quarterly* 53:2 (April 1983), 161-168.

272 Michael R. Kronenfeld and James A. Thompson. "The Impact of Inflation on Journal Costs," *Library Journal* 106:7 (April 1,1981), 714-717.

273 George D'Elia and Mary K. Chelton. "Paperback Books," *Library Journal* 107:16 (September 15, 1982), 1718-1721.

274 Patsy Hansel and Robert Burgin. "Hard Facts about Overdues," *Library Journal* 108:4 (February 15, 1983), 349-352.

275 Robert Dale Karr. "Becoming a Library Director," *Library Journal* 108:4 (February 15, 1983), 343-346. **(38, 39, 46, 52, 53, 54)**

276 Mary V. Gaver. "The Science Collection—New Evidence To Consider," *Junior Libraries* (later *School Library Journal*) 7:6 (February 1961), 4-7.

277 Dorothy G. Petersen. "Teachers' Professional Reading," *School Library Journal* 9:8 (April 1963), 24-27.

278 Linda Kraft. "Lost Herstory: The Treatment of Women in Children's Encyclopedias," *School Library Journal* 19:5 (January 1973), 26-35.

279 John Stewig and Margaret Higgs. "Girls Grow Up: A Study of Sexism in Children's Literature," *School Library Journal* 19:5 (January 1973), 44-49.

280 W. Bernard Lukenbill. "Fathers in Adolescent Novels," *School Library Journal* 20:6 (February 1974), 26-30.

281 Jacqueline C. Mancall and M. Carl Drott. "Tomorrow's Scholars: Patterns of Facilities Use," *School Library Journal* 20:7 (March 1980), 99-103.

282 John McCrossan. "Education of Librarians Employed in Small Public Libraries," *Journal of Education for Librarianship* 7:4 (Spring 1967), 237-245. **(53, 175, 196, 197)**

283 Gail Schlachter and Dennis Thomison. "The Library Science Doctorate: A Quantitative Analysis of Dissertations and Recipients," *Journal of Education for Librarianship* 15:2 (Fall 1974), 95-111.

284 Constance Rinehart and Rose Mary Magrill. "Characteristics of Applicants for Library Science Teaching Positions," *Journal of Education for Librarianship* 16:3 (Winter 1976), 173-182.

285 George W. Whitbeck. "Grade Inflation in the Library School—Myth or Reality," *Journal of Education for Librarianship* 17:4 (Spring 1977), 214-237. **(91)**

286 Charles H. Davis. "Computer Programming for Librarians," *Journal of Education for Librarianship* 18:1 (Summer 1977), 41-52.

287 Helen M. Gothberg. "A Study of the Audio-Tutorial Approach to Teaching Basic Reference," *Journal of Education for Librarianship* 18:3 (Winter 1978), 193-202.

288 J. Periam Danton. "British and American Library School Teaching Staffs: A Comparative Inquiry," *Journal of Education for Librarianship* 19:2 (Fall 1978), 97-129.

289 Lucille Whalen. "The Role of the Assistant Dean in Library Schools," *Journal of Education for Librarianship* 20:1 (Summer 1979), 44-54.

290 A. Neil Yerkey. "Values of Library School Students, Faculty and Librarians: Premises for Understanding," *Journal of Education for Librarianship* 21:2 (Fall 1980), 122-134. **(35)**

291 Judith B. Katz. "Indicators of Success: Queens College Department of Library Science," *Journal of Education for Librarianship* 19:2 (Fall 1978), 130-139.

292 Lawrence Auld, Kathleen H. Heim and Jerome Miller. "Market Receptivity for an Extended M.L.S.," *Journal of Education for Librarianship* 21:3 (Winter 1981), 235-245.

293 John Richardson, Jr. and Peter Hernon. "Theory vs. Practice: Student Preferences," *Journal of Education for Librarianship* 21:4 (Spring 1981), 287-300,

294 Richard I. Blue and James L. Divilbiss. "Optimizing Selection of Library School Students," *Journal of Education for Librarianship* 21:4 (Spring 1981), 301-312.

295 David H. Jonassen and Gerald G. Hodges. "Student Cognitive Styles: Implications for Library Educators," *Journal of Education for Librarianship* 22:3 (Winter 1982), 143-153.

296 Mary Kingsbury. "How Library Schools Evaluate Faculty Performance," *Journal of Education for Librarianship* 22:4 (Spring 1982), 219-238.

297 John W. Lee and Raymond L. Read. "The Graduate Business Student and the Library," *College and Research Libraries* 33:5 (September 1972), 403-407.

298 Carol Steer. "Authors Are Studied," *Canadian Library Journal* 39:3 (June 1982), 151-155.

299 Rashid Tayyeb. "Implementing AACR 2—A National Survey," *Canadian Library Journal* 39:6 (December 1982), 373-376.

300 Dick Matzek and Scott Smith. "Online Searching in the Small College Library—The Economics and the Results," *Online* (March 1982), 21-29.

301 Mary Lee Bundy. "Metropolitan Public Library Use," *Wilson Library Bulletin* 41:9 (May 1967), 950-961. **(122, 233)**

302 John Shipman. "Signifying Renewal as Well as Change: One Library's Experience with the Center for Research Libraries," *Library Acquisitions: Practice and Theory* 2:5 (1978), 243-248.

303 Nathan R. Einhorn. "The Inclusion of the Products of Reprography in the International Exchange of Publications," *Library Acquisitions: Practice and Theory* 2:5 (1978), 227-236

304 Nancy J. Williamson. "Education for Acquisitions Librarians: A State of the Art Review," *Library Acquisitions: Practice and Theory* 2:3-4 (1978), 199-208.

305 Janet L. Flowers. "Time Logs for Searchers: How Useful?" *Library Acquisitions: Practice and Theory* 2:2 (1978), 77-83. **(210)**

306 D.N. Wood. "Current Exchange of Serials at the British Library Lending Division," *Library Acquisitions: Practice and Theory* 3:2 (1979), 107-113.

307 Robert Goehlert. "Journal Use Per Monetary Unit: A Reanalysis of Use Data," *Library Acquisitions: Practice and Theory* 3:2 (1979), 91-98.

308 Margaret Landesman and Christopher Gates. "Performance of American Inprint Vendors: A Comparison at the University of Utah," *Library Acquisitions: Practice and Theory* 4:3-4 (1980), 187-192.

309 Kenton Pattie and Mary Ernst. "Chapter II Grants: Libraries Gain," *School Library Journal* 29:5 (January 1983), 17-19. **(224)**

310 John Erlandson and Yvonne Boyer. "Acquistions of State Documents," *Library Acquisitions: Practice and Theory* 4:2 (1980), 117-127.

311 George V. Hodowanec. "Analysis of Variables Which Help To Predict Book and Periodical Use," *Library Acquisitions: Practice and Theory* 4:1 (1980), 75-85.

312 Darrell L. Jenkins. "Acquiring Acquisitions Librarians," *Library Acquisitions: Practice and Theory* 5:2 (1981), 81-87. **(91, 92)**

313 Steven E. Maffeo. "Invoice Payment by Library Acquisitions: A Controlled Time Study," *Library Acquisitions: Practice and Theory* 5:2 (1981), 67-71.

314 Joyce G. McDonough, Carol Alf O'Connor and Thomas A. O'Connor. "Moving the Backlog: An Optimum Cycle for Searching OCLC," *Library Acquisitions: Practice and Theory* 6:3 (1982), 265-270.

315 Paul B. Wiener. "Recreational Reading Services in Academic Libraries: An Overview," *Library Acquisitions: Practice and Theory* 6:1 (1982), 59-70.

316 Peter Hernon. "Use of Microformatted Government Publications," *Microform Review* 11:4 (Fall 1982), 237-252. **(233)**

317 Charles R. McClure. "Online Government Documents Data Base Searching and the Use of Microfiche Documents Online by Academic and Public Depository Librarians," *Microfilm Review* 10:4 (Fall 1981), 245-259. **(225, 226, 229, 230)**

318 Peter Hernon and George W. Whitbeck. "Government Publications and Commercial Microform Publishers: A Survey of Federal Depository Libraries," *Microform Review* 6:5 (September 1977), 272-284.

319 Robert F. Jennings and Hathia Hayes. "The Use of Microfiche Copies of Children's Trade Books in Selected Fourth-Grade Classrooms," *Microform Review* 3:3 (July 1974), 189-193.

320 E.R. Norten. "New Books in Microform: A Survey," *Microform Review* 1:4 (October 1972), 284-288.

321 Renata Tagliacozzo, Manfred Kochen and Lawrence Rosenberg. "Orthographic Error Patterns of Author Names in Catalog Searches," *Journal of Library Automation* 3:2 (June 1970), 93-101.

322 Lorne R. Buhr. "Selective Dissemination of MARC: A User Evaluation," *Journal of Library Automation* 5:1 (March 1972), 39-50.

323   Gerry D. Guthrie and Steven D. Slifko. "Analysis of Search Key Retrieval on a Large Bibliographic File," *Journal of Library Automation* 6:2 (June 1972), 96-100.

324   Alan L. Landgraf and Frederick G. Kilgour. "Catalog Records Retrieved by Personal Author Using Derived Search Keys," *Journal of Library Automation* 6:2 (June 1973), 103-108.

325   Martha E. Williams. "Data Element Statistics for the MARC II Data Base," *Journal of Library Automation* 6:2 (June 1976), 89-100.

326   Michael D. Cooper and Nancy A. DeWath. "The Cost of On-Line Bibliographic Searching," *Journal of Library Automation* 9:3 (September 1976), 195-209.

327   Edward John Kazlauskas. "The Application of the Instrumental Development Process to a Module on Flowcharting," *Journal of Library Automation* 9:3 (September 1976), 234-244.

328   Lawrence K. Legard and Charles P. Bourne. "An Improved Title Word Search Key for Large Catalog Files," *Journal of Library Automation* 9:4 (December 1976), 318-327.

329   Ryan E. Hoover. "Patron Appraisal of Computer-Aided On-Line Bibliographic Retrieval Services," *Journal of Library Automation* 9:4 (December 1976), 335-350.

330   T.D.C. Kuch. "Analysis of the Literature of Library Automation through Citations in the *Annual Review of Information Science and Technology*," *Journal of Library Automation* 10:1 (March 1977), 82-84.

331   Isobel Jean Mosley. "Cost-Effectiveness Analysis of the Automation of a Circulation System," *Journal of Library Automation* 10:3 (September 1977), 240-254. **(224)**

332   Michael D. Cooper and Nancy A. DeWath. "The Effect of User Fees on the Cost of On-Line Searching in Libraries," *Journal of Library Automation* 10:4 (December 1977), 304-319.

333   James W. Bourg, Douglas Lacy, James Llinas and Edward T. O'Neill. "Developing Corporate Author Search Keys," *Journal of Library Automation* 11:2 (June 1978), 106-125.

334   Cynthia C. Ryans. "A Study of Errors Found in Non-MARC Cataloging in a Machine-Assisted System," *Journal of Library Automation* 11:2 (June 1978), 125-132.

335   Joselyn Druschel. "Cost Analysis of an Automated and Manual Cataloging and Book Processing System," *Journal of Library Automation* 14:1 (March 1981), 24-49.

336 Kunj B. Bastogi and Ichiko T. Morita. "OCLC Search Key Usage Patterns in a Large Research Library," *Journal of Library Automation* 14:2 (June 1981), 90-99.

337 Georgia L. Brown. "AACR 2: OCLC's Implementation and Database Conversion," *Journal of Library Automation* 14:3 (September 1981), 161-173.

338 James R. Martin. "Automation and the Service Attitudes of ARL Circulation Managers," *Journal of Library Automation* 14:3 (September 1981), 190-194.

339 University of Oregon Library. "A Comparison of OCLC, RLG/RLIN and WLN," *Journal of Library Automation* 14:3 (September 1981), 215-217. **(121)**

340 Terence Crowley. "Comparing Fiche and Film: A Test of Speed," *Journal of Library Automation* 14:4 (December 1981), 292-294. **(233)**

341 Public Service Satellite Consortium. "Cable Library Survey Results," *Journal of Library Automation* 14:4 (December 1981), 304-313. **(221)**

342 Dennis Reynolds. "Entry of Local Data on OCLC: The Options and Their Impact on the Processing of Archival Tapes," *Information Technology and Libraries* 1:1 (March 1982), 5-14.

343 Joseph Ford. "Network Service Centers and Their Expanding Role," *Information Technology and Libraries* 1:1 (March 1982), 28-35. **(95, 96, 120)**

344 Carolyn A. Johnson. "Retrospective Conversion of Three Library Collections," *Information Technology and Libraries* 1:2 (June 1982), 133-139.

345 Lynn L. Magrath. "Computers in the Library: The Human Element," *Information Technology and Libraries* 1:3 (September 1982), 266-270.

346 Izabella Taler. "Automated and Manual ILL: Time Effectiveness and Success Rate," *Information Technology and Libraries* 1:3 (September 1982), 277-280. **(97)**

347 Martha E. Williams, Stephen W. Barth and Scott E. Preece. "Summary of Statistics for Five Years of the MARC Data Base," *Journal of Library Automation* 12:4 (December 1979), 314-337.

348 Susan U. Golden and Gary A. Golden. "Access to Periodicals: Search Key versus Keyword," *Information Technology and Libraries* 2:1 (March 1983), 26-32.

349 Ray R. Larson and Vicki Graham. "Monitoring and Evaluating MELVYL," *Information Technology and Libraries* 2:1 (March 1983), 93-104.

350 Barbara E. Carr. "Improving the Periodicals Collection through an Index Correlation Study," *Reference Services Review* 9:4 (October/December 1981), 27-31.

351 I.N. Sengupta. "Impact of Scientific Serials on the Advancement of Medical Knowledge: An Objective Method of Analysis," *International Library Review* 4:2 (April 1972), 169-195.

352 June L. Stewart. "The Literature of Politics: A Citation Analysis," *International Library Review* 2:3 (July 1970), 329-353.

353 I.N. Sengupta. "The Literature of Microbiology," *International Library Review* 6:3 (July 1974), 353-369.

354 I.N. Sengupta. "The Literature of Pharmacology," *International Library Review* 6:4 (October 1974), 483-504.

355 A.W. Hafner. "Citation Characteristics of Physiology Literature, 1970-72," *International Library Review* 8:1 (January 1976), 85-115.

356 Hans Hanan Wellisch. "Script Conversion Practices in the World's Libraries," *International Library Review* 8:1 (January 1976), 55-84.

357 Christine Anderson Brock and Gayle Smith Edelman. "Teaching Practices of Academic Law Librarians," *Law Library Journal* 71:1 (February 1978), 96-107. **(35, 36, 49, 55, 73, 74, 75, 159, 164)**

358 Charles B. Wolfe. "Current Problems Facing State Law Libraries," *Law Library Journal* 71:1 (February 1978), 108-114). **(18, 154, 236)**

359 Mindy J. Myers. "The Impact of Lexis on the Law Firm Library: A Survey," *Law Library Journal* 71:1 (February 1978), 158-169. **(226, 227, 230, 231)**

360 Nancy P. Johnson. "Legal Periodical Usage Survey: Method and Application," *Law Library Journal* 71:1 (February 1978), 177-186.

361 Ann M. Carter. "Budgeting in Private Law Firm Libraries," *Law Library Journal* 71:1 (February 1978), 187-194. **(36, 128)**

362 James F. Bailey, III and Oscar M. Trelles, II. "Autonomy, Librarian Status, and Librarian Tenure in Law School Libraries: The State of the Art, 1978," *Law Library Journal* 71:3 (August 1978), 425-462. **(18, 19, 20, 21, 22, 23, 33, 36, 50, 55, 70, 72, 74, 75, 125, 126, 127, 128, 129, 130, 158, 192, 198)**

363 Frank Wm. Goudy. "Funding Local Public Libraries: FY 1966 to FY 1980," *Public Libraries* 21:2 (Summer 1982), 52-54. **(16)**

364 Guy Garrison. "A Look At Research on Public Library Problems in the 1970's," *Public Libraries* 19:1 (Spring 1980), 4-8. **(76, 77)**

365 Terry L. Weech. "School and Public Library Cooperation—What We Would Like To Do, What We Do," *Public Libraries* 18:2 (Summer 1979), 33-34. **(98, 102, 103, 106, 107)**

366 Patricia L. Piper and Cecilia Hing Ling Kwan. "Cataloging and Classification Practices in Law Libraries: Results of a Questionnaire," *Law Library Journal* 71:3 (August 1978), 481-483.

367 Christian M. Boissonnas. "The Quality of OCLC Bibliographic Records: The Cornell Law Library Experience," *Law Library Journal* 72:1 (Winter 1979), 80-85.

368 Kent Schrieffer and Linnea Christiani. "Ballots at Boalt," *Law Library Journal* 72:3 (Summer 1979), 497-512.

369 Ermina Hahn. "Survey of Technical Services Practices at Fifty Large Law School Libraries," *Law Library Journal* 73:3 (Summer 1980), 715-725.

370 Lana Caswell Garcia. "Legal Services Law Librarianship—An Investigation of Salary and Benefits in a Pioneer Field," *Law Library Journal* 73:3 (Summer 1980), 731-733.

371 Reynold J. Kosek. "Faculty Status and Tenure for Nondirector, Academic Law Librarians" a section within "Status of Academic Law Librarians," *Law Library Journal* 73:4 (Fall 1980), 892-905. **(169, 171)**

372 Martha C. Adamson and Gloria J. Zamora. "Authorship Characteristics in *Law Library Journal*: A Comparative Study," *Law Library Journal* 74:3 (Summer 1981), 527-533.

373 David G. Badertscher. "An Examination of the Dynamics of Change in Information Technology as Viewed from Law Libraries and Information Centers," *Law Library Journal* 75:2 (Spring 1982), 198-211.

374 Donald J. Dunn. "The Law Librarian's Obligation To Publish," *Law Library Journal* 75:2 (Spring 1982), 225-231.

375 Audio-Visual Committee, American Association of Law Libraries. "Summary of Audio-Visual Materials Used in Legal Education: Audio-Visual Committee Report—June 1967," *Law Library Journal* 60:3 (August 1967), 272-276.

376 Cameron Allen. "Duplicate Holding Practices of Approved American Law School Libraries." *Law Library Journal* 62:2 (May 1969), 191-200.

377 Margaret Shediac. "Private Law Libraries Special Interest Section 1980 Salary Survey," *Law Library Journal* 74:2 (Spring 1981), 444-457. **(11, 19, 24, 165)**

378 Bettie H. Scott. "Price Index for Legal Publications," *Law Library Journal* 75:1 (Winter 1982), 171-174.

379 Silvia A. Gonzalez. "County Law Library Survey," *Law Library Journal* 74:3 (Summer 1981), 654-691. **(73)**

380 Silvia A. Gonzalez. "Survey of State Law Libraries," *Law Library Journal* 74:1 (Winter 1981), 160-201. **(55, 72, 73)**

381 Silvia A. Gonzalez. "Survey of Court Law Libraries," *Law Library Journal* 74:2 (Spring 1981), 458-494. **(73)**

382 David A. Thomas. "1980 Statistical Survey of Law School Libraries and Librarians," *Law Library Journal* 74:2 (Spring 1981), 359-443. **(9, 11, 12, 70, 72)**

383 Marija Hughes. "Sex-Based Discrimination in Law Libraries," *Law Library Journal* 64:1 (February 1971), 13-22. **(39, 54, 59, 68, 71, 125)**

384 Oscar M. Trelles. "Law Libraries and Unions," *Law Library Journal* 65:2 (May 1972), 158-180. **(171)**

385 Claudia Sumler, Kristine Barone and Art Goetz. "Getting Books Faster and Cheaper: A Jobber Acquisitions Study," *Public Libraries* 19:4 (Winter 1980), 103-105.

386 Vernon A. Rayford. "A Black Librarian Takes a Look at Discrimination: by a Law School Library Survey," *Law Library Journal* 65:2 (May 1972), 183-189. **(119, 206)**

387 Audio-Visual Committee, American Association of Law Libraries. "The Use of Audio-Visual Teaching Aids and Library Microforms in American Legal Education," *Law Library Journal* 66:1 (February 1973), 84-87. **(223)**

388 Cameron Allen. "Whom We Shall Serve: Secondary Patrons of the University Law School Library," *Law Library Journal* 66:2 (May 1973), 160-171.

389 O. James Werner. "The Present Legal Status and Conditions of Prison Law Libraries," *Law Library Journal* 66:3 (August 1973), 259-269. **(79, 125, 151, 152, 235, 236, 237)**

390 George S. Grossman. "Clinical Legal Education and the Law Library," *Law Library Journal* 67:1 (February 1974), 60-78. **(131, 137)**

391 Kurt Schwerin and Igor I. Kavass. "Foreign Legal Periodicals in American Law Libraries 1973 Union List," *Law Library Journal* 67:1 (February 1974), 120-126.

392 Bethany J. Ochal. "County Law Libraries," *Law Library Journal* 67:2 (May 1974), 177-234. **(11, 17, 18, 122, 164, 228, 236)**

393 Peter Enyingi. "Subject Cataloging Practices in American Law Libraries: A Survey," *Law Library Journal* 68:1 (February 1975), 11-17.

394 Sandra Sadow and Benjamin R. Beede. "Library Instruction in American Law Schools," *Law Library Journal* 68:1 (February 1975), 27-32.

395 Michael L. Richmond. "Attitudes of Law Librarians to Theft and Mutilation Control Methods," *Law Library Journal* 68:1 (February 1975), 60-81.

396 Ellin B. Christianson. "Mergers in the Publishing Industry, 1958-1970," *Journal of Library History, Philosophy and Comparative Librarianship* 7:1 (January 1972), 5-32.

397 Eugene E. Graziano. "Interlibrary Loan Analysis: Diagnostic for Scientific Serials Backfile Acquisitions," *Special Libraries* 53:5 (May/June 1962), 251-257.

398 John E. James. "Library Technician Program: The Library Technician Graduates' Point of View," *Special Libraries* 62:6 (July/August 1971), 268-278. **(202, 203)**

399 James M. Matarazzo. "Scientific Journals: Page or Price Explosion?" *Special Libraries* 63:2 (February 1972), 53-58.

400 Julie L. Moore. "Bibliographic Control of American Doctoral Dissertations," *Special Libraries* 63:7 (July 1972), 285-291.

401 Robert T. Bottle and William W. Chase. "Some Characteristics of the Literature on Music and Musicology," *Special Libraries* 63:10 (October 1972), 469-476.

402 William P. Koughan and John A. Timour. "Are Hospital Libraries Meeting Physicians' Information Needs?" *Special Libraries* 64:5/6 (May/June 1972), 222-227.

403 Jean M. Ray. "Who Borrows Maps from a University Library Map Collection —And Why?" *Special Libraries* 65:3 (March 1974), 104-109.

404 Ching-Chih Chen. "How Do Scientists Meet Their Information Needs?" *Special Libraries* 65:7 (July 1974), 272-280.

405 Katherine C. Owen. "Productive Journal Titles in the Pharmaceutical Industry," *Special Libraries* 65:10/11 (October/November 1974), 430-439.

406 Stanley A. Elman. "Cost Comparison of Manual and On-Line Computerized Literature Searching," *Special Libraries* 66:1 (January 1975), 12-18.

407 Jerome P. Fatcheric. "Survey of Users of a Medium-Sized Technical Library," *Special Libraries* 66:5/6 (May/June 1975), 245-251.

408 Bahaa El-Hadidy. "Bibliographic Control among Geoscience Abstracting and Indexing Services," *Special Libraries* 66:5/6 (May/June 1975), 260-265.

409 Ruth W. Wender. "Hospital Journal Title Usage Study," *Special Libraries* 66:11 (November 1975), 532-537.

410 Thelma Freides. "Bibliographic Gaps in the Social Science Literature," *Special Libraries* 67:2 (February 1976), 68-75.

411 Eileen E. Hitchingham. "MEDLINE Use in a University without a School of Medicine," *Special Libraries* 67:4 (April 1976), 188-194.

412   David Hull and Henry D. Fearnley. "The Museum Library in the United
      States: A Sample," *Special Libraries* 67:7 (July 1976), 289-298.   **(18, 79, 164,
      172)**

413   Amelia Breiting, Marcia Dorey and Deirdre Sockbeson. "Staff Development
      in College and University Libraries," *Special Libraries* 67:7 (July 1976),
      305-309.   **(8, 25, 62, 183)**

414   Arley L. Ripin and Dorothy Kasman. "Education for Special Librarianship:
      A Survey of Courses Offered in Accredited Programs," *Special Libraries*
      67:11 (November 1976), 504-509.

415   George W. Black, Jr. "Selected Annaul Bound Volume Production," *Special
      Libraries* 67:11 (November 1976), 534-536.

416   Howard Fosdick. "An SDC-Based On-Line Search Service: A Patron
      Evaluation Survey and Implications," *Special Libraries* 68:9 (September
      1977), 305-312.

417   Diane M. Nelson. "Methods of Citation Analysis in the Fine Arts," *Special
      Libraries* 68:11 (November 1977), 390-395.

418   Annette Corth. "Coverage of Marine Biology Citations,"*Special Libraries*
      68:12 (December 1977), 439-446.

419   Jean K. Martin. "Computer-Based Literature Searching: Impact on Interli-
      brary Loan Service," *Special Libaries* 69:1 (January 1978), 1-6.

420   Jean M. Ray. "Who Borrows Maps from a University Library Map Collection
      —and Why? Report II," *Special Libraries* 69:1 (January 1978), 13-20.

421   Robert Goehlert. "Periodical Use in an Academic Library: A Study of
      Economists and Political Scientists," *Special Libraries* 69:2 (February 1978),
      51-60.

422   Sandra J. Springer, Robert A. Yokel, Nancy M. Lorenzi, Leonard T. Sigell
      and E. Don Nelson. "Drug Information to Patient Care Areas via Television:
      Preliminary Evaluation of Two Years' Experience," *Special Libraries* 69:4
      (April 1978), 155-163.

423   Martha J. Bailey. "Requirement for Middle Managerial Positions," *Special
      Libraries* 69:9 (September 1978), 323-331.   **(37, 50, 92, 116)**

424   Carolyn L. Warden. "An Industrial Current Awareness Service: A User
      Evaluation Study," *Special Libraries* 69:12 (December 1978), 459-467.

425   Charles H. Davis. "Programming Aptitude as a Function of Undergraduate
      Major," *Special Libraries* 69:12 (December 1978), 482-485.

426   Jean Mace Schmidt. "Translation of Periodical Literature in Plant Patholo-
      gy," *Special Libraries* 70:1 (January 1979), 12-17.

427 Susan Dingle-Cliff and Charles H. Davis. "Collection Overlap in Canadian Addictions Libraries," *Special Libraries* 70:2 (February 1979), 76-81.

428 John J. Knightly. "Overcoming the Cirterion Problem in the Evaluation of Library Performance," *Special Libraries* 70:4 (April 1979), 173-178. **(152)**

429 Ruth W. Wender. "Counting Journal Title Usage in the Health Sciences," *Special Libraries* 70:5/6 (May/June 1975), 219-226.

430 John Steuben. "Interlibrary Loan of Photocopies of Articles under the New Copyright Law," *Special Libraries* 70:5/6 (May/June 1979), 227-232.

431 John Kok and Edward G. Strable. "Moving Up: Librarians Who Have Become Officers of Their Organization," *Special Libraries* 71:1 (January 1980), 5-12. **(3)**

432 Rebecca J. Jensen, Herbert D. Asbury and Radford G. King. "Costs and Benefits to Industry of Online Literature Searches," *Special Libraries* 71:7 (July 1980), 291-299.

433 C. Margaret Bell. "The Applicability of OCLC and Inforonics in Special Libraries," *Special Libraries* 71:9 (September 1980), 398-404.

434 A. Neil Yerkey. "The Psychological Climate of Librarianship: Values of Special Librarians," *Special Libraries* 72:3 (July 1981), 195-200. **(207, 210)**

435 Virgil P. Diodato. "Author Indexing," *Special Libraries* 72:4 (October 1981), 361-369.

436 Judith M. Pask. "Bibliographic Instruction in Business Libraries," *Special Libraries* 72:4 (October 1981), 370-378. **(162, 235)**

437 Ann T. Dodson, Paul P. Philbin and Kunj B. Rastogi. "Electronic Interlibrary Loan in the OCLC Library: A Study of its Effectiveness," *Special Libraries* 73:1 (January 1982), 12-20.

438 Gloria J. Zamora and Martha C. Adamson. "Authorship Characteristics in *Special Libraries*: A Comparative Study," *Special Libraries* 73:2 (April 1982), 100-107.

439 Robert K. Poyer. "Time Lag in Four Indexing Services," *Special Libraries* 73:2 (April 1982), 142-146.

440 Pauline R. Hodges. "Keyword in Title Indexes: Effectiveness of Retrieval in Computer Searches," *Special Libraries* 74:1 (January 1983), 56-60.

441 D.K. Varma. "Increased Subscription Costs and Problems of Resource Allocation," *Special Libraries* 74:1 (January 1983), 61-66.

442 Michael Halperin and Ruth A. Pagell. "Searchers' Perceptions of Online Database Vendors," *Special Libraries* 74:2 (April 1973), 119-126.

443 Michael E.D. Koenig. "Education for Special Librarianship," *Special Libraries* 74:2 (April 1983), 182-196.

444 Powell Niland and William H. Kurth. "Estimating Lost Volumes in a University Library Collection," *College and Research Libraries* 37:2 (March 1976), 128-136.

445 Rush G. Miller. "The Influx of Ph.D.s into Librarianship: Intrusion or Transfusion?" *College and Research Libraries* 37:2 (March 1976), 158-165. **(49, 192)**

446 Steven Leach. "The Growth Rates of Major Academic Libraries: Rider and Purdue Reviewed," *College and Research Libraries* 37:6 (November 1976), 531-542.

447 T. Saracevic, W.M. Shaw, Jr. and P.B. Kantor. "Causes and Dynamics of User Frustration in an Academic Library," *College and Research Libraries* 38:1 (January 1977), 7-18.

448 R.W. Meyer and Rebecca Panetta. "Two Shared Cataloging Data Bases: A Comparison," *College and Research Libraries* 38:1 (January 1977), 19-24.

449 Peter Hernon and Maureen Pastine. "Student Perceptions of Academic Librarians," *College and Research Libraries* 38:2 (March 1977), 129-139.

450 Catherine V. Von Schon. "Inventory 'By Computer'," *College and Research Libraries* 38:2 (March 1977), 147-152.

451 David C. Genaway and Edward B. Stanford. "Quasi-Departmental Libraries," *College and Research Libraries* 38:3 (May 1977), 187-194. **(224)**

452 Elizabeth W. Matthews. "Trends Affecting Community College Library Administrators," *College and Research Libraries* 38:3 (May 1977), 210-217. **(32, 38, 41, 58, 59, 73, 123, 126, 221)**

453 Lawrence J. Perk. "Secondary Publications in Education: A Study of Duplication," *College and Research Libraries* 38:3 (May 1977), 221-226.

454 Geraldine Murphy Wright. "Current Trends in Periodical Collections," *College and Research Libraries* 38:3 (May 1977), 234-240. **(33, 123)**

455 Lawrence J. Perk and Noelle Van Pulis. "Periodical Usage in an Education-Psychology Library," *College and Research Libraries* 38:4 (July 1977), 304-308.

456 Egill A. Halldorsson and Marjorie E. Murfin. "The Performance of Professionals and Nonprofessionals in the Reference Interview," *College and Research Libraries* 38:5 (September 1977), 385-395. **(153)**

457 Susan A. Lee. "Conflict and Ambiguity in the Role of the Academic Library Director," *College and Research Libraries* 38:5 (September 1977), 396-403. **(33)**

458 Glenn R. Wittig. "Dual Pricing of Periodicals," *College and Research Libraries* 38:5 (September 1977), 412-418.

459 Miriam A. Drake. "Attribution of Library Costs," *College and Research Libraries* 38:6 (November 1977), 514-519. **(13)**

460 Harry M. Kriz. "Subscriptions vs. Books in a Constant Dollar Budget," *College and Research Libraries* 39:2 (March 1978), 105-109.

461 Charles J. Popovich. "The Characteristics of a Collection for Research in Business/Management," *College and Research Libraries* 39:2 (March 1978), 117.

462 Jean A. Major. "The Visually Impaired Reader in the Academic Library," *College and Research Libraries* 39:3 (May 1978), 191-196. **(231)**

463 Herbert S. White and Karen Momenee. "Impact of the Increase in Library Doctorates," *College and Research Libraries* 39:3 (May 1978), 207-214. **(48, 50, 58, 190)**

464 James Michalko and Toby Heidtmann. "Evaluating the Effectiveness of an Electronic Security System," *College and Research Libraries* 39:4 (July 1978), 263-267.

465 William M. McClellan. "Judging Music Libraries," *College and Research Libraries* 39:4 (July 1978), 281-286. **(80, 81, 82)**

466 Rita Hoyt Smith and Warner Granade. "User and Library Failures in an Undergraduate Library," *College and Research Libraries* 39:6 (November 1978), 467-473.

467 Linda Ann Hulbert and David Stewart Curry. "Evaluation of an Approval Plan," *College and Research Libraries* 39:6 (November 1978), 485-491.

468 Julia F. Baldwin and Robert S. Rudolph. "The Comparative Effectiveness of a Slide/Tape Show and a Library Tour," *College and Research Libraries* 40:1 (January 1979), 31-35.

469 Melissa D. Trevvett. "Characteristics of Interlibrary Loan Requests at the Library of Congress," *College and Research Libraries* 40:1 (January 1979), 36-43.

470 Elaine Zaremba Jennerich and Bessie Hess Smith. "A Bibliographic Instruction Program in Music," *College and Research Libraries* 40:3 (May 1979), 226-233.

471 William J. Maher and Benjamin F. Shearer. "Undergraduate Use Patterns of Newspapers on Microfilm," *College and Research Libraries* 40:3 (May 1979), 254-260.

472 Larry Hardesty, Nicholas P. Lovrich, Jr. and James Mannon. "Evaluating Library-Use Instruction," *College and Research Libraries* 40:4 (July 1979), 309-317.

473 Seymour H. Sargent. "The Uses and Limitations of Trueswell," *College and Research Libraries* 40:5 (September 1979), 416-425.

474 Patricia Stenstrom and Ruth B. McBride." Serial Use by Social Science Faculty: A Survey," *College and Research Libraries* 40:5 (September 1979), 426-431.

475 Elaine C. Clever. "Using Indexes as 'Memory Assists'," *College and Research Libraries* 40:5 (September 1979), 444-449.

476 William E. McGrath, Donald J. Simon and Evelyn Bullard. "Ethnocentricity and Cross-Disciplinary Circulation," *College and Research Libraries* 40:6 (November 1979), 511-518.

477 Michael Gorman and Jami Hotsinpiller. "ISBD: Aid or Barrier to Understanding," *College and Research Libraries* 40:6 (November 1979), 519-526.

478 Jinnie Y. Davis and Stella Bentley. "Factors Affecting Faculty Perceptions of Academic Libraries," *College and Research Libraries* 40:6 (November 1979), 527-532.

479 Dennis J. Reynolds. "Regional Alternatives for Interlibrary Loan: Access to Unreported Holdings," *College and Research Libraries* 41:1 (January 1980), 33-42.

480 Ronald Rayman and Frank William Goudy. "Research and Publication Requirements in University Libraries," *College and Research Libraries* 41:1 (January 1980), 43-48. **(10, 76)**

481 John N. Olsgaard and Jane Kinch Olsgaard. "Authorship in Five Library Periodicals," *College and Research Libraries* 41:1 (January 1980), 49-53.

482 Albert F. Maag. "Design of the Library Director Interview: The Candidate's Perspective," *College and Research Libraries* 41:2 (March 1980), 112-121. **(34, 56, 57, 93, 94)**

483 Thomas M. Gaughan. "Resume Essentials for the Academic Librarian," *College and Research Libraries* 41:2 (March 1980), 122-127.

484 Harold B. Shill. "Open Stacks and Library Performance," *College and Research Libraries* 41:3 (May 1980), 220-225.

485 Robert L. Turner, Jr. "Femininity and the Librarian—Another Test," *College and Research Libraries* 41:3 (May 1980), 235-241. **(209)**

486 Ray L. Carpenter. "College Libraries: A Comparative Analysis in Terms of the ACRL Standards," *College and Research Libraries* 42:1 (January 1981), 7-18. **(14, 20, 22, 23, 79, 159, 165, 211, 213, 214)**

487 George V. Hodowanec. "An Acquisition Rate Model for Academic Libraries," *College and Research Libraries* 39:6 (September 1978), 439-442.

488 Roland Person. "Long-Term Evaluation of Bibliographic Instruction: Lasting Encouragement," *College and Research Libraries* 42:1 (January 1981), 19-25.

489 Laslo A. Nagy and Martha Lou Thomas. "An Evaluation of the Teaching Effectiveness of Two Library Instructional Videotapes," *College and Research Libraries* 42:1 (January 1981), 26-30.

490 David N. King and John C. Ory. "Effects of Library Instruction on Student Research: A Case Study," *College and Research Libraries* 42:1 (January 1981), 31-41.

491 Herbert S. White. "Perceptions by Educators and Administrators of the Ranking of Library School Programs," *College and Research Libraries* 42:3 (May 1981), 191-202.

492 Russ Davidson, Connie Capers Thorson and Margo C. Trumpeter. "Faculty Status for Librarians in the Rocky Mountain Region: A Review and Analysis," *College and Research Libraries* 42:3 (May 1981), 203-213. **(10, 27)**

493 M. Kathy Cook. "Rank, Status, and Contribution of Academic Librarians as Perceived by the Teaching Faculty at Southern Illinois University, Carbondale," *College and Research Libraries* 42:3 (May 1981), 214-223. **(132)**

494 John N. Olsgaard and Jane Kinch Olsgaard. "Post-MLS Educational Requirements for Academic Librarians," *College and Research Libraries* 42:3 (May 1981), 224-228. **(52, 194)**

495 Ronald Rayman. "Employment Opportunities for Academic Librarians in the 1970's: An Analysis of the Past Decade," *College and Research Libraries* 42:3 (May 1981), 229-234.

496 Martha C. Adamson and Gloria J. Zamora. "Publishing in Library Science Journals: A Test of the Olsgaard Profile," *College and Research Libraries* 42:3 (May 1981), 235-241.

497 Charles Sage, Janet Klass, Helen H. Spalding and Tracey Robinson. "A Queueing Study of Public Catalog Use," *College and Research Libraries* 42:4 (July 1981), 317-325.

498 Doris Cruger Dale. "Cataloging and Classsification Practices in Community College Libraries," *College and Research Libraries* 42:4 (July 1981), 333-339.

499 Dana Weiss. "Book Theft and Book Mutilation in a Large Urban University Library," *College and Research Libraries* 42:4 (July 1981), 341-347.

500 Raymond L. Carpenter. "Two-Year College Libraries: A Comparative Analysis in Terms of the ACRL Standards," *College and Research Libraries* 42:5 (September 1981), 407-415. **(14, 21, 22, 79, 84, 162, 166, 211, 214, 215)**

501 Paul D. Luyben, Leonard Cohen, Rebecca Conger and Selby U. Gration. "Reducing Noise in a College Library," *College and Research Libraries* 42:5 (September 1981), 470-481. **(122, 234, 235)**

502 Prabha Sharma. "A Survey of Academic Librarians and Their Opinions Related to Nine-Month Contracts and Academic Status Configurations in Alabama, Georgia and Mississippi," *College and Research Libraries* 42:6 (November 1981), 561-570. **(10, 27, 179, 189, 194)**

503 Priscilla Geahigan, Harriet Nelson, Stewart Saunders and Lawrence Woods. "Acceptability of Non-Library/Information Science Publications in the Promotion and Tenure of Academic Librarians," *College and Research Libraries* 42:6 (November 1981), 571-575.

504 Barbara Moore, Tamara J. Miller and Don L. Tolliver. "Title Overlap: A Study of Duplication in the University of Wisconsin System Libraries," *College and Research Libraries* 43:1 (January 1982), 14-21.

505 Gary A. Golden, Susan U. Golden and Rebecca T. Lenzini. "Patron Approaches to Serials: A User Study," *College and Research Libraries* 43:1 (January 1982), 22-30.

506 Thomas T. Surprenant. "Learning Theory, Lecture, and Programmed Instruction Text: An Experiment in Bibliographic Instruction," *College and Research Libraries* 43:1 (January 1982), 31-37.

507 Larry Hardesty, Nicholas P. Lovrich, Jr. and James Mannon. "Library-Use Instruction: Assessment of the Long-Term Effects," *College and Research Libraries* 43:1 (January 1982), 38-46.

508 Robert Swisher and Peggy C. Smith. "Journals Read by ACRL Academic Librarians, 1973 and 1978," *College and Research Libraries* 43:1 (January 1982), 51-58.

509 William Caynon. "Collective Bargaining and Professional Development of Academic Librarians," *College and Research Libraries* 43:2 (March 1982), 133-139. **(170)**

510 Barbara J. Smith. "Background Characteristics and Education Needs of a Group of Instruction Librarians in Pennsylvania," *College and Research Libraries* 43:3 (May 1982), 199-207.

511 Gloria S. Cline. "*College and Research Libraries*: Its First Forty Years," *College and Research Libraries* 43:3 (May 1982), 208-232.

512 John B. Harer and C. Edward Huber. "Copyright Policies in Virginia Academic Library Reserve Rooms," *College and Research Libraries* 43:3 (May 1982), 233-241.

513 Laurie S. Linsley. "Academic Libraries in an Interlibrary Loan Network," *College and Research Libraries* 43:4 (July 1982), 292-299.

514 Timothy D. Jewell. "Student Reactions to a Self-Paced Library Skills Workbook Program: Survey Evidence," *College and Research Libraries* 43:5 (September 1982), 371-378.

515 Mary Baier Wells. "Requirements and Benefits for Academic Librarians: 1959-1979," *College and Research Libraries* 43:6 (November 1982), 450-458. **(190, 191, 193)**

516 Marjorie A. Benedict, Jacquelyn A. Gavryck and Hanan C. Selvin. "Status of Academic Librarians in New York State," *College and Research Libraries* 44:1 (January 1983), 12-19. **(29)**

517 Carol Truett. "Services to Developmental Education Students in the Community College: Does the Library Have a Role?" *College and Research Libraries* 44:1 (January 1983), 20-28. **(117, 132, 144, 145)**

518 Gene K. Rinkel and Patricia McCandless. "Application of a Methodology Analyzing User Frustration," *College and Research Libraries* 44:1 (January 1983), 29-37.

519 Jo Bell Whitlatch. "Library Use Patterns Among Full- and Part-Time Faculty and Students," *College and Research Libraries* 44:2 (March 1983), 141-152.

520 Madeleine Stern. "Characteristics of the Literature of Literary Scholarship," *College and Research Libraries* 44:4 (July 1983), 199-209.

521 Philip Schwarz. "Demand-Adjusted Shelf Availability Parameters: A Second Look," *College and Research Libraries* 44:4 (July 1983), 210-219.

522 Paul M. Anderson and Ellen G. Miller. "Participative Planning for Library Automation: The Role of the User Opinion Survey," *College and Research Libraries* 44:4 (July 1983), 245-254. **(5)**

523 Raymond W. Barber and Jacqueline C. Mancall. "The Application of Bibliometric Techniques to the Analysis of Materials for Young Adults," *Collection Management* 2:3 (Fall 1978), 229-245.

524 Kenneth C. Kirsch and Albert H. Rubenstein. "Converting from Hard Copy to Microfilm: An Administrative Experiment," *Collection Management* 2:4 (Winter 1978), 279-302.

525 Herbert Goldhor. "U.S. Public Library Adult Non-Fiction Book Collections in the Humanities," *Collection Management* 3:1 (Spring 1979), 31-43.

526 Sally F. Williams. "Construction and Application of a Periodical Price Index," *Collection Management* 2:4 (Winter 1978), 329-344.

527 Mary Jane Pobst Reed. "Identification of Storage Candidates among Monographs," *Collection Management* 3:2/3 (Summer/Fall 1979), 203-214.

528 Ung Chon Kim. "Participation of Teaching Faculty in Library Book Selection," *Collection Management* 3:4 (Winter 1979), 333-352.

529 Glenn R. Lowry. "A Heuristic Collection Loss Rate Determination Methodology: An Alternative to Shelf-Reading," *Collection Management* 4:1/2 (Spring/Summer 1982), 73-83.

530 Stewart Saunders. "Student Reliance on Faculty Guidance in the Selection of Reading Materials: The Use of Core Collections," *Collection Management* 4:4 (Winter 1982), 9-23.

531 Ralph M. Daehn. "The Measurement and Projection of Shelf Space," *Collection Management* 4:4 (Winter 1982), 25-39. **(237)**

532 Igor I. Kavass. "Foreign and International Law Collections in Selected Law Libraries of the United States: Survey, 1972-73," *International Journal of Law Libraries* 1:3 (November 1973), 117-133.

533 Robert J. Garen. "Library Orientation on Television," *Canadian Library Journal* 24:2 (September 1967), 124-126.

534 D.W. Miller. "Non-English Books in Canadian Public Libraries," *Canadian Library Journal* 27:2 (March/April 1970), 123-129.

535 Robert H. Blackburn. "Canadian Content in a Sample of Photocopying," *Canadian Library Journal* 27:5 (September/October 1970), 332-340. **(149, 150)**

536 Peter H. Wolters and Jack E. Brown. "CAN/SDI System: User Reaction to a Computer Information Retrieval System for Canadian Scientists and Technologists," *Canadian Library Journal* 28:1 (January/ February), 20-23.

537 M. Jamil Qureshi. "Academic Status, Salaries and Fringe Benefits in Community College Libraries of Canada," *Canadian Library Journal* 28:1 (January/February 1971), 41-45. **(27, 157, 192)**

538 George J. Snowball. "Survey of Social Sciences and Humanities Monograph Circulation by Random Sampling of the Stack," *Canadian Library Journal* 28:5 (September/October 1971), 352-361.

539 Roop K. Sandhu and Harjit Sandhu. "Job Perception of University Librarians and Library Students," *Canadian Library Journal* 28:6 (November/ December 1971), 438-445. **(176, 177, 178)**

540 Brian Dale and Patricia Dewdney. "Canadian Public Libraries and the Physically Handicapped," *Canadian Library Journal* 29:3 (May/June 1972), 231-236. **(232)**

541 R.G. Wilson. "Interlibrary Loan Experiments at the University of Calgary," *Canadian Library Journal* 30:1 (January/February 1973), 38-40.

542 Peter Simmons. "Studies in the Use of the Card Catalogue in a Public Library," *Canadian Library Journal* 31:4 (August 1974), 323-337.

543 L.J. Amey and R.J. Smith. "Combination School and Public Libraries: An Attitudinal Study," *Canadian Library Journal* 33:3 (June 1976), 251-261. **(100, 101, 102, 103, 104, 105)**

544 John Wilkinson. "The Library Market for Canadian Juvenile Fiction: A Further Analysis," *Canadian Library Journal* 34:1 (February 1977), 5-15.

545 Larry Orten and John Wiseman. "Library Service to Part-time Students," *Canadian Library Journal* 34:1 (February 1977), 23-27. **(146)**

546 Esther L. Sleep. "Whither the ISSN? A Practical Experience," *Canadian Library Journal* 34:4 (August 1977), 265-270.

547 Sarah Landy. "Why Johnny Can Read...but Doesn't," *Canadian Library Journal* 34:5 (October 1977), 379-387.

548 Sharon Mott. "An Edmonton High School Reduces Book Losses," *Canadian Library Journal* 35:1 (February 1978), 45-49.

549 Fotoula Pantazis. "Library Technicians in Ontario Academic Libraries," *Canadian Library Journal* 35:2 (April 1978), 77-91. **(159, 160, 203, 204)**

550 Dorothy Ryder. "Canadian Reference Sources—A 10 Year Overview," *Canadian Library Journal* 35:4 (August 1978), 289-293.

551 Laurent-G. Denis. "Full-time Faculty Survey Describes Educators," *Canadian Library Journal* 36:3 (June 1979), 107-121.

552 Marie Foster. "Philosophy of Librarianship," *Canadian Library Journal* 36:3 (June 1979), 131-137.

553 Kenneth H. Plate and Jacob P. Seigel. "Career Patterns of Ontario Librarians," *Canadian Library Journal* 36:3 (June 1979), 143-148.

554 Mavis Cariou. "Liaison Where Field and Faculty Meet," *Canadian Library Journal* 36:3 (June 1979), 155-163.

555 Norman Horrocks. "Encyclopedias and Public Libraries: A Canadian Survey," *Canadian Library Journal* 38:2 (April 1981), 79-83.

556 Stephen B. Lawton. "Diffusion of Automation in Post-Secondary Institutions," *Canadian Library Journal* 38:2 (April 1980), 93-97. **(4, 5)**

557 Mary Ann Wasylycia-Coe. "Profile: Canadian Chief Librarians by Sex," *Canadian Library Journal* 38:3 (June 1981), 159-163. **(32, 37, 40, 58, 67)**

558 Margaret Currie, Elaine Goettler and Sandra McCaskill. "Evaluating the Relationship between Library Skills and Library Instruction," *Canadian Library Journal* 39:1 (February 1982), 35-37.

559 Esther L. Sleep. "Periodical Vandalism: A Chronic Condition," *Canadian Library Journal* 39:1 (February 1982), 39-42.

560 Kenneth Setterington. "The Ph.D. in Library Administration: A Report of Research," *Library Research* (after Spring 1983 called *Library and Information Science Research*) 5:2 (Summer 1983), 177-194.

561 Robert F. Rose. "Identifying a Core Collection of Business Periodicals for Academic Libraries," *Collection Management* 5:1/2 (Spring/Summer 1983), 73-87.

562 Raymond Kilpela. "A Profile of Library School Deans, 1960-81," *Journal of Education for Librarianship* 23:3 (Winter 1983), 173-191.

563 Charlene Renner and Barton M. Clark. "Professional and Nonprofessional Staffing Patterns in Departmental Libraries," *Library Research* 1 (1979), 153-170. **(160, 161, 162)**

564 Jacqueline C. Mancall and M. Carl Drott. "Materials Used by High School Students in Preparing Independent Study Projects: A Bibliometric Approach," *Library Research* 1 (1979), 223-236.

565 Alan R. Samuels. "Assessing Organizational Climate in Public Libraries," *Library Research* 1 (1979), 237-254. **(25, 119, 120, 124)**

566 Diane Mittermeyer and Lloyd J. Houser. "The Knowledge Base for the Administration of Libraries," *Library Research* 1 (1979), 255-276.

567 Michael V. Sullivan, Betty Vadeboncoeur, Nancy Shiotani and Peter Stangl. "Obsolescence in Biomedical Journals: Not an Artifact of Literature Growth," *Library Research* 2 (1980-81), 29-46.

568 Robert V. Williams. "Sources of the Variability in Level of Public Library Development in the United States: A Comparative Analysis," *Library Research* 2 (1980-81), 157-176. **(85)**

569 Bluma C. Peritz. "The Methods of Library Science Research: Some Results from a Bibliometric Survey," *Library Research* 2 (1980-81), 251-268.

570 Nancy Van House DeWath. "Fees for Online Bibliographic Search Services in Publicly-Supported Libraries," *Library Research* 3 (1981), 29-45.

571 Bluma C. Peritz. "Citation Characteristics in Library Science: Some Further Results from a Bibliometric Survey," *Library Research* 3 (1981), 47-65.

572 Gary Moore. "Library Long-Range Planning: A Survey of Current Practices," *Library Research* 3 (1981), 155-165. **(115, 116)**

573 Larry Hardesty. "Use of Library Materials at a Small Liberal Arts College," *Library Research* 3 (1981), 261-282.

574 Stewart Saunders, Harriet Nelson and Priscilla Geahigan. "Alternatives to the Shelflist Measure for Determining the Size of a Subject Collection," *Library Research* 3 (1981), 383-391.

575 P. Robert Paustian. "Collection Size and Interlibrary Loan in Large Academic Libraries," *Library Research* 3 (1981), 393-400.

576 Daniel O. O'Connor. "Evaluating Public Libraries Using Standard Scores: The Library Quotient," *Library Research* 4 (1982), 51-70. **(149, 153)**

577 Snunith Shoham. "A Cost-Preference Study of the Decentralization of Academic Library Services," *Library Research* 4 (1982), 175-194. **(12)**

578 A.S. Pickett. "San Franscisco State College Library Technical Services Time Study," *Library Resources and Technical Services* 4:1 (Winter 1960), 45-46.

579 Rosamond H. Danielson. "Cornell's Area Classification: A Space-Saving Device for Less-Used Books," *Library Resources and Technical Services* 5:2 (Spring 1961), 139-141.

580 Miriam C. Maloy. "Reclassification for the Divisional Plan," Library Resources and Technical Services 6:3 (Summer 1962), 239-242.

581 Andre Nitecki. "Costs of a Divided Catalog," *Library Resources and Technical Services* 6:4 (Fall 1962), 351-355.

582 Donald V. Black. "Automatic Classification and Indexing, for Libraries?" *Library Resources and Technical Services* 9:1 (Winter 1965), 35-52.

583 Perry D. Morrison. "Use of Library of Congress Classsification Decisions in Academic Libraries—An Empirical Study," *Library Resources and Technical Services* 9:2 (Spring 1965), 235-242.

584 Manuel D. Lopez. "Subject Catalogers Equal to the Future?" *Library Resources and Technical Services* 9:3 (Summer 1965), 371-375.

585 Ashby J. Fristoe. "The Bitter End," *Library Resources and Technical Services* 10:1 (Winter 1966), 91-95.

586 Ole V. Groos. "Less-Used Titles and Volumes of Science Journals: Two Preliminary Notes," *Library Resources and Technical Services* 10:3 (Summer 1966), 289-290.

587 Paula M. Strain. "A Study of the Usage and Retention of Technical Periodicals," *Library Resources and Technical Services* 10:3 (Summer 1966), 295-304.

588 William R. Nugent. "Statistics of Collection Overlap at the Libraries of the Six New England State Universities," *Library Resources and Technical Services* 12:1 (Winter 1968), 31-36.

589 Walter R. Stubbs and Robert N. Broadus. "The Value of the Kirkus Service for College Libraries," *Library Resources and Technical Services* 13:2 (Spring 1969), 203-205.

590 Barton R. Burkhalter and LaVerne Hoag. "Another Look at Manual Sorting and Filing: Backwards and Forwards," *Library Resources and Technical Services* 14:3 (Summer 1970), 445-454.

591 "More on DC Numbers on LC Cards: Quantity and Quality," *Library Resources and Technical Services* 14:4 (Fall 1970), 517-527.

592   Carol A. Nemeyer. "Scholarly Reprint Publishing in the United States: Selected Findings from a Recent Survey of the Industry," *Library Resources and Technical Services* 15:1 (Winter 1971), 35-48.

593   Betty J. Mitchell and Carol Bedoian. "A Systematic Approach to Performance Evaluation of Out-of-Print Book Dealers: The San Fernando Valley State College Experience," *Library Resources and Technical Services* 15:2 (Spring 1971), 215-222.

594   Barbara Schrader and Elaine Orsini. "British, French and Australian Publications in the National Union Catalog: A Study of NPAC's Effectiveness," *Library Resources and Technical Services* 15:3 (Summer 1971), 345-353.

595   Joel Levis. "Canadian Publications in the English Language: CBI vs. *Canadiana*," *Library Resources and Technical Services* 15:3 (Summer 1971), 354-358.

596   Zubaidah Isa. "The Entry-Word in Indonesian Names and Titles," *Library Resources and Technical Services* 15:3 (Summer 1971), 393-398.

597   Richard J. Hyman. "Access to Library Collections: Summary of a Documentary and Opinion Survey on the Direct Shelf Approach and Browsing," *Library Resources and Technical Services* 15:4 (Fall 1971), 479-491.

598   Robert L. Mowery. "The Cryptic Other," *Library Resources and Technical Services* 16:1 (Winter 1972), 74-78.

599   Ann Craig Turner. "Comparative Card Production Methods," *Library Resources and Technical Services* 16:3 (Summer 1972), pp. 347-358.

600   Edmund G. Hamann. "Expansion of the Public Card Catalog in a Large Library," *Library Resources and Technical Services* 16:4 (Fall 1972), 488-496.

601   Ernest R. Perez. "Acquisitions of Out-of-Print Materials," *Library Resources and Technical Services* 17:1 (Winter 1973), 42-59.

602   E. Dale Cluff and Karen Anderson. "LC Card Order Experiment Conducted at University of Utah Marriott Library," *Library Resources and Technical Services* 17:1 (Winter 1973), 70-72.

603   Betty J. Mitchell. "Methods Used in Out-of-Print Acquisition; A Survey of Out-of-Print Book Dealers," *Library Resources and Technical Services* 17:2 (Spring 1973), 211-215.

604   George Piternick. "University Library Arrearages," *Library Resources and Technical Services* 13:1 (Winter 1969), 102-114.

605   Nancy E. Brodie. "Evaluation of a KWIC Index for *Library Literature*," *Journal of the American Society for Information Science* 21:1 (January-February 1970), 22-28.

606 William S. Cooper. "The Potential Usefulness of Catalog Access Points Other than Author, Title and Subject," *Journal of the American Society for Information Science* 21:2 (March-April 1970), 112-127.

607 Barbara F. Frick and John M. Ginski. "Cardiovascular Serial Literature: Characteristics, Productive Journals, and Abstracting/Indexing Coverage," *Journal of the American Society for Information Science* 21:5 (September-October 1970), 338-344.

608 Ching-Chih Chen. "The Use Patterns of Physics Journals in a Large Academic Research Library," *Journal of the American Society for Information Science* 23:4 (July-August 1972), 254-265.

609 Janet Friedlander. "Clinician Search for Information," *Journal of the American Society for Information Science* 24:1 (January-February 1973), 65-69.

610 Tefko Saracevic and Lawrence J. Perk. "Ascertaining Activities in a Subject Area through Bibliometric Analysis," *Journal of the American Society for Information Science* 24:3 (March-April 1973), 120-134.

611 Ruth Kay Maloney. "Title versus Title/Abstract Text Searching in SDI Systems," *Journal of the American Society for Information Science* 25:6 (November-December 1974), 370-373.

612 Gladys B. Dronberger and Gerald T. Kowitz. "Abstract Readability as a Factor in Information Systems," *Journal of the American Society for Information Science* 26:2 (March-April 1975), 108-111.

613 Jerry R. Byrne. "Relative Effectiveness of Titles, Abstracts and Subject Headings for Machine Retrieval from the COMPENDEX Services," *Journal of the American Society for Information Science* 26:4 (July-August 1975), 223-229.

614 Joseph D. Smith and James E. Rush. "The Relationship between Author Names and Author Entries in a Large On-Line Union Catalog as Retrieved Using Truncated Keys," *Journal of the American Society for Information Science* 28:2 (March 1977), 115-120.

615 Marcia J. Bates. "Factors Affecting Subject Catalog Search Success," *Journal of the American Society for Information Science* 28:3 (May 1977), 161-169.

616 Terry Noreault, Matthew Koll and Michael J. McGill. "Automatic Ranked Output from Boolean Searches in SIRE," *Journal of the American Society for Information Science* 28:6 (November 1977), 333-339.

617 Chai Kim and Eui Hang Shin. "Sociodemographic Correlates of Intercounty Variations in the Public Library Output," *Journal of the American Society for Information Science* 28:6 (November 1977), 359-365. **(15)**

618 Harold E. Bamford, Jr. "Assessing the Effect of Computer Augmentation on Staff Productivity," *Journal of the American Society for Information Science* 30:3 (May 1979), 136-142. **(4, 5)**

619 Charles H. Davis and Deborah Shaw. "Collection Overlap as a Function of Library Size: A Comparison of American and Canadian Public Libraries," *Journal of the American Society for Information Science* 30:1 (January 1979), 19-24.

620 M. Carl Drott and Belver C. Griffith. "An Empirical Examination of Bradford's Law and the Scattering of Scientific Literature," *Journal of the American Society for Information Science* 29:5 (September 1978), 238-246.

621 James D. Anderson. *"Ad hoc* and Selective Translations of Scientific and Technical Journal Articles: Their Characteristicsand Possible Predictability," *Journal of the American Societyfor Information Science* 29:3 (May 1978), 130-135.

622 Richard C. Anderson, Francis Narin and Paul McAllister. "Publication Ratings versus Peer Ratings of Universities," *Journal of the American Society for Information Science* 29:2 (March 1978), 91-103.

623 Dennis R. Eichesen. "Cost-Effectiveness Comparison of Manual and On-line Retrospective Bibliographic Searching," *Journal of the American Society for Information Science* 29:2 (March 1978), 56-66.

624 Topsy N. Smalley. "Comparing *Psychological Abstracts* and *Index Medicus* for Coverage of the Journal Literature in a Subject Area in Psychology," *Journal of the American Society for Information Science* 31:3 (May 1980), 144-146.

625 Paul R. McAllister, Richard C. Anderson and Francis Narin. "Comparison of Peer and Citation Assessment of the Influence of Scientific Journals," *Journal of the American Society for Information Science* 31:3 (May 1980), 148-152.

626 Jerry Specht. "Patron Use of an Online Circulation System in Known-Item Searching," *Journal of the American Society for Information Science* 31:5 (September 1980), 335-346.

627 Guilbert C. Hentschke and Ellen Kehoe. "Serial Acquisition as a Capital Budgeting Problem," *Journal of the American Society for Information Science* 31:5 (September 1980), 357-362.

628 G. Edward Evans and Claudia White Argyres. "Approval Plans and Collection Development in Academic Libraries," *Library Resources and Technical Services* 18:1 (Winter 1974), 35-50.

629 Doris E. New and Retha Zane Ott. "Interlibrary Loan Analysis as a Collection Development Tool," *Library Resources and Technical Services* 18:3 (Summer 1974), 275-283.

630 H. William Axford. "The Validity of Book Price Indexes for Budgetary Projections," *Library Resources and Technical Services* 19:1 (Winter 1975), 5-12.

631 Geza A. Kosa. "Book Selection Tools for Subject Specialists in a Large Research Library: An Analysis," *Library Resources and Technical Services* 19:1 (Winter 1975), 13-18.

632 George P. D'Elia. "The Determinants of Job Satisfaction among Beginning Librarians," *Library Quarterly* 49:3 (July 1979), 283-302. **(206, 207)**

633 Tim LaBorie and Michael Halperin. "Citation Patterns in Library Science Dissertations," *Journal of Education for Librarianship* 16:4 (Spring 1976), 271-283.

634 Anne Woodsworth and Victor R. Neufeld. "A Survey of Physician Self-education Patterns in Toronto. Part 1: Use of Libraries," *Canadian Library Journal* 29:1 (January-February 1972), 38-44.

635 Richard Eggleton. "The ALA Duplicates Exchange Union—A Study and Evaluation," *Library Resources and Technical Services* 19:2 (Spring 1975), 148-163.

636 Katherine H. Packer and Dagobert Soergel. "The Importance of SDI for Current Awareness in Fields with Severe Scatter of Information," *Journal of the American Society for Information Science* 30:3 (May 1979), 125-135.

637 Doris M. Carson. "The Act of Cataloging," *Library Resources and Technical Services* 20:2 (Spring 1976), 149-153.

638 Robert L. Mowery. "The Cutter Classification: Still at Work," *Library Resources and Technical Services* 20:2 (Spring 1976), 154-156.

639 Kelly Patterson, Carol White and Martha Whittaker. "Thesis Handling in University Libraries," *Library Resources and Technical Services* 21:3 (Summer 1977), 274-285.

640 Sandra L. Stokley and Marion T. Reid. "A Study of Performance of Five Book Dealers Used by Louisiana State University Library," *Library Resources and Technical Services* 22:2 (Spring 1978), 117-125.

641 Hans H. Wellisch. "Multiscript and Multilingual Bibliographic Control: Alternatives to Romanization," *Library Resources and Technical Services* 22:2 (Spring 1978), 179-190.

642 Bert R. Boyce and Mark Funk. "Bradford's Law and the Selection of High Quality Papers," *Library Resources and Technical Services* 22:4 (Fall 1978), 390-401.

643 Susan Dingle-Cliff and Charles H. Davis. "Comparison of Recent Acquisitions and OCLC Find Rates for Three Canadian Special Libraries," *Journal of the American Society for Information Science* 32:1 (January 1981), 65-69.

644 Rose Mary Juliano Longo and Ubaldino Dantas Machado. "Characterization of Databases in the Agricultural Sciences," *Journal of the American Society for Information Science* 32:2 (March 1981), 83-91.

BIBLIOGRAPHY OF ARTICLES

645   Edward S. Warner. "The Impact of Interlibrary Access to Periodicals on Subscription Continuation/Cancellation Decision Making," *Journal of the American Society for Information Science* 32:2 (March 1981), 93-95.

646   Charles T. Payne and Robert S. McGee. "Comparisons of LC Proofslip and MARC Tape Arrival Dates at the University of Chicago Library," *Journal of Library Automation* 3:2 (June 1970), 115-121.

647   Wanda V. Dole and David Allerton. "University Collections: A Survey of Costs," *Library Acquistions: Practice and Theory* 6:2 (1982), 25-32.

648   Silvia A. Gonzalez. "1976 Statistical Survey of Law Libraries Serving a Local Bar," *Law Library Journal* 70:2 (May 1977), 222-237. **(71, 80)**

649   Carole J. Mankin and Jacqueline D. Bastille. "An Analysis of the Differences between Density-of-Use Ranking and Raw-Use Ranking of Library Journal Use," *Journal of the American Society for Information Science* 32:3 (May 1981), 224-228.

650   Katherine W. McCain and James E. Bobick. "Patterns of Journal Use in a Departmental Library: A Citation Analysis," *Journal of the American Society for Information Science* 32:4 (July 1981), 257-267.

651   Manfred Kochen, Victoria Reich and Lee Cohen. "Influence on [sic] Online Bibliographic Services on Student Behavior," *Journal of the American Society for Information Science* 32:6 (November 1981), 412-420.

652   Mark P. Carpenter and Francis Narin. "The Adequacy of the *Science Citation Index* (SCI) as an Indicator of International Scientific Activity," *Journal of the American Society for Information Science* 32:6 (November 1981), 430-439.

653   Chai Kim. "Retrieval Languages of Social Sciences and Natural Sciences: A Statistical Investigation," *Journal of the American Society for Information Science* 33:1 (January 1982), 3-7.

654   Ann H. Schabas. "Postcoordinate Retrieval: A Comparison of Two Indexing Languages," *Journal of the American Society for Information Science* 33:1 (January 1982), 32-37.

655   Miranda Lee Pao. "Collaboration in Computational Musicology," *Journal of the American Society for Information Science* 33:1 (January 1982), 38-43.

656   Robert K. Poyer. "*Science Citation Index*'s Coverage of the Preclinical Science Literature," *Journal of the American Society for Information Science* 33:5 (September 1982), 333-337.

657   Stephen M. Lawani and Alan E. Bayer. "Validity of Citation Criteria for Assessing the Influence of Scientific Publications: New Evidence with Peer Assessment," *Journal of the American Society for Information Science* 34:1 (January 1983), 59-66.

658 Edward G. Summers, Joyce Matheson and Robert Conry. "The Effect of Personal, Professional and Psychological Attributes, and Information Seeking Behavior on the Use of Information Sources by Educators," *Journal of the American Society for Information Science* 34:1 (January 1983), 75-85.

659 Bluma C. Peritz. "A Note on 'Scholarliness' and 'Impact,'" *Journal of the American Society for Information Science* 34:5 (September 1983), 360-362.

660 Michael D. Cooper. "Response Time Variations in an Online Search System," *Journal of the American Society for Information Science* 34:6 (November 1983), 374-380.

661 Richard S. Marcus. "An Experimental Comparison of the Effectiveness of Computers and Humans as Search Intermediaries," *Journal of the American Society for Information Science* 34:6 (November 1983), 381-404.

662 Michael J. Simonds, "Work Attitudes and Union Membership," *College and Research Libraries* 36:2 (March 1975), 136-142.

663 Jerold Nelson. "Faculty Awareness and Attitudes toward Academic Library Reference Services: A Measure of Communication," *College and Research Libraries* 34:5 (September 1973), 268-275.

664 Andre Nitecki, "Polish Books in America and the Farmington Plan," *College and Research Libraries* 27:6 (November 1966), 439-449.

665 Leslie R. Morris. "Projections of the Number of Library School Graduates," *Journal of Education for Librarianship* 22:4 (Spring 1982), 283-291.

666 Thomas J. Galvin and Allen Kent. "Use of a University Library Collection," *Library Journal* 102:20 (November 1977), 2317-2320. [For further and more complete information see Allen Kent, et al. *Use of Library Materials: The University of Pittsburgh Study.* New York: Marcel Dekker, 1979.]

667 Allen Kent. "Library Resource Sharing Networks: How To Make a Choice," *Library Acquisitions: Practice and Theory* 2 (1978), 69-76. [For further and more complete information see Allen Kent, et al. *Use of Library Materials: The University of Pittsburgh Study.* New York: Marcel Dekker, 1979.]

668 Leigh S. Estabrook and Kathleen M. Heim. "A Profile of ALA Personal Members," *American Libraries* 11:11 (December 1980), 654-659. [For a fuller and more complete description of this study see Kathleen M. Heim and Leigh S. Estabrook. *Career Profiles and Sex Discrimination in the Library Profession.* Chicago: American Library Association, 1983.] **(80)**

669 Mary Lee DeVilbiss. "The Approval-Built Collection in the Medium-Sized Academic Library," *College and Research Libraries* 36:6 (November 1975), 487-492.

670 Thomas P. Fleming and Frederick G. Kilgour. "Moderately and Heavily Used Biomedical Journals," *Bulletin of the Medical Library Association* 52:1 (January 1964), 234-241.

671 Richard J. Hyman. "Medical Interlibrary Loan Patterns," *Bulletin of the Medical Library Association* 53:2 (April 1965), 215-224.

672 L. Miles Raisig, Meredith Smith, Renata Cuff and Frederick G. Kilgour. "How Biomedical Investigators Use Library Books," *Bulletin of the Medical Library Association* 54:2 (April 1966), 104-107.

673 Helen Crawford. "Centralization vs. Decentralization in Medical School Libraries," *Bulletin of the Medical Library Association* 54:2 (April 1966), 199-205. **(12, 13, 17, 123, 125)**

674 Peter Stangl and Frederick G. Kilgour. "Analysis of Recorded Biomedical Book and Journal Use in the Yale Medical Library," *Bulletin of the Medical Library Association* 55:3 (July 1967), 290-300.

675 Peter Stangl and Frederick G. Kilgour. "Analysis of Recorded Biomedical Book and Journal Use in the Yale Medical Library," *Bulletin of the Medical Library Association* 55:3 (July 1967), 301-315.

676 Gwendolyn S. Cruzat. "Keeping Up with Biomedical Meetings," *Bulletin of the Medical Library Association* 56:2 (April 1968), 132-137.

677 Joan B. Woods, Sam Pieper and Shervert H. Frazier. "Basic Psychiatric Literature: I. Books," *Bulletin of the Medical Library Association* 56:3 (July 1968), 295-309.

678 Joan B. Woods, Sam Pieper and Shervert H. Frazier. "Basic Psychiatric Literature: II. Articles and Article Sources," *Bulletin of the Medical Library Association* 56:4 (October 1968), 404-427.

679 Reva Pachefsky. "Survey of the Card Catalog in Medical Libraries," *Bulletin of the Medical Library Association* 57:1 (January 1969), 10-20.

680 Janet Barlup. "Mechanization of Library Procedures in the Medium-sized Medical Library: VII. Relevancy of Cited Articles in Citation Indexing," *Bulletin of the Medical Library Association* 57:3 (July 1969), 260-263.

681 Wilhelm Moll. "Basic Journal List for Small Hospital Libraries," *Bulletin of the Medical Library Association* 57:3 (July 1969), 267-271.

682 Lois Ann Colainni and Robert F. Lewis. "Reference Services in U.S. Medical School Libraries," *Bulletin of the Medical Library Association* 57:3 (July 1969), 272-274. **(78, 79, 159, 164, 211, 212)**

683 Vern M. Pings and Joyce E. Malin. "Access to the Scholarly Record of Medicine by the Osteopathic Physicians of Southeastern Michigan," *Bulletin of the Medical Library Association* 58:1 (January 1970), 18-22.

684 D.J. Goode, J.K. Penry and J.F. Caponio. "Comparative Analysis of *Epilepsy Abstracts* and a MEDLARS Bibliography," *Bulletin of the Medical Library Association* 58:1 (January 1970), 44-50.

685 Robert Oseasohn. "Borrower Use of a Modern Medical Library by Practicing Physicians," *Bulletin of the Medical Library Association* 59:1 (January 1970), 58-59.

686 Joan M.B. Smith. "A Periodical Use Study at Children's Hospital of Michigan," *Bulletin of the Medical Library Association* 58:1 (January 1970), 65-67.

687 Jean K. Miller. "Mechanization of Library Procedures in the Medium-sized Medical Library: XI. Two Methods of Providing Selective Dissemination of Information to Medical Scientists," *Bulletin of the Medical Library Association* 58:3 (July 1970), 378-397.

688 Stella S. Gomes. "The Nature and the Use and Users of the Midwest Regional Medical Library," *Bulletin of the Medical Library Association* 58:4 (October 1970), 559-577.

689 Donald A. Windsor. "Publications on a Drug before the First Report of Its Administration to Man," *Bulletin of the Medical Library Association* 59:3 (July 1971), 433-437.

690 Charles L. Bowden and Virginia M. Bowden. "A Survey of Information Sources Used by Psychiatrists," *Bulletin of the Medical Library Association* 59:4 (October 1971), 603-608.

691 Ruth E. Fenske. "Mechanization of Library Procedures in the Medium-sized Medical Library: XIV. Correlations between National Library of Medicine Classification Numbers and MeSH Headings," *Bulletin of the Medical Library Association* 60:2 (April 1972), 319-324.

692 Anne Brearley Piternick. "Measurement of Journal Availability in a Biomedical Library," *Bulletin of the Medical Library Association* 60:4 (October 1972), 534-542.

693 Isabel Spiegel and Janet Crager. "Comparison of SUNY and MEDLINE Searches," *Bulletin of the Medical Library Association* 61:2 (April 1973), 205-209.

694 Fred W. Roper. "Special Programs in Medical Library Education, 1957-1971: Part II: Analysis of the Programs," *Bulletin of the Medical Library Association* 61:4 (October 1973), 387-395.

695 Norma Jean Lodico. "Physician's Referral Letter Bibliographic Service: A New Method of Disseminating Medical Information," *Bulletin of the Medical Library Association* 61:4 (October 1973), 422-432. **(137)**

696 Wilhelm Moll. "MEDLINE Evaluation Study," *Bulletin of the Medical Library Association* 62:1 (January 1974), 1-5.

697 Pamela Tibbetts. "A Method for Estimating the In-House Use of the Periodical Collection in the University of Minnesota Bio-Medical Library," *Bulletin of the Medical Library Association* 62:1 (January 1974), 37-48.

698   Joan Ash. "Library Use of Public Health Materials: Description and Analysis," *Bulletin of the Medical Library Association* 62:2 (April 1974), 95-104.

699   Ching-Chih Chen. "Current Status of Biomedical Book Reviewing: Part I. Key Biomedical Reviewing Journals with Quantitative Significance," *Bulletin of the Medical Library Association* 62:2 (April 1974), 105-112.

700   Ching-Chih Chen. "Current Status of Biomedical Book Reviewing: Part II. Time Lag in Biomedical Book Reviewing," *Bulletin of the Medical Library Association* 62:2 (April 1974), 113-119.

701   George Scheerer and Lois E. Hines. "Classification Systems Used in Medical Libraries," *Bulletin of the Medical Library Association* 62:3 (July 1974), 272-280.

702   Jo Ann Bell. "The Academic Health Sciences Library and Serial Selection," *Bulletin of the Medical Library Association* 62:3 (July 1974), 281-290.

703   Ching-Chih Chen. "Current Status of Biomedical Book Reviewing: Part III. Duplication Patterns in Biomedical Book Reviewing," *Bulletin of the Medical Library Association* 62:3 (July 1974), 296-301.

704   Ching-Chih Chen. "Current Status of Biomedical Book Reviewing: Part IV. Major American and British Biomedical Book Publishers," *Bulletin of the Medical Library Association* 62:3 (July 1974), 302-308.

705   M. Sandra Wood and Robert S. Seeds. "Development of SDI Services from a Manual Current Awareness Service to SDILINE," *Bulletin of the Medical Library Association* 62:4 (October 1974), 374-384.

706   Margaret Butkovich and Robert M. Braude. "Cost-Performance of Cataloging and Card Production in a Medical Center Library," *Bulletin of the Medical Library Association* 63:1 (January 1975), 29-34.

707   Donald A. Windsor. "Science-Speciality Literatures: Their Legendary-Contemporary Parity, Based on the Transmission of Information between Generations," *Bulletin of the Medical Library Association* 63:2 (April 1975), 209-215.

708   Helen J. Brown, Jean K. Miller and Diane M. Pinchoff. "Study of the Information Dissemination Service—Health Sciences Library, State University of New York at Buffalo," *Bulletin of the Medical Library Association* 63:3 (July 1975), 259-271.

709   Rachel K. Goldstein and Dorothy R. Hill. "The Status of Women in the Administration of Health Science Libraries," *Bulletin of the Medical Library Association* 63:4 (October 1975), 386-395.   **(38, 40, 42, 47, 49, 54)**

710   Janet G. Schnall and Joan W. Wilson. "Evaluation of a Clinical Medical Librarianship Program at a University Health Sciences Library," *Bulletin of the Medical Library Association* (July 1976), 278-283.   **(141, 142)**

711 Anne B. Piternick. "Effects of Binding Policy and Other Factors on the Availability of Journal Issues," *Bulletin of the Medical Library Association* 64:3 (July 1976), 284-292.

712 Richard B. Fredericksen and Helen N. Michael. "Subject Cataloging Practices in North American Medical School Libraries," *Bulletin of the Medical Library Association* 64:4 (October 1976), 356-366.

713 Paul M. McIlvaine and Malcolm H. Brantz. "Audiovisual Materials: A Survey of Bibliographic Controls in Distributors' Catalogs," *Bulletin of the Medical Library Association* 65:1 (January 1977), 17-21.

714 Bette Greenberg, Robert Breedlove and Wendy Berger. "MEDLINE Demand Profiles: An Analysis of Requests for Clinical and Research Information," *Bulletin of the Medical Library Association* 65:1 (January 1977), 22-28.

715 Renata Tagliacozzo. "Estimating the Satisfaction of Information Users," *Bulletin of the Medical Library Association* 65:2 (April 1977), 243-249.

716 Ruth W. Wender, Ester L. Fruehauf, Marilyn S. Vent and Constant D. Wilson. "Determination of Continuing Medical Education Needs of Clinicians from a Literature Search Study: Part I. The Study," *Bulletin of the Medical Library Association* 65:3 (July 1977), 330-337.

717 Ruth W. Wender, Ester L. Fruehauf, Marilyn S. Vent and Constant D. Wilson. "Determination of Continuing Medical Education Needs of Clinicians from a Literature Search Study: Part II. Questionnaire Results," *Bulletin of the Medical Library Association* 65:3 (July 1977), 338-341. **(143, 144)**

718 Donald J. Morton. "Analysis of Interlibrary Requests by Hospital Libraries for Photocopied Journal Articles," *Bulletin of the Medical Library Association* 65:4 (October 1977), 425-432,

719 Patrick W. Brennen and W. Patrick Davey. "Citation Analysis in the Literature of Tropical Medicine," *Bulletin of the Medical Library Association* 66:1 (January 1978), 24-30.

720 Theresa C. Strasser. "The Information Needs of Practicing Physicians in Northeastern New York State," *Bulletin of the Medical Library Association* 66:2 (April 1978), 200-209.

721 Inci A. Bowman, Elizabeth K. Eaton and J. Maurice Mahan. "Are Health Science Faculty Interested in Medical History? An Evaluative Case Study," *Bulletin of the Medical Library Association* 66:2 (April 1978), 228-231. **(132, 137)**

722 Maurice C. Leatherbury and Richard A. Lyders. "Friends of the Library Groups in Health Sciences Libraries," *Bulletin of the Medical Library Association* 66:3 (July 1978), 315-318. **(109, 110, 112, 113)**

723 Bette Greenberg, Sara Battison, Madeleine Kolisch and Martha Leredu. "Evaluation of a Clinical Medical Librarian Program at the Yale Medical Library," *Bulletin of the Medical Library Association* 66:3 (July 1978), 319-326. **(141, 142, 143)**

724 Gloria Werner. "Use of On-Line Bibliographic Retrieval Services in Health Sciences Libraries in the United States and Canada," *Bulletin of the Medical Library Association* 67:1 (January 1979), 1-14.

725 B. Tommie Usdin. "Core Lists of Medical Journals: A Comparison," *Bulletin of the Medical Library Association* 67:2 (April 1979), 212-217.

726 John A. Timour. "Brief Communications: Use of Selected Abstracting and Indexing Journals in Biomedical Resource Libraries," *Bulletin of the Medical Library Association* 67:3 (July 1979), 330-335.

727 Rachel K. Goldstein and Dorothy R. Hill. "The Status of Women in the Administration of Health Sciences Libraries: A Five-Year Follow-Up Study, 1972-1977," *Bulletin of the Medical Library Association* 68:1 (January 1980), 6-15. **(43, 48, 49, 55, 56, 66)**

728 Richard T. West and Maureen J. Malone. "Communicating the Results of NLM Grant-supported Library Projects," *Bulletin of the Medical Library Association* 68:1 (January 1980), 33-39. **(76, 78)**

729 James A. Thompson and Michael R. Kronenfeld. "The Effect of Inflation on the Cost of Journals on the Brandon List," *Bulletin of the Medical Library Association* 68:1 (January 1980), 47-52.

730 Carol C. Spencer. "Random Time Sampling with Self-observation for Library Cost Studies: Unit Costs of Reference Questions," *Bulletin of the Medical Library Association* 68:1 (January 1980), 53-57.

731 Justine Roberts. "Circulation versus Photocopy: Quid pro Quo?" *Bulletin of the Medical Library Association* 68:3 (July 1980), 274-277. **(150)**

732 Dick R. Miller and Joseph E. Jensen. "Dual Pricing of Health Sciences Periodicals: A Survey," *Bulletin of the Medical Library Association* 68:4 (October 1980), 336-347.

733 Jacqueline D. Bastille. "A Simple Objective Method for Determining a Dynamic Journal Collection," *Bulletin of the Medical Library Association* 68:4 (October 1980), 357-366.

734 Mary H. Mueller. "An Examination of Characteristics Related to Success of Friends Groups in Medical School Rare Book Libraries," *Bulletin of the Medical Library Association* 69:1 (January 1981), 9-13. **(110, 111, 112, 113, 114, 115)**

735 Scott Davis, Lincoln Polissar and Joan W. Wilson. "Continuing Education in Cancer for the Community Physician: Design and Evaluation of a Regional

Table of Contents Service," *Bulletin of the Medical Library Association* 69:1 (January 1981), 14-20. **(137, 138, 139)**

736 Gary D. Byrd. "Copyright compliance in Health Sciences Libraries: A Status Report Two Years after the Implementation of PL 94-553," *Bulletin of the Medical Library Association* 69:2 (April 1981), 224-230. **(30, 31, 32)**

737 Ester L. Baldinger, Jennifer P.S. Nakeff-Plaat and Margaret S. Cummings. "An Experimental Study of the Feasibility of Substituting Chemical Abstracts Online for the Printed Copy in a Medium-Sized Medical Library," *Bulletin of the Medical Library Association* 69:2 (April 1981), 247-251.

738 Doris R.F. Dunn. "Dissemination of the Published Results of an Important Clinical Trial: An Analysis of the Citing Literature," *Bulletin of the Medical Library Association* 69:3 (July 1981), 301-306. **(140, 145)**

739 Cynthia H. Goldstein. "A Study of Weeding Policies in Eleven TALON Resource Libraries," *Bulletin of the Medical Library Association* 69:3 (July 1981), 311-316.

740 K. Suzanne Johnson and E. Guy Coffee. "Veterinary Medical School Libraries in the United States and Canada, 1977-78," *Bulletin of the Medical Library Association* 70:1 (January 1982), 10-20. **(70, 72, 84, 86, 87, 123, 128, 130, 160, 164, 228, 229, 231, 235, 238)**

741 Suzanne F. Grefsheim, Robert H. Larson, Shelley A. Bader and Nina W. Matheson. "Automation of Internal Library Operations in Academic Health Sciences Libraries: A State of the Art Report," *Bulletin of the Medical Library Association* 70:2 (April 1982), 191-200.

742 Elizabeth R. Lenz and Carolyn F. Walz. "Nursing Educators' Satisfaction with Library Facilities," *Bulletin of the Medical Library Association* 70:2 (April 1982), 201-206.

743 Ruth Traister Morris, Edwin A. Holtum and David S. Curry. "Being There: The Effect of the User's Presence on MEDLINE Search Results," *Bulletin of the Medical Library Association* 70:3 (July 1982), 298-304.

744 James K. Cooper, Diane Cooper and Timothy P. Johnson. "Medical Library Support in Rural Areas," *Bulletin of the Medical Library Association* 71:1 (January 1983), 13-15.

745 Susan Crawford. "Health Science Libraries in the United States: I. Overview of the Post-World War II Years," *Bulletin of the Medical Library Association* 71:1 (January 1983), 16-20. **(81, 83, 88, 162, 165)**

746 Susan Crawford and Alan M. Rees. "Health Sciences Libraries in the United States: II. Medical School Libraries, 1960-1980," *Bulletin of the Medical Library Association* 71:1 (January 1983), 21-29. **(88)**

747 Susan Crawford. "Health Science Libraries in the United States: III. Hospital Health Science Libraries, 1969-1979," *Bulletin of the Medical Library Association* 71:1 (January 1983), 30-36. **(15, 89, 162, 165, 211, 212)**

748   Mark E. Funk and Carolyn Anne Reid. "Indexing Consistency in MED-LINE," *Bulletin of the Medical Library Association* 71:2 (April 1983), 176-183.

749   Michael R. Kronenfeld and Sarah H. Gable. "Real Inflation of Journal Prices: Medical Journals, U.S. Journals and Brandon List Journals," *Bulletin of the Medical Library Association* 71:4 (October 1983), 375-379.

750   Jane McCarthy. "Survey of Audiovisual Standards and Practices in Health Sciences Libraries," *Bulletin of the Medical Library Association* 71:4 (October 1983), 391-395. **(84, 89, 222, 223, 224)**

751   Rajia C. Tobia and David A. Kronick. "A Clinical Information Consultation Service at a Teaching Hospital," *Bulletin of the Medical Library Association* 71:4 (October 1983), 396-399.

752   Elizabeth R. Ashin. "Library Service to Dental Practitioners," *Bulletin of the Medical Library Association* 71:4 (October 1983), 400-402. **(132, 133, 140)**

753   Peter P. Olevnik. "Non-Formalized Point-of-Use Library Instruction: A Survey," *Catholic Library World* 50:5 (December 1978), 218-220.

754   Susan A. Stussy. "Automation in Catholic College Libraries," *Catholic Library World* 53:3 (October 1981), 109-111. **(5)**

755   R.M. Longyear. "Article Citations and 'Obsolescence' in Musicological Journals," *Notes* 33:3 (March 1977), 563-571.

756   Ann Basart. "Criteria for Weeding Books in a University Music Library," *Notes* 36:4 (June 1980), 819-836.

757   Richard P. Smiraglia and Arsen R. Papakhian. "Music in the OCLC Online Union Catalog: A Review," *Notes* 38:2 (December 1981), 257-274.

758   William Gray Potter. "When Names Collide: Conflict in the Catalog and AACR 2," *Library Resources and Technical Services* 24:1 (Winter 1980), 3-16.

759   Rose Mary Magrill and Constance Rinehart. "Selection for Preservation: A Service Study," *Library Resources and Technical Services* 24:1 (Winter 1980), 44-57.

760   Sally Braden, John D. Hall and Helen H. Britton. "Utilization of Personnel and Bibliographic Resources for Cataloging by OCLC Participating Libraries," *Library Resources and Technical Services* 24:2 (Spring 1980), 135-154.

761   Cynthia C. Ryans. "Cataloging Administrators' Views on Cataloging Education," *Library Resources and Technical Services* 24:4 (Fall 1980), 343-351.

762   Thomas Schadlich. "Changing from Sears to LC Subject Headings," *Library Resources and Technical Services* 24:4 (Fall 1980), 361-363.

763 Elizabeth L. Tate. "For Our 25th Anniversary...," *Library Resources and Technical Services* 25:1 (January/March 1981), 3-7.

764 Barbara Moore. "Patterns in the Use of OCLC by Academic Library Cataloging Departments," *Library Resources and Technical Services* 25:1 (January/March 1981), 30-39. **(225)**

765 Judith J. Johnson and Clair S. Josel. "Quality Control and the OCLC Data Base: A Report on Error Reporting," *Library Resources and Technical Services* 25:1 (January/March 1981), 40-47.

766 Edward T. O'Neill and Rao Aluri. "Library of Congress Subject Heading Patterns in OCLC Monographic Records," *Library Resources and Technical Services* 25:1 (January/March 1981), 63-80.

767 Elizabeth H. Groot. "A Comparison of Library Tools for Monograph Verification," *Library Resources and Technical Services* 25:2 (April/June 1981), 149-161.

768 Elizabeth G. Mikita. "Monographs in Microform: Issues in Cataloging and Bibliographic Control," *Library Resources and Technical Services* 25:4 (October/December 1981), 352-361.

769 Lee R. Nemchek. "Problems of Cataloging and Classification in Theater Librarianship," *Library Resources and Technical Services* 25:4 (October/December 1981), 374-385.

770 John Hostage. "AACR 2, OCLC, and the Card Catalog in the Medium-Sized Library," *Library Resources and Technical Services* 26:1 (January/March 1982), 12-20.

771 Robert H. Hassell. "Revising the Dewey Music Schedules: Tradition vs. Innovation," *Library Resources and Technical Services* 26:2 (April/June 1982), 192-203.

772 Patricia Dwyer Wanninger. "Is the OCLC Database Too Large? A Study of the Effect of Duplicate Records in the OCLC System," *Library Resources and Technical Services* 26:4 (October/December 1982), 353-361.

773 Stephen R. Salmon. "Characteristics of Online Public Catalogs," *Library Resources and Technical Services* 27:1 (January/March 1983), 36-67.

774 Thomas E. Nisonger. "A Test of Two Citation Checking Techniques for Evaluating Political Science Collections in University Libraries," *Library Resources and Technical Services* 27:2 (April/June 1983), 163-176.

775 John Rutledge and Willy Owen. "Changes in the Quality of Paper in French Books, 1860-1914: A Study of Selected Holdings of the Wilson Library, University of North Carolina," *Library Resources and Technical Services* (April/June 1983), 177-187.

776   Jim Williams and Nancy Romero. "A Comparison of the OCLC Database
      and *New Serial Titles* as an Information Resource for Serials," *Library
      Resources and Technical Services* 27:2 (April/June 1983), 177-187.

777   Mary E. Clack and Sally F. Williams. "Using Locally and Nationally
      Produced Periodical Price Indexes in Budget Preparation," *Library Re-
      sources and Technical Services* 27:4 (October/December 1983), 345-356.

778   Victoria Cheponis Lessard and Jack Hall. "Vocational Technical Collection
      Building: Does it Exist?" *Collection Building* 4:2 (1982), 6-18.

779   Virginia Witucke. "The Reviewing of Children's Science Books," *Collection
      Building* 4:2 (1982) 19-30.

780   Margaret F. Stieg. "The Information Needs of Historians," *College and
      Research Libraries* 42:6 (November 1981), 549-560.

781   Howard D. White. "Library Censorship and the Permissive Minority,"
      Library Quarterly 51:2 (1981), 192-207.

782   Judith Serebnick. "Book Reviews and the Selection of Potentially Controver-
      sial Books in Public Libraries," *Library Quarterly* 51:4 (1981), 390-409.

783   Richard W. Scamell and Bette Ann Stead. "A Study of Age and Tenure as it
      Pertains to Job Satisfaction," *Journal of Library Administration* 1:1 (Spring
      1980), 3-18.   **(201)**

784   Robert M. Hayes. "Citation Statistics as a Measure of Faculty Research
      Productivity," *Journal of Education for Librarianship* 23:3 (Winter 1983),
      151-172.

785   William Skeh Wong and David S. Zubatsky. "The First-Time Appointed
      Academic Library Director 1970-1980: A Profile," *Journal of Library Admin-
      istration* 4:1 (Spring 1983), 41-70.   **(38, 45, 47, 51, 52, 65, 68, 69, 117, 118)**

786   James Rice, Jr. "An Assessment of Student Preferences for Method of
      Library Orientation," *Journal of Library Administration* 4:1 (Spring 1983),
      87-93.

787   Frank William Goudy. "Affirmative Action and Library Science Degrees: A
      Statistical Overview, 1973-74 through 1980-81," *Journal of Library Adminis-
      tration* 4:3 (Fall 1983), 51-60.

788   Thomas G. English. "Librarian Status in the Eighty-Nine U.S. Academic
      Institutions of the Association of Research Libraries: 1982," *College and
      Research Libraries* 44:3 (May 1983), 199-211.   **(10, 26, 28, 158)**

789   Nathan M. Smith and Veneese C. Nelson. "Burnout: A Survey of Academic
      Reference Librarians," *College and Research Libraries* 44:3 (May 1983),
      245-250.   **(181, 201)**

790 Floris W. Wood. "Reviewing Book Review Indexes," *Reference Services Review* (April/June 1980), 47-52.

791 Herbert Goldhor. "Public Library Circulation up 3%; Spending Jumps 11%," *American Libraries* 14:8 (September 1983), 534. **(16, 23)**

792 Laura N. Gasaway and Steve Margeton. "Continuing Education for Law Librarianship," *Law Library Journal* 70:1 (February 1977), 39-52. **(188, 189)**

793 Michael L. Renshawe. "The Condition of the Law Librarian in 1976," *Law Library Review* 69:4 (November 1976), 626-640. **(37, 86, 197)**

794 Susanne Patterson Wahba. "Women in Libraries," *Law Library* Journal 69:2 (May 1976), 223-231. **(179, 208, 209)**

795 Jean Finch and Lauri R. Flynn. "An Update on Faculty Libraries," *Law Library Journal* 73:1 (Winter 1980), 99-106. **(146, 147, 148, 229, 230)**

796 Robert D. Swisher, Peggy C. Smith and Calvin J. Boyer. "Educational Change Among ACRL Academic Librarians," *Library Research* (*Library and Information Science Research* since Spring 1983) 5:2 (Summer 1983), 195-205. **(186, 189, 195, 196)**

797 Michael D. Cooper. "Economies of Scale in Academic Libraries," *Library Research* (*Library and Information Science Research* after Spring 1983) 5:2 (Summer 1983), 207-219. **(23, 107)**

798 Virgil Diodato. "Faculty Workload: A Case Study," *Journal of Education for Librarianship* 23:4 (Spring 1983), 286-295.

799 Jerry D. Saye. "Continuing Education and Library School Faculty," *Journal of Education for Librarianship* 24:1 (Summer 1983), 3-16.

800 Maurice P. Marchant and Carolyn F. Wilson. "Developing Joint Graduate Programs for Librarians," *Journal of Education for Librarianship* 24:1 (Summer 1983), 30-37. **(63, 64)**

801 Barbara L. Stein and Herman L. Totten. "Cognitive Styles: Similarities Among Students," *Journal of Education for Librarianship* 24:1 (Summer 1983), 38-43.

802 Marilyn J. Markham, Keith H. Stirling and Nathan M. Smith. "Librarian Self-Disclosure and Patron Satisfaction in the Reference Interview," *RQ* 22:4 (Summer 1983), 369-374.

803 June L. Engle and Elizabeth Futas. "Sexism in Adult Encyclopedias," *RQ* 23:1 (Fall 1983), 29-39.

804 David F. Kohl. "Circulation Professionals: Management Information Needs and Attitudes," *RQ* 23:1 (Fall 1983), 81-86. **(180, 181, 182, 184, 185, 186, 187, 188)**

805   Kevin Carey. "Problems and Patterns of Periodical Literature Searching at an Urban University Research Library," *RQ* 23:2 (Winter 1983), 211-218.

806   Beverly P. Lynch and Jo Ann Verdin. "Job Satisfaction in Libraries: Relationships of the Work Itself, Age, Sex, Occupational Group, Tenure, Supervisory Level, Career Commitment and Library Department," *Library Quarterly* 53:4 (October 1983), 434-447.   **(198, 199, 200, 201, 215, 216)**

807   Louise W. Diodato and Virgil P. Diodato. "The Use of Gifts in a Medium Sized Academic Library," *Collection Management* 5:1/2 (Spring/Summer 1983), 53-71.

AUTHOR INDEX
TO BIBLIOGRAPHY OF ARTICLES

Note: The index is arranged alphabetically, word by word. All characters or groups of characters separated by spaces, dashes, hyphens, diagonal slashes or periods are treated as separate words. Acronyms not separated by spaces or punctuation are alphabetized as though they are single words, while initials separated by spaces or punctuation are treated as if each letter is a complete word. Personal names beginning with capital Mc, M' and Mac are all listed under Mac as though the full form were used, and St. is alphabetized as if spelled out.

ABOUT THE AUTHORS

DAVID F. KOHL is currently Undergraduate Librarian and Assistant Director for Undergraduate Libraries and Instructional Services at the University of Illinois-Urbana, with the rank of Associate Professor. Dr. Kohl did his graduate work at the University of Chicago. He has taught library administration at the University of Illinois Graduate School of Library and Information Science and has published numerous articles and monographs on library management and automation. His wide range of service in library management includes active participation in the ARL/OMS Library Consultant Program, the Washington State University's Managing for Productivity Program, and the Assessment Center Program for Potential Managers, sponsored jointly by the University of Washington Graduate Library School and the Washington State Library.

BERNARD KREISSMAN served with the Air Force in World War II, received his M.L.S. from Columbia University in 1954, and earned his Ph.D. from the University of Nebraska in 1962. He has worked as the Supervisor of the Main Reading Room of the New York Public Library; Assistant Director of Libraries, the University of Nebraska; Chief Librarian, the City College of the City University of New York; and University Librarian, the University of California, Davis. Dr. Kreissman has served on numerous committees of the American Library Association and its constituent Divisions including a term on the Board of the Library Administration and Management Association; he has been elected President of the New York Library Club, Convenor of the Archons of Colophon and President of the California Library Association; he has served as library consultant in New York, New Jersey, Maryland, Wisconsin, and most recently as UNESCO Consultant to the Universidad de Oriente in Venezuela; and he has been a member of a score of academic accrediting teams with the Middle States Association and with the Western Association of Schools and Colleges. Kreissman has published two literary studies, and he is currently co-editor of *Advances in Library Administration and Organization*.

DATE DUE